1|s 4|16

Consumption and Public Life
Series Editors: Frank Trentmann and Richard Wilk

Titles include:

Mark Bevir and Frank Trentmann (*editors*)
GOVERNANCE, CITIZENS AND CONSUMERS
Agency and Resistance in Contemporary Politics

Magnus Boström and Mikael Klintman
ECO-STANDARDS, PRODUCT LABELLING AND GREEN CONSUMERISM

Jacqueline Botterill
CONSUMER CULTURE AND PERSONAL FINANCE
Money Goes to Market

Daniel Thomas Cook (*editor*)
LIVED EXPERIENCES OF PUBLIC CONSUMPTION
Encounters with Value in Marketplaces on Five Continents

Nick Couldry, Sonia Livingstone and Tim Markham
MEDIA CONSUMPTION AND PUBLIC ENGAGEMENT
Beyond the Presumption of Attention

Anne Cronin
ADVERTISING, COMMERCIAL SPACES AND THE URBAN

Stephen Kline
GLOBESITY, FOOD MARKETING AND FAMILY LIFESTYLES

Amy E. Randall
THE SOVIET DREAM WORLD OF RETAIL TRADE AND CONSUMPTION IN THE 1930s

Roberta Sassatelli
FITNESS CULTURE
Gyms and the Commercialisation of Discipline and Fun

Kate Soper, Martin Ryle and Lyn Thomas (*editors*)
THE POLITICS AND PLEASURES OF SHOPPING DIFFERENTLY
Better than Shopping

Kate Soper and Frank Trentmann (*editors*)
CITIZENSHIP AND CONSUMPTION

Lyn Thomas (*editor*)
RELIGION, CONSUMERISM AND SUSTAINABILITY
Paradise Lost?

Harold Wilhite
CONSUMPTION AND THE TRANSFORMATION OF EVERYDAY LIFE
A View from South India

Consumption and Public Life
Series Standing Order ISBN 978-1-4039-9983-2 Hardback
978-1-4039-9984-9 Paperback
(*outside North America only*)

You can receive future titles in this series as they are published by placing a standing order. Please contact your bookseller or, in case of difficulty, write to us at the address below with your name and address, the title of the series and the ISBN quoted above.

Customer Services Department, Macmillan Distribution Ltd, Houndmills, Basingstoke, Hampshire RG21 6XS, England

---

Globesity, Food Marketing and Family Lifestyles

Stephen Kline
Simon Fraser University, Canada

palgrave
macmillan

First published 2011 by
PALGRAVE MACMILLAN

Palgrave Macmillan in the UK is an imprint of Macmillan Publishers Limited, registered in England, company number 785998, of Houndmills, Basingstoke, Hampshire RG21 6XS.

Palgrave Macmillan in the US is a division of St Martin's Press LLC, 175 Fifth Avenue, New York, NY 10010.

Palgrave Macmillan is the global academic imprint of the above companies and has companies and representatives throughout the world.

Palgrave® and Macmillan® are registered trademarks in the United States, the United Kingdom, Europe and other countries.

ISBN 978–0–230–53740–8   hardback

This book is printed on paper suitable for recycling and made from fully managed and sustained forest sources. Logging, pulping and manufacturing processes are expected to conform to the environmental regulations of the country of origin.

A catalogue record for this book is available from the British Library.

Library of Congress Cataloging-in-Publication Data

Kline, Stephen.
Globesity, food marketing, and family lifestyles / Stephen Kline.
       p. cm.
Summary: "This book examines the public controversies surrounding lifestyle risks in the consumer society. Comparing news coverage of the globesity pandemic in Britain and the USA, it illustrates the way moral panic brought children's food marketing to the centre of the policy debates about consumer lifestyles"— Provided by publisher.
       ISBN 978–0–230–53740–8
     1. Obesity—United States.   2. Obesity—Great Britain.   3. Lifestyles— United States.   4. Lifestyles—Great Britain.   5. Food—United States— Marketing.   6. Food—Great Britain—Marketing.   I. Title.
       RC628.K55 2011
       362.196'398—dc22   2010034138

10 9 8 7 6 5 4 3 2 1
20 19 18 17 16 15 14 13 12 11

Transferred to Digital Printing 2011

Contents

List of Figures

Acknowledgements

Systems thinking makes for a restless mind. In the process of writing this book I found myself attempting to knit together some of the ravelled threads woven through my interdisciplinary career as a researcher. It started when as a graduate student I began to reflect upon the biases of TV news and its relationship to democratic social change which is predicated on open and transparent communication about the evils we confront. My comparative studies of Canada, the US and Britain made me aware of the different ways journalists commented on hazards, war and social movements that threatened the moral order – ultimately shaping both public opinion and the policy agenda. Later on, as an environmentalist, I became troubled by the unnecessary havoc wrought on the natural world by 'un-reflexive modernity'. Like other greens, I have long dreamt of and worked towards a socio-ecological awareness of the environment that could help change capitalism's destructive relationship with nature. I have also long believed that the problems of distributional justice required better analysis of the system of social relations which dynamized the mediated markets. To this end I have studied marketing communication as the privileged discourse that both intensifies and distorts the negotiations between producers and consumers in the globalizing marketplace. Recognizing that children today become citizens in the context of media-saturated households in which they are addressed daily by marketers who target them, I have also been interested in the impact of toy and food marketing directed at them. And as a father, I have had to confront TV and its profound disturbance of the family system. This led me also to reflect on the ways children negotiate domestic consumerism caught between parents, schools and peers. In this book I have attempted to weave together these four threads woven through my career – the importance of democratic journalism, the changing public debates about environmentalism, the problem of regulating the mediated marketplace and the dynamics of consumer socialization – through a case study of child obesity.

In retrospect this synthetic ambition may have been presumptuous. The changing discourses on children's consumer empowerment in the risk society are at the same time scientifically sophisticated, contradictory and illusive. What started as a simple investigation into fast food marketing and children's capacity to make healthy lifestyle choices quickly broadened into a five-year long empirical inquiry into the multiple layers of social communication shaping domestic consumption in the risk society. Child obesity turned out to be a very robust social system problematic because the question of mitigation leads in different directions – to the food marketers that target them (and the regulators that license them to do so), to the parents that provision the household with unhealthy snacks, to the schools that fail to teach them about the nutritional and health risks associated with consumption and to health sciences that approached obesity as a medical rather than a family and lifestyle issue. In short I could find no single thread that neatly provided an overarching narrative for the study of globesity.

That said, while writing this book, I have gained a greater appreciation of the pivotal part played by journalism in market democracy: the news still sets the discursive agenda of reflexive modernity, in this case by galvanizing a moral panic about the place of children's unhealthy food consumption. I have also come to recognize the importance of epidemiology as a new risk science. Among other things, this book therefore zooms in on the role that the health sciences came to play in the controversy over the media-saturated lifestyles of millennial children – in the press debates, the policy debates and ultimately within family life. As a media analyst and children's culture researcher, I was initially surprised to find myself reading studies of children's media use conceived and written from a medical point of view. Although the tradition goes back to studies of violence, many of my colleagues in media studies had abandoned the 'effects models' as crass and unsophisticated. It took me a while to appreciate the importance of epidemiology to the study of consumerism. It took me even longer to understand the paradoxical nature of the medicalization of lifestyle risks implicit in the discursive politics of the globesity pandemic.

Globesity manifested weight gain equally as a consumerist and a medical issue. Because they lack both information about food risks and the rational capacity to interpret food advertising, children fail the test of 'informed consent' making fast food and sedentary lifestyle the poster child of a moral panic. Child obesity became the new tobacco, and in so doing the press proved their merit in making the public aware of health problems associated with the market system. The consequences therefore of moral panic are both negative and positive: it distorted lifestyle risk communication while it precipitated lifestyle risk policymaking. Mitigating globesity was a cultural systems problem as much as a medical one. The conditions in which children attain the capacity to choose healthy and balanced lifestyles for themselves involves marketers, parents, teachers and governments. To break the hold of neoliberalism, policymakers forged a more nuanced understanding of the social dynamics of children's consumer empowerment. In the UK food marketing was deemed a lifestyle risk factor.

Much of the empirical research reported here was supported by a grant from the CIHR undertaken with Alec Ostry and Ryna Levy-Milne. I was also lucky enough to receive an International Fellowship with the Cultures of Consumption project to help me launch the study of globesity in the news. Discussions with Frank Trentmann and other colleagues associated with the programme were fundamental in providing the motivation for writing this book. My collaborations with Ines de la Ville and all the colleagues I have met through events at the European Centre for the Children's Products at the University of Poitier have been crucial in forging a critical analysis of the responsibility of marketers. I have also collaborated on both the comparative advertising analysis and the surveys of children's responses to it with David Marshall and Stephenie O'Donahoe at Edinburgh University. In addition to these colleagues, a number of excellent young researchers have helped me gather and process the evidence that is presented here. To Kym Stewart and Lindsay Nielson my grateful thanks for managing the project team and infusing the studies with practical wisdom as well as order. Additionally, Sonja Weaver, Sarah Bearchell, Nicola Harper, Cindy Mulligan and Daniel Kline have all made the arduous task of the news analysis, the ad studies, the survey research with parents and children and focus groups in schools easier.

My interest in the communication of risk in mediated markets was initially inspired by my friend and colleague, William Leiss. Long may we continue to discuss these issues. My partner and colleague Jackie Botterill has provided insight, humour and encouragement throughout the research and writing. And yes, this is the last book, I promise – but only if you read beyond the acknowledgements. To my daughter Meghan who has so willingly helped by copy editing the first draft, I dedicate this book. You provided the sustaining light at the end of the tunnel.

Preface

The ideology of progress has long underscored improvements in children's education and care. During the nineteenth century, child advocates improved children's welfare by reducing their exploitation as labour, mandating state schooling and providing play spaces for their leisure. But in the twentieth century public health has broadened the scope of the politics of children's well-being. Responding to concerns associated with illness and malnutrition among working-class children, Britain's Education (Provision of Meals) Act of 1906 foreshadowed the growing concern with health by mandating schools to provide free meals to the poor. When World War I again exposed the relationship between poverty and malnutrition among young soldiers, the British government again set out to improve nutrition and fitness of poor children. Over the years, schools have been integrated into pubic health policy by monitoring children's growth, providing checkups and first aid, administering mass inoculations and teaching health education. Immediately after World War II the debate about poor children's continuing bad health was renewed with greater vigour. In Britain the parliament passed the School Milk Act in 1946 while in the US Congress enacted the National School Lunch Act 'as a measure of national security, to safeguard the health and well-being of the Nation's children'.

The mounting concern with children's health in the twentieth century became the progressives' mantra for the baby boom generation. Yet watching them become mesmerized by TV, American commentators began to worry about their children's increasingly sedentary lives. Many observers feared that children's fascination with the screen was turning them into sedentary screenagers. Exercise physiologists measured the declining energy expenditures of the first TV generation, recommending fitness classes in schools to save the nation. Public health goals were integrated into mass education too, bringing vitamins, food groups and regular exercise into the standard curriculum. Media literacy was introduced into the curriculum in the 1970s as an inoculation against mass culture. Yet these interventions seemed to be failing precisely as the child population gained in both affluence and power to shape their own lives. Despite fitness campaigns and health education, research showed that the activity levels of children began to decline across the population. At the same time, nutritionists noted that children's diets included more sugared cereals, energy-dense snacks and fast foods that were advertised on TV. By late twentieth century, anxieties about children's declining health began to re-emerge as a key issue for the public health community as the incidence of overweight increased.

Canaries in the supermarket

A recent Zazou ad provides a cautionary tale for the would-be parent of the consumerist millennium. The ad is set inside the sonically manicured supermarket where shoppers move slowly and quietly, gazing at rows of cans and boxes. Into this scene move a chic but genial French father and mild-mannered son on a seemingly routine post-feminist quest for their groceries. But the familiar surface of food shopping is threatened when the sweet smiling boy looks up to his father to make a request for some 'bonbons'. Half ignoring, half admonishing, the father continues filling the shopping basket. But the boy is not dissuaded. He next grabs a package of sweets from the well-stocked shelves, usurping his father's control over the basket. And now, slowly, the deeper truth of this promotional morality tale is revealed as the embarrassed dad quietly returns the package to the shelf. Judgemental shoppers stop to watch with bemusement and apprehension as the child's tantrum tactics escalate out of control. First he cries, then shouts, then flays the ground with his fists as the father looks at the camera in sheepish exasperation. The final scene climaxes with the child writhing on the floor, screams piercing the muzak-tinged complacency of the supermarket. The cool female voice over intones: 'Use Zazou condoms. Fun, Sexy, Safe', which drives home the message that raising a family has lost its charm in the consumer culture.

The implications of Zazou's ad is lost on no one because it dramatized so well the problem of managing consumer socialization in the risk society. Its dystopian vista is one in which shopping has become tedious, and where children are spoilt, disruptive and demanding. Indeed family life has degenerated into a constant struggle over health and social control. And why? Because advertisers badger vulnerable children into unhealthy eating habits until they pester their parents to exhaustion. I believe this ad articulates perfectly the underlying anxiety about lifestyle risks to children, which like the speck of dust in the pearl, galvanized the discursive politics of globesity. In the risk society, the daily practices of familial consumption are crucial to both environmental sustainability and human well-being. So parents fret about their children's consumer socialization mindful that it is not just pleasure but danger that lurks in the supermarket. In 1997 the WHO gave that anxiety a name – obesity.

Growing evidence of the declining health of children in an age of affluence and scientific progress implied that something was drastically wrong with our consumerist lifestyles. Children's weight gain was a symptom of a deeper cultural malaise. In the world press the globesity epidemic was seized upon as a paradoxical malady which struck the poor in developed countries and the rich in developing ones. By 2004, the front pages of newspapers showed sagging bodies as a constant reminder of the health risks associated with our sedentary lifestyles. Shouldn't children's status as a special class of consumers entitle them to state protection from the 'potential' harm done by food marketing targeted at them, clamoured a growing number of children's advocates.

I became interested in the public hand-wringing over children's obesogenic lifestyles precipitated by the globesity pandemic in both the US and the UK because it seemed to augur a reversal in the progressive project of childhood. Millennial children were seemingly less healthy than the baby boomers that spawned them. With their weight gain, the long march to modernity seems to have gone into a tailspin. As a student of the ongoing debates about children's consumer lifestyles, while on a Fellowship at Birkbeck College, I undertook a project monitoring child globesity in the press. I found that in the ensuing moral panic, fast food had become 'the new tobacco', in which the incidence of overweight among children had become symptomatic of their unhealthy lifestyles. Journalists reported a raft of medical studies which suggested an epidemic rise in children's BMIs which suggested that food marketing was responsible for the declining health of children. Caught between the industry's rights to market to them and the parents' responsibilities for keeping children healthy, the marketing of food on TV confronted British policymakers with a profound challenge to their neoliberal policies. The public controversy provoked by the crisis only abated when the British government banned what became known as HFSS (High Fat, Salt and Sugar) food ads from children's TV day-parts – a policy response at odds with the affluent world's drift towards neoliberalism.

The growing public awareness of lifestyle risks associated with the weight gain in the child populations of the western world is at the heart of this story, which traces what I call the discursive politics of the 'globesity pandemic' in the press between 1997 and 2007 in North America and the UK. I use the word 'pandemic' because the scientific analysis of risk factors associated with population weight gain among millennial children became the 'code red' for the growing realization that children's changing lifestyles have consequences for their health and well-being. And the word 'globesity' to capture the idea that this medical prognosis for their media saturated lifestyles quickly became political. Combined, advocacy science and moral panic became the driving forces behind a new mobilization to protect millennial children in the mediated marketplace.

This analysis of risk communication is undertaken with three objectives in mind. The first goal is to resituate the long-standing academic controversies about the 'vulnerability of children' within Ulrich Beck's sociological speculations about the role of eco-sciences in the risk society. Beck's theory has linked the promise of reflexive modernization to the application of risk analysis to the various problems that have plagued the global expansion of market democracy – particularly environmentalism. This case study sets out to contribute to Beck's insight into the role that ecological advocacy played in the politics of environmentalism by documenting the growing importance of the sciences of *lifestyle risk analysis* within health advocacy and mitigation politics that followed the WHO's championing of globesity. Because all lifestyle risk factors, but especially dietary ones, are matters of consumer choice, risk reduction requires changing the patterns of daily domestic consumption. In the consumer society, I argue, the prospects for human well-being depend on governmental responses to global warming and GMOs to be sure, but also on our ability to communicate about the various forms of consumer risk taking that is undertaken daily in the media-saturated family – from the car they drive to the food they eat. This component of risk taking transacted through consumption – lifestyle risks – augurs an emerging politics of risk communication.

The second goal is to explore the current dynamics governing the communication of lifestyle risks within three crucial institutional domains – in the mass-mediated policymaking process, in the regulation of TV food marketing and in the familial dynamics of consumer socialization. In each of these dominant institutions I find strong evidence of the growing relevance of scientific risk discourses. Medical research provided a new kind of evidence about the risks to children in the mediated marketplace that galvanized the moral panic about overweight children based on a growing parental discomfort with the fast food and sedentary lifestyles of the millennial child. Although this moral panic about 'globesity' was based on a narrow and disputed interpretation of the empirical evidence, it was politically consequential in both the US and the UK. As this case study attempts to show, the public attention given to overweight children simply re-ignited these deeply held anxieties surrounding children's empowerment in the consumer culture renewing one of the most profound challenges to neoliberalism that exists – the vulnerable child consumer.

The third goal therefore is to examine the implications of this new way of thinking about children's consumer empowerment. The moral panic about child obesity brought into the open the uncertain responsibilities for life-style risk reduction in the current matrix of socialization – caught between parents, peers, schools and marketers. With health advocates pointing at fast food marketers and the industry blaming obesity on irresponsible parenting, the state was forced to undertake a lifestyle risk analysis which could evaluate the contribution of each threat. By highlighting the systemic interplay of precautionary discourse, the moral panic about globesity exposed the overlapping responsibilities of schools, parents and marketers for ensuring children's health and well-being. In this sense, I argue, children's special status as 'vulnerable' consumers in the 'risk society' has made them canaries in the coal mines of twenty-first century lifestyle politics. But I also believe that the controversy about children's consumerism raises some important unresolved questions about the competing systems of risk communication in the mediated marketplace. It will take more than the removal of Coke machines from the schools and a ban on food advertising on children's television to ensure that children have sufficient market competences to match their consumer empowerment.

1
Introduction: Growing Up in the Risk Society

A recent McDonald's TV commercial opens with two scenes showing a spoilt young boy engaged in typical domestic mischief. Tired of painting a tree at his easel, he prefers to draw the same picture on his bedroom wall. Bored with art, he then decides to play golf with his father's clubs in the middle of the living room where his strokes endanger the bourgeois neatness. The message embedded in these brief visions of contemporary life are clear: children are bored, out of control and incapable of making appropriate choices. Because they are 'free from responsibility' in the modern world they also need the understanding guidance of a caring parent. And, as if we didn't get this idea, the camera zooms in on the mother's chagrined face. As she anxiously watches his playful antics the male voice-over intones 'Kids don't always make the best choices.' But of course the parable of modern childrearing does not stop here. We then see the no-longer-distressed mother taking her son for something to eat. The last scene shows the mother and son smiling and chatting as they enjoy their 'healthy' meal at McDonald's. The announcer now explains, 'At McDonald's they can't go wrong. They can choose their favourite happy meal food and a drink like milk or juice ... new apple slices with caramel dip.'

The problematic nature of children's free choice has indeed preoccupied, and divided, scholars since Benjamin Spock's best-selling *Baby and Child Care* (1964) established medical expertise as the sine qua non of childrearing. This parenting manual advocated a less repressive approach that abandoned punishment in favour of loving support for children's development as autonomous self-regulating and self-expressive 'individuals'. As the war economy gave way to a rapidly expanding commercial culture, its progressive parenting values were woven into public discourses about managing food, leisure, play and entertainment for the baby boom generation. As sociologists Berger, Berger and Kellner (1974) later suggested, 'these new modern worlds of childhood' could be easily grasped by comparing their fundamental values with those of the pre-war years. The gentle revolution sought to cultivate young individuals who were 'used to being treated as uniquely valuable persons, accustomed to having their opinions respected by all significant persons around them, and generally unaccustomed to harshness, suffering or for that matter, any kind of intense frustration' (1974: 173).

The introduction of television into American households was therefore initially heralded as the next way station on the long march of progressive childhood. Its broad reach into every home prophesied a powerful tool of mass education. Optimism was especially strong among modern educators who imagined that television's 'window unto the world' would provide the post-war generation with universal access to the Western legacy of cultural and scientific knowledge. This idea was soon challenged. When granted freedom to explore and learn the empowered baby boomer did not always choose wisely: parents discovered that children's play time was now spent largely in front of the screen. As Spigel (1998) notes, post-war enthusiasm waned as parents began to wonder whether commercial TV was a magic kingdom or a vast commercialized spectacle cultivating a spoilt, aggressive and uncivilized generation of young couch potatoes?

The hope that TV gave children access to the best and brightest the world had to offer was quickly obliterated by anxieties about the child mesmerized by mindless cartoons punctuated by messages from paying sponsors selling Burp Guns and Barbies. Children have of course been targeted by marketers since the 1920s, but as James McNeal (1964) pointed out, there were three reasons why children were increasingly being integrated into marketing: insofar as they purchased goods, because they can influence their parents' purchasing behaviour, and because they are future consumers-in-the-making. The vast wasteland debate propelled food and toy advertising into the forefront of the struggle over childhood. As marketers targeted children, they also vied with parental aspirations for children's leisure, play and lifestyles. Parents began to see that the invisible hand of marketing was also leaving smudgy fingerprints on the screen: the cereals it promoted were too sweet and the toys were too war-like for many parents. Alarmist academics decried the generational 'crisis' pointing to moral decline, the rise of violence, sedentary children and the fragmentation of family life as evidence of the unravelling of modernity.

A central issue in academic debates about childhood in the post-war years concerns why the public exhibits such a predisposition to anxiety in a period of growing affluence. Some believe it is bound up with the ideology of childhood innocence. Since Rousseau, childhood has been considered a time of vulnerability: swaddled in a naive trust in the goodness of the world, many parents believed that children need to be protected from influences outside the family. Nostalgia for this vision of domestic innocence was compounded by the rapidity of social change induced by mounting affluence. As Jackson and Scott commented: 'Because children are thus constituted as protected species and childhood as a protected state, both become loci of risk anxiety: guarding children entails keeping danger at bay: preserving childhood entails guarding against anything which threatens it' (1999: 86). Parents feel they can protect children by guarding them from the commercialized world – and in the process denying them the prerogatives of consumer choice until they are adults. During the late 1970s the tensions between the ideologies of progressive parenting, democratic media and mass marketing began to focus public attention on children's vulnerability, as Dan Cook remarks, while the 'new forms of electronic media together with the flow and forces of capital converged in the last quarter century fomenting a post-modern childhood inseparable from media use and media surveillance' (Cook 2000: 82).

Direct-to-child marketing emerged as the catalyst of the ensuing policy debate. A small group of market communication scholars began to undertake research on children's consumerism (Ward and Wackman 1972; Gorn and Goldberg 1974; Goldberg et al. 1978; Atkin 1975; Rossiter and Robertson 1974; Robertson and Rossiter 1977) focusing on advertising's impact. Acknowledging a growing body of research that showed that children's preferences and requests are influenced by food marketers, in 1974, the Federal Communication Commission (FCC) limited the amount of advertising to 9.5 minutes and called for separation ('bumpers') of programming and advertising content. In 1978, Action for Children's Television (ACT) called on the FCC for an outright ban on children's advertising, arguing that research showed that the young were developmentally incapable of understanding advertising's intent to sell (Ward et al. 1977). As Martin (1997) notes, the anti-commercialization critics used children's immaturity as the basis of their lobbying effort for if children are unaware of the persuasive intent of advertising, all advertisements aimed at them are, by definition, unfair and/or misleading. The rhetorical battle lines were thus drawn up around children's rights as consumers (Ward 1972, 1974; Wackman et al. 1977; Engle 2004). On one side of this debate were media moguls who proposed that deregulated markets enabled the young to choose their own pleasures (freed from the constraints imposed on them by their parents). On the other side were the protectionist parenting groups who wished to legally buffer vulnerable children from the evils of commercial exploitation.

The American ideology of fair market competition takes precedence in all US commercial and constitutional law. Commercial free speech is constitutionally warranted as long as the information that sellers provide is truthful, not misleading and meets community standards (Federal Trade Commission (FTC) 1978, 1981). But conditions apply to commercial speech, for markets are efficient only when consumers are fully informed about the qualities of products available to them, and when they are capable of making rational decisions based on the costs, benefits and risks associated with their use. Since the assumption of rational informed choice cannot be assumed in all young children, Federal Trade Commissioner Azcuenaga (1997) has argued that it was appropriate for US governments to regulate advertising in the interests of 'ensuring informed choice as the sine qua non of fair markets'. Child protection is in the interest of markets as well as children!

As I have argued in *Out of the Garden* (1993), the anti-commercialization movement's attempt to limit advertisers' growing influence on children was cast aside by Ronald Reagan's deregulation of children's TV advertising. Imbued by a neoliberal conception of a deregulated media marketplace, Congress passed the FTC Improvements Act of 1980, which curtailed the agencies' authority to restrict advertising on television. Shortly thereafter Ronald Reagan appointed a neoconservative to the FTC who further deregulated children's TV in the interests of commercial free speech and children's rights as consumers. Although this policy put a temporary lid on critics' insistence on children's special status as vulnerable consumers, Grossbart and Crosby (1984) presciently warned that such political decisions would not end the controversy about child-targeted marketing: 'Children's advertising is not a dead issue. … The FTC's defeat will do little to alleviate their concern or eliminate the possibility of direct action by concerned parents to mitigate advertising's effects.' As we shall see, how could it be otherwise when children's health was what was at stake (Mello 2010).

Towards a case study of the globesity pandemic

In June 1997, the World Health Organization (WHO) began a health promotion initiative somewhat out of keeping with its usual reports on global malnutrition, violence and viral epidemics. A press conference launched a report titled *Preventing and Managing the Global Epidemic* that reviewed prevalence, consequences and public health policies related to what WHO defined as one of the most easily prevented afflictions in the modern world. Citing mounting evidence that over 50 per cent of adults in the US and Britain were overweight, WHO set out to focus world attention on this emerging health crisis which presaged rising incidence of cardiovascular disease (CVD) and diabetes 2 among the overweight populations of the developing, as well as affluent, world. Like most other scientific shots across the bow of public opinion, the report received little attention from the press otherwise preoccupied with Monica Lewinski and the death of Lady Di.

At the outset of the millennium a second report issued by WHO (2000) proclaimed that obesity was now an epidemic. This august medical body warned that the overconsumption of energy-dense foods coupled with 'sedentary lifestyles' were a greater global health issue than malnutrition: 'At the other end of the malnutrition scale, obesity is one of today's most blatantly visible – yet most neglected – public health problems'. Paradoxically coexisting with undernutrition, excessive weight is found in populations in many parts of the world. 'If immediate action is not taken, millions will suffer from an array of serious health disorders' they concluded. The press responded to this shocking evidence of a mounting public health crisis: nutrition and starvation in Africa and Asia were becoming less important health issues than eating too much of the wrong foods. Soon an expanding chorus of health professionals rallied to the cause proclaiming the obesity epidemic was especially visible in the US and Britain where nearly 65 per cent of the adult population was now considered either overweight or obese.

By 2002 the WHO report (2002) further demonized food as a 'risk factor' in the epidemic rise of BMI, warning that during the last 15 years the incidence and severity of childhood obesity rose from 5 to 15 per cent (and of overweight children to 40 per cent). The WHO report remarked that children's habitual consumption of soft drinks and sweetened snacks is a considerable health risk worldwide. The Western press picked up on these signs of a 'globesity epidemic' pointing to soft drinks and fast food as the new scourge of our consumer culture. Obesity became the science story of the year. The medical community rallied behind the WHO's call for governments to immediately confront the affluent world's sedentary lifestyles and energy-dense diets. Schlosser's *Fast Food Nation* (2001) and later Spurlock's blockbuster documentary *Supersize Me* (2003) gave renewed expression to the growing suspicion of 'big food'. Children's ambiguous legal status as immature consumers gave moral force to the arguments of a coalition of health and parenting advocates who lobbied hard to stop 'big food' industries from promoting unhealthy foods in Britain and the US.

The scientific discussion of health risks associated with excessive weight gain then moved from the back to the front pages as health advocates, ministers and corporate spokespersons debated the causes and cures for obese kids. Citing reports analysing the rising incidence of adiposity and the inadequacy of the TV diet, their calls to action were grounded in the centuries-old legal conception of the child as 'a not-yet competent and highly vulnerable social actor who is at risk' in the mediated marketplace. Proclaiming child obesity a pandemic, journalists increasingly turned their spotlights on children as the key 'at risk population' writing polemics against the irresponsibility of the soft drinks industry and the tyranny of 'fast food' marketing. Moral panic is the term many commentators use to describe the discursive politics of changing youth lifestyles in the press (Thompson 1998; Critcher 2006). But, as I hope to show, in the risk society, panic is not just about generating unnecessary anxiety about a new threat to our well-being but an integral part of the promotional communication dynamics engulfing consumer socialization and lifestyle choices of the young.

The role of science journalism is crucial in the democratic public policy process, not only to ensure the public awareness of the risks but to inform a policymaking process that can prevent and mitigate the hazard (Leiss and Powell 1996; Leiss 2001). I decided therefore, to explore the globesity pandemic as a case study of the discursive politics of what Ulrich Beck (1992) so appropriately called the Risk Society. Although he focused on ecological issues, I was interested in the way the anxieties about children's health, coupled with uncertainty about who is responsible for their risky lifestyle choices, served to reignite the simmering debates about commercial

TV as an environmental health hazard. The case study that I embarked on set out to examine the press, regulatory and familial discourses on 'children's weight gain' on three levels of analysis. Firstly, through a discourse analysis of the press coverage I sought to trace the part played by new forms of risk analysis and health advocacy in setting the media agenda and framing public perceptions of obesity. Secondly, through a review of the policy analysis of food marketing to children I attempt to show the part played by medical researchers in the determination of exposure risks associated with food advertising and its effects on children's weight status. And thirdly, by exploring moral panic's impact on the negotiations about domestic consumption, I set out to explore the ways in which British Columbian families managed to minimize the lifestyle risks associated with children's empowerment within the media-saturated household.

Bad news: Risk analysis, news and evolving environmentalism

During the 1970s TV news increasingly reported on the growing ideological struggle between the discourses produced by corporate capitalism and those of an emerging generation of social critics who vied for public attention within the proscenium of mass media (Gitlin 1987). Then as now, America was at war, and its promised affluence was troubled by economic uncertainty and the growing threat of pollution and resource depletion. Environmentalism – the new political buzzword – was the corrective for the increasingly negative impacts of industrial modes of production on health and the eco-system. Increasingly the environmental movement used the same marketing techniques as the corporate world to get their voice heard. In the emerging ecological rhetoric, the very sustainability of life on our planet hinged on understanding the complex and vulnerable super system that is biological as well as technological, that is economic as well as cultural. Like the phantom at opening night at the opera, the dystopian theology of environmentalism circulating in TV news began to challenge the 'happy consciousness' of consumerism promoted by TV advertising. Environmentalism, perhaps more than Marxism, became the ideological counterpoint to optimistic discourses of corporate advertising.

In the light of the growing strength of the environmental movement Ulrich Beck (1995) proposed a critical sociology of what he called reflexive modernization. His vision for a sustainable form of industrialization rested on the belief that the better scientists understand the unseen forces governing our world, the more we will be able to avoid disturbing them. Risk analysis – a procedure for evaluating policy alternatives based on statistical comparison of probabilities of measurable outcomes – had long been used by actuaries in setting insurance rates, engineers designing fail-safe Moon landers and epidemiologists studying health risks of exposure to pesticides (Talib 2007). In the 1970s, the same statistical techniques that helped economists document the risks to life for insurance purposes and doctors to estimate the cancer risks of smoking were being applied to the assessment of environmental 'hazards' such as acid rain and DDT (Fischhoff et al. 1981). Beck's writings awakened social theory to the important policy debates arising from the scientific management of the socioecological changes brought about by industrialization. But risk perception studies repeatedly documented how the general public differs considerably from scientific and governmental experts in their understanding of the threats they face (Slovic 1992). Personal circumstances and limited information about the causes of those risks or what can be done about them coloured the perceptions of relative risks compared with the sober estimates of risk scientists. In many cases, the public was simply ignorant of the probability of hazardous outcomes that particular risks pose. Citizens also seemed to filter the risk agenda through a culturally biased screen, deploying risk heuristics that underestimate the likelihood of some personal health risks, like smoking and cancer, while exaggerating those that involve catastrophic consequences, such as airplane crashes (Kasperson 1992). People perceived dread risks that are beyond human control as disproportionately troubling, especially where they posed a threat to children (Slovic and Weber 2002). Although mounting environmental controversy does seem to have produced greater public awareness of ecological issues, many commentators remain sceptical about the ability of market democracies to manage them given the difficulty of explaining probabilistic science to the public (Fischhoff 2005).

Although Beck had little faith in these corporate risk experts, he was not a pessimist. He saw the 1990s as the early stages of 'reflexive modernization' because he believed that continuing public disputes fomented by the exposure of previously unacknowledged environmental risks – pesticides, resource depletion, habitat destruction, pollution, waste, genetic modification of seed crops, global warming – were a turning point in modernity. In prophetic films from the *China Syndrome* to *The Day after Tomorrow* filmmakers helped environmentalist pessimism gain a foothold in common parlance. Expanding upon the Frankenstein motif, Hollywood scripted humankind's most brilliant inventions in the role of tools of our destruction. Narratives often unfolded as battles between corporate scientists and their environmentalist opponents. The corporate scientist tries to cover up the underlying truth about their planetary destruction with platitudes and falsifying statistics. In contrast, the visionary environmental scientist, the hero, who sees through the massaged half-truths of industrialization, questions the world's outdated faith in technological progress, corporate arrogance and elites who unwittingly or maliciously deny the truth. The discursive politics of greening became well established in popular culture (Gibbins and Reimer, 1999).

By the 1990s, the media coverage of the mounting conflicts over global wealth, racial tensions, generation gaps, urban degeneration, pollution, habitat destruction and resource depletion had undermined the prospect of infinite expansionism replacing it with the protectionist rhetoric of ecological sustainability. Looking anxiously forward to climate change, every day seemed to reveal a new safety risk, a new disease, a new environmental hazard that threatens our well-being in the global village – as well as life on our planet. Beck assumed that these public controversies precipitated by ecological advocacy provided a positive shift in the way modernity sought to bring the world into control. Insofar as risk analysis provided better estimates of the system-wide ecological consequences of unchecked industrialization, there was hope for human progress. Yet as Frank Furedi (1997) argued, given that the media's coverage of threats was as likely to increase public anxiety as much as raise awareness about hazards, mitigation policy was often grounded in fear rather than risk science.

Advocacy science and risk communication

Public relations (PR) is an ancient communication practice which blends politics and persuasion in strategic social influence. Politicians' daily efforts at 'managing consent' by either getting their story out (or by stopping a hostile one) has made spin doctoring an accepted part of democratic politics during the twentieth century. According to Stuart Ewen (1996), since the 1950s most large corporations endeavoured, through formal or informal lobbying of the press, to promote their corporate self-interest. After Love Canal and the Exxon Valdez disaster, PR departments became essential for getting out the corporation's version of environmental issues (Greenberg 1989). Press secretaries organized pseudo-events and fed (dis)-information, trial balloons, rumour and opinion to journalists while a journalist's daily rounds included looking for whistle-blowers, receiving manila envelopes, engaging in friendly gossip, schmoozing and backroom trading of secrets (Kline 1984). Advocates, from Greenpeace to anti-smoking lobbyists, launched highly effective pro-social media campaigns that attacked corporate irresponsibility – becoming innovators in public relations staging spectacular events to attract the camera. Thanks to films like *Wag the Dog*, the codependency between the boys on the bus and the back-room spin doctors has earned notoriety among media critics and acceptance among journalists.

Adopting the PR approach, throughout the 1980s environmental advocates consolidated their relationships with journalists as they intensified their public communication efforts (Davis 2000; Terkildsen et al. 1998). In a context of whistle-blowing and industrial counterclaims, maintaining their legitimacy within the fray of risk controversy taught many government scientists to become media smart too. Advocacy science is the term that I think best captures the array of PR tactics used by corporate, mandated and public interest groups as they battled over the environment and health. Just as leaks and whistle-blowing have become essential to investigative journalism, so too, public advocacy has become an accepted part of the environmental and public health communication arsenal (Anderson et al. 2005; Hayes et al. 2007). Not only ministers but also governmental scientists got trained in public communication about environment and health. But science advocacy is evidence based. In support of their missions many organizations commissioned and published 'independent' research reports and position papers to support their arguments or expose the limits of their opponents' science. Their most useful scientific facts were carefully distilled in executive summaries that could be easily assimilated by reporters (Woloshin and Schwartz 2002). The film *Thank You for Smoking* provides a fictionalized, but credible, account of the raging battle over news coverage of health risks: backstage of the newsroom, professional communicators vie to improve coverage of their interests.

The politicization of risk advocacy

The success of ecological advocacy was a central tenet of Beck's analysis of the politics of the environmental movement (Beck 1995, 1998). Beck's prognosis for a sustainable eco-democracy (implied in his term 'reflexive modernity') rested on the political influence of scientific advocacy within environmental decision making. Beck argued that because environmental hazards are produced by and benefit specific interests while their risky outcomes are system wide, invisible and hard to measure, environmental management had become extremely controversial. By mobilizing scientific opposition in the public realm the ecology movement, he argued, forced the mandated scientists of the modern state to realize that environmental problems are both commonplace – and extremely difficult to resolve. Increasingly reported in the news, these scientific controversies undermined the beliefs of those who ignored the challenge of establishing a sustainable form of industrialization. Beck therefore welcomed the politicization of 'scientific' risk assessment because he believed that ultimately the risk controversies it provoked would not only inform government decision makers about the unseen and long-term threats the world faces but would foster more sustainable policies.

And history has proved him partially right. The ecological crisis of the 1970s forced governments to include risk-assessment procedures in a more transparent decision-making process. As risk science became a part of the mitigation of ecological disasters, environmental ideology could no longer be kept backstage, guarded by administrators. Instead, as Beck pointed out, environmental politics must be transacted in the limelight of democratic media. Over the years most democratic states passed legislation creating complex regimes of risk assessment and management. Measured empirically by risk analysts, the unseen systemic 'consequences of industrial expansion' were made visible through the multiple political struggles over the environment and health. In some cases governments banned known risks to health and environment entirely (lead in gasoline, PCBs, atomic waste and CFCs). Other risks were managed by identifying the toxin, standard setting and monitoring to ensure the safer production, distribution and disposal of risks (i.e. food safety, pharmaceuticals, pesticides, air travel, CO_2 emission levels, etc.). Other initiatives included product labelling and mandated warnings for both environmental hazards (floods, storms, earthquakes) and legal products (toys, seat belts, alcohol, tobacco warnings, food and prescription drugs).

The discursive politics of risk communication

While agreeing that 'the idea of risk has recently risen to prominence in political debate, and has become the regular coinage of exchange on public policy', the anthropologist Mary Douglas (Douglas 1994: x) held a less optimistic view of the widening gap between the governmental attempts to manage environmental risk and the public's confusion about risks they face in a consumer culture. The chaotic and unpredictable character of the world is not new according to Douglas. Faced with changing weather, failed crops and plagues and pestilence, prior societies feared difficult-to-comprehend threats to their well-being too. Like we do today, they wondered why those risks occurred. Douglas's more sceptical view of the communication dynamics emerging in the risk society today derives from her anthropological study of the politics of witchcraft, plagues and famine in tribal and mediaeval societies. Just as today, these threats were debated in the public forum, not as abstract science but as moral issues that invoked taboos, blame and sanctioning of likely causes. Although risk science can play an important role in convincing the public that a particular hazard is newsworthy, scientific abstractions about tolerable risks mumbled by government bureaucrats may fail to mollify those morally outraged by a little-known threat to human life. The problem with Beck's prognosis then is that it puts too much faith in the politics of eco-science, while forgetting that 'in all places at all times the universe is moralized and politicized' in the context of societal values and market interactions (Douglas 1994: 5).

Beck's hopes for a more rational management of the industrial ecosystem is based on three assumptions about the implications of the politicization of risk analysis which are all suspect when the dynamics of risk communication are taken into account. As William Leiss (2001) points out, risk analysis makes visible some of the little-understood 'eco-systemic' processes; but it rarely suggests what we can do about them. Examining numerous risk controversies, Leiss's work on risk analysis highlights the multiple problems of communicating risk science to the public (Leiss and Chociolko 1994; Leiss and Powell 1996). The discursive politics of risk reduction is always precautionary; based on probabilities and predictive models its findings can never be stated as simple facts or absolute solutions. Communicating 'uncertainty' is hard enough, but in the context of politicized advocacy sciences it has become well-nigh impossible. Perhaps it is not the unwillingness of citizens to accept some risks, he argues, so much as the failure of governments to manage risk communication 'properly and fairly apportioning responsibility' that explains why conflict and controversy shadowed environmental management of industrial risk taking.

The inability of risk analysts to agree on the measurement of 'invisible' interacting forces that make specific practices risky remains a root problem. Leiss's case studies show that it is often not the risk analysis per se but the question of responsibility for risk reduction that leads scientific controversies to degenerate into PR battles over liability for the harm done to environment and public health. As blame is tested with class action lawsuits, public inquiries and risk assessment processes, the legitimacy of the science is shaken amid the stage-managed battles between corporate flaks and environmental advocates who vie in the limelight for the control of media spin. The limited success of risk mitigation therefore may not only be attributed to a governmental reluctance to hold corporations responsible for the unintended by-products of industrialization but also to the difficulties of communicating about scientific controversy in a media democracy. The precautionary principle is a rational criterion suggested by risk analysis. But it is hard to prevent 'harm' to someone when the 'certainty' of predicted outcomes is scientifically contested.

For even if those risk factors are agreed upon by science, disputes remain about how to fairly mitigate them without further destabilizing the socio-ecological system. Risk mitigation is especially controversial because it raises questions of who is to blame for causing those risks. As Leiss explains in *Risk and Responsibility*, risk assessment provoked environmental controversy during the 1970s because 'all of us in the modern society have a direct and vital interest in the proper allocation of responsibility for risky activity'. The democratic state had a clear mandate to manage the risks because as Leiss explains 'we cannot maintain our current system of material well being without engaging in some risk taking' (Leiss and Chociolko 1994: 5). But the public also had to accept the implications of the assignment of responsibility. Sometimes whistle-blowers emerge from the shadows of a bureaucracy to reveal counter-evidence; and sometimes investigative journalists mobilize sympathy for the 'exceptional' victims, but a precautionary policy is almost always contested by the opposing evidence produced by corporate or consumer advocates. Fought out within the proscenium of television, risk communication often degenerates into politicized spectacles staged between corporate and environmental advocates who each brandish their own partisan 'truths' (Leiss 2001).

Tulloch and Lupton (2003) have therefore questioned the implicit faith in risk analysis from a psychological point of view. One can be optimistic about the increasing deployment of risk science, if public controversy raises public awareness of the risks. But using in-depth surveys in Britain and Australia, Tullock and Lupton found that their interviewees exhibit an extremely limited conception of risk science and the role that it plays in public life. Interviewees were vague and confused about relative risk, blurring ecological impacts of development with health risk factors ranging from drinking tap water and driving a car to buying a house and getting married. People did not base their perception of risk on scientific knowledge of the ecosystem, but rather were mobilized by self-interest, anxiety about the future and a growing cynicism about the modern state's ability to manage social change. Their interviewees did recognize the negative consequences of many consumer behaviours but failed to engage in prevention. Many individuals report voluntarily taking risks for pleasure or convenience. They drink and drive, smoke and fail to recycle because risk taking is a habitual practice and, in some cases, an acceptable part of daily experience. Although generally fearful of the environmental consequences of development, many of their deepest concerns arise from the risks they confront in their daily lives – their eating, driving and leisure activities rather than the ones fought over in environmental risk-assessment panels. They also saw zero-tolerance policies enacted by government as infringements on personal freedom.

Lifestyle politics and climate of opinion

Perhaps the most uncertain aspect of risk analysis therefore is its discursive politics. For even if the experts agree on what needs to be done, the democratic state can't always bring about the adjustments in public perception and behaviour that are required – either among politicians, industrialists or citizens – without effective risk communication. No better example of the problems of communicating about environmental risks can be found than in the current controversy over climate change. Like most environmental issues, global warming emerged gradually out of the shadows of arcane risk analysis of glacier chemistry and changing marine biology, which implied that rising temperatures and changing CO_2 levels implicated the human forcing of climate change. And, like most risk analyses, the evidence is complex, equivocal and highly controversial. In a series of high-profile governmental conferences, first in Brazil and then in Kyoto, a group of environmental scientists were able to move climate issues gradually up the environmental policy agenda. To address the issue a group of climate scientists, the International Panel on Climate Change (IPCC), was commissioned to develop better models to predict global weather patterns. Their consensus findings were presented to the press with considerable fanfare despite the fact that some of the findings were speculative.

Although many meteorologists agreed with the IPCC's consensus reports on possible global warming, other equally august climatologists (often supported by oil and automotive industries) argued that the theory of human CO_2 forcing cannot be justified on the evidence. Bush refused to sign the Kyoto accord with an unproven verdict in mind while Al Gore's film toured the world dramatizing the IPCC's probabilistic predictions which became magnified on the wide screen. The film *Day After Tomorrow* expressed the changing public perceptions of climate risks by vividly visualizing the possible consequences of continuing to ignore these predictions. Increasingly the questions asked by the press were not how fast the ice caps were melting but how to get the car makers to make fuel-efficient cars, the oil industry to provide biofuels, recalcitrant governments to set realistic targets and ordinary consumers to use public transit.

The discursive struggle between climate advocates and deniers brought climate issues into daily conversation of the world. The news agenda too gradually shifted from speculation about causes of climate change to who should pay how much to stop it. At my own university, global warming deniers and doomsayers go head to head daily on faculty email lists, questioning everything from the rates of CO_2 absorption to the evidence about the impact of automobiles on temperature. Public cynicism was provoked recently when the backstage of science was revealed by stolen emails leading to accusations of 'forecast fudging' which derailed the international negotiations at Copenhagen 2010. To some degree this is to be expected: there is no single indicator of systemic weather change and no accepted mechanism to explain the changing patterns of storm formation, solar irradiation, CO_2 accumulation or oceanic currents. Yet even if scientists agreed on the mechanisms by which climate change occurs, the problem of stopping global warming is permanently bogged down in the political questions concerning global allocation of responsibility for mitigation and harm reduction.

In this way, environmental controversies convey a political as well as scientific message to citizens: they serve to remind the anxious public that Western governments are poorly equipped to measure or manage the many unintended and long-term consequences of the profoundly intertwined ecological and global economic relations without sweeping lifestyle changes. The automobile, once symbolic of the social mobility and personal freedom of post-war affluence, became a risk factor materially connected to America's congested and polluted cities, global oil imperialism and the threat of global climate change. We encounter these risks whether we own a car or take public transit. Children growing up in a polluted city suffer from asthma, whether their parents drive or not. Yet no one knows how to reverse the deeply entrenched pattern of car culture etched into daily lifestyles. Thus the modern state seems incapable of managing the discursive politics of risk so as to achieve a sustainable industrial ecosystem. And so after the recent meeting in Copenhagen, the world anxiously waits as the developing world's embrace of consumerism promises to be both the engine of economic growth and the end of life on the planet. Only one thing is sure: the scientific uncertainty of risk analysis is now part of the story.

Beck recognized that the affluent marketplace had not only become a complex system for the distribution of the material benefits – goods – but also for 'the bads' – the habitat destruction, social conflict and health problems which have unwittingly accompanied industrialization. When risk analysis reveals that particular 'goods' may also be 'bads', the public clamours for clarification of who is responsible for the danger to the environment – the corporations that made and distributed them or the consumers that bought them. In Beck's view, the democratic state holds ultimate responsibility for ensuring that risk analysis serves the collective good by standard setting, testing and notifying the public of risks – that is by imposing state-mandated risk management on the industrial economy. But if the industrial economy is a system of risk distribution, what Beck has overlooked is that like the distribution of goods, the market bifurcates responsibility for risks into spheres of production and consumption. Risk taking can be assigned to both the producer (of environmental) or consumer (of lifestyle) risks. Take for example the currently stalled attempts to slow the rate of global warming. Clearly responsibility for changing a car-based culture cannot be assigned only to the industries that produce and fuel cars. Are SUV makers more responsible for their CO_2 emissions or SUV drivers? Yet the market policies which regulate the distribution of goods have not fully accounted for the fair 'distribution' of the risks. It is for this reason that most risk controversies result in protracted discursive struggles between corporate and consumer interests in which risk analysis plays a marginal role and the assignment of blame a decisive one.

Smoke and mirrors: Analysing lifestyle risk controversies

In market democracies, lifestyle risks are distributed within the specific context of a consumer marketplace in which corporate power and advocacy spin discursively contest the ideas of responsibility for prevention, mitigation and harm reduction. Clearly some of the responsibility for a hazard accrues to the corporation that makes and distributes a risky good – and some to the individual who buys and uses them. Both responsibilities are subject to market regulation. But domestic consumption, unlike industrial production, is not governed by the laws of corporate liability. Rather, personal risk taking is embedded in the cultural and moral discourses of informed consent. When the risks are declared, consumers are free to engage in risk taking willingly, even though they know their consumption and use can harm the environment (waste disposal) or themselves (alcohol). Since the production and consumption of risks are obviously linked through the institutional arrangements which control the marketplace, all risks implicate the state and its administration of the economy. Yet worried about the economic consequences of market regulation, neoliberal governments have grown increasingly reluctant to regulate the producers of environmental risks without convincing evidence of harm done, putting more responsibility for harm reduction upon the risk-informed choices of consumers.

Anthony Giddens (1998) has therefore called Beck's optimism about reflexive modernization into question, in the light of the everyday domestic context of risk taking in the consumer society. Giddens notes the powerful cultural resistance to 'reflexive modernization' arising from anxiety and confusion that surrounds everyday lifestyle choices in the consumer culture. Social progress depends not only on environmental regulation forged by government but on the lifestyle choices consumers voluntarily make through their long-term use of risky goods and services. Whether it be face creams, extreme skiing or anxiety-reducing drugs, airline holidays or prescription pharmaceuticals, consumers must increasingly engage in a complex risk calculus, weighing up anticipated pleasures with threatened perils associated with their modern way of living. Giddens's argument highlights how risk is interwoven with the everyday problems of identity construction and lifestyle management contemporary individuals face in their status as consumers and citizens. Lifestyle patterns are notoriously difficult to change because they are grounded in routines of consumption that give meaning and identity to everyday life. Consumerism as a way of life and the individual choices of consumers whose right it is in a market democracy to make informed risk decisions also taint the prospects for a sustainable future (Fox 1999).

The hallmark dispute about the responsibility for consumer risk taking is the long controversy about the health risks associated with tobacco. For years tobacco consumption was normalized and widely accepted (except perhaps for Canadian children whose right to smoke was taken away in 1908 on moral grounds). Thanks to the PR savvy of Edward Bernays women in the interwar period understood cigarettes as liberty sticks, symbols of their freedom and suffragette rights. Nations gave young soldiers free cigarettes to help them adjust to the manly expectations of soldiering during World War II. Children appeared in Hollywood movies puffing cigarettes. Billboards proclaimed that 'doctors recommend cigarettes as milder'. It was only when epidemiologists found the first evidence of a relationship between cancer and smoking in 1950 that things began to change. For over half a century since, policymakers have wrestled with the questions of how to manage the health risks associated with tobacco consumption given its legal distribution in the market. By 1954 smokers were in court seeking compensation for health damages. They pointed to the endless advertising campaigns, declaring that the risks had been obscured and not fully disclosed. Although the manufacturers were not found liable, package warnings were mandated. Over the next 20 years, the issue continued to be fought out in the US courts, where smokers' advocates claimed that the responsibility for ill health lay with cigarette makers who failed to fully disclose the risks. Yet even when smokers understand those risks, medical research showed they don't always avoid them. The supreme court judges therefore refused to assign liability to the cigarette makers without compelling scientific proof of deception, in large part because smoking was deemed a voluntary action undertaken with adequate knowledge of the risks – thanks to mandated Surgeon General warnings on packages.

The Surgeon General's report released in 1964 not only confirmed these health concerns existed but issued calls to ban advertising promoting the sale of these 'risky products' to young people. So in 1966 the protracted struggle over the rights of consumers to smoke and the rights of merchandisers to market their brands began to focus on young smokers (Gostin et al. 1997). The legal principle of informed consent in the marketplace is accepted as the basis for liability for lifestyle risks for adults. But uncertainties surrounded youth smoking because it wasn't clear at what age the ability to understand the long-term health risks was achieved. Pressure mounted and governments around the world began restricting sale of tobacco to those under 18 years, deeming youth incapable of appreciating risks fully. The growing evidence of health risks associated with second-hand smoke, further forced governments to recognize that the individual choices of consumers could pose risks for others. The health consequences of parental smoking, for example, emphasized the hazards to both the unborn child and children growing up in a smoking household. Second, because the costs of health care for lifestyle risks are paid for collectively, the increased risks to individuals is experienced as a collective increase in the costs of health care. What this means is that the risky choices of individuals (especially where medical care is heavily state subsidized) can be costly to the state.

The long battle fought over consumer access to tobacco reminds us that the idea of voluntary risk taking is formed within historically patterned cultural, political and legal frameworks. With the issue of informed consent front and centre in the debates about youth smoking, the North American tobacco industry reluctantly accepted a voluntary ban on its TV advertising in the early 1970s. Meanwhile, TV screens were filled with anti-smoking messages that accused the tobacco manufacturers of selling 'addictive' substances to the youth. Tobacco, and the lifestyle risks associated with smoking, established the template for market self-regulation of risky products: 'risk labelling' and 'informed consent' became the twin principles for managing lifestyle risk distribution in the marketplace (Food and Drug Administration (FDA) 2004).

Milking the mad cows: Science advocacy, PR and risk agenda setting

Each lifestyle risk issue is embedded in a unique policy context defined historically around the regulation of that product (tobacco, drugs, poisons, cribs, seat belts etc). William Leiss (1996) therefore championed the case study approach for making sense of the discursive politics of risk controversy. His reading of the press coverage of debates about GMOs, BSE, EMF, Avian Flu demonstrates that attention has shifted from habitat destruction, pollution and species decimation to the threats to health and environment from toxic products distributed legally in the marketplace. The exemplary case of lifestyle risk controversy is the Bovine Spongiform Encephalitis (BSE) 'epidemic'. This new threat spilled onto the front pages when cows exhibited similar behavioural symptoms to a sheep disease called scrapie known from the late 1700s. Sheep with this disease lacked coordination and gradually wasted away. In the mid 1980s, the British Ministry of Agriculture noted considerable numbers of cattle stumbling and falling on their way to the abattoir. When later autopsied, their brains were found to be perforated like a sponge – a symptom recently connected with the presence of folded prions in brain material of scrapie sheep.

This cattle epidemic appeared first as a science story in the back pages of newspapers. John Wilesmith, an epidemiologist at the Central Veterinary Lab, began to suspect that the mechanism of transmission was through cattle feed. As an agricultural scientist, he was aware that for reasons of cost, many feedstocks for cattle included rendered sheep offal and waste, feathers from poultry and cow brain stems. Putting the facts together, he proposed that rendered sheep brains in cattle feed enabled the folded prion to transmit from one species to another. Prions it turns out are not destroyed in the rendering process. Given this means of transmission, might the same factors present risks of transmission to humans who consume meat or milk from exposed cattle, he wondered? He made his speculations public, and now the press was interested.

Worried about the economic consequences of an epidemic in cattle, the ministry of agriculture called Wilesmith's speculation about the link between BSE (a cattle disease) and vCJD (a human disease) a 'groundless fear' stirred up by press sensationalism. Consumers after all did not eat dairy cattle, and the number of vCJD cases in Britain was miniscule. This was scientifically correct and in keeping with the notion of governmental suppression of risks. Responding to the criticism, the minister of Agriculture, John Gummer, even decided to appear eating hamburgers with his four-year-old daughter at an agribusiness event in 1992. This did little, however, to make the public's anxiety about a possible link between the cow disease and human health go away. As the *Guardian* writers chivvied, 'Take a secretive civil service culture, marinade with mendacious politicians and stir in greedy farmers. Stuff with complacency and incompetence, season with buck-passing and cover-ups. You have the recipe for the noxious catastrophe of mad cow disease.'

Food politics and advocacy science

When they involve food, children and dreaded diseases, lifestyle risks are not easily managed by PR stunts. They tend to insult investigative journalists and provoke responsible scientists to whistle-blowing. The 'mad cow epidemic' therefore became the code word for hopeless attempts to mollify public apprehension under the weight of agribusiness lobbying. More importantly, the facts released by the ministry indicated that they had failed to understand or stop the epidemic. The press set out to dig up the truth about this dreaded risk associated with food. While in 1992 there were only 1000 cattle exhibiting scrapie symptoms, by 1996 over 180,000 cases had been identified in Britain. Anxiety about beef, we must remember, was based on the speculation that pathogens could be transmitted through the food chain from scrapie sheep to BSE cows to vCJD humans. As cattle fell ill, the risks of human exposure increased proportionately. The detection of vCJD among children in 1995 further undermined the public's confidence. On 20 March 1996, the Thatcher government reluctantly reversed its position admitting the possibility of a link between BSE in cattle and vCJD. Despite the low incidence of vCJD (perhaps 80 confirmed cases in the UK), it is estimated that up to 8 million cows were 'burned at the steak'. Export bans were imposed, and a special task force launched to get the scientific evidence needed to understand prion transmission. On the pages of the *Guardian* (1998), Rawnsley's journalistic ridicule portrayed the management of BSE as the hallmark disaster of the industrialized food chain:

> First, a freemarket dogma is pursued to a fatal conclusion. In the name of deregulation, farmers seeking to harvest the maximum profit were allowed to buy cheap feed. ... Cows were turned into cannibals and sent for slaughter in abattoirs which were sloppily regulated. ... Then, Ministers and civil servants react to warnings about health risks by ridiculing the scientists who are raising the alarm. When the evidence becomes too compelling for Whitehall to ignore, they respond belatedly and furtively. And when the crisis grows too serious to be concealed any longer, they still carry on misleading the public.
>
> (Rawnsley 1998)

Moral panic is hardly negative communication once the press gets its teeth into the story. If the amount of media coverage is taken as an indicator, then BSE became the most visible epidemic of the century. If anxiety about eating beef is an effective measure of risk perception, then vCJD is now more feared than many more risky behaviours (smoking and driving, for example). Its brain wasting properties are far more dreaded than alcohol poisoning and AIDS, even by children. Moreover, if consumer preference is a measure of the economic effect of risk controversy, then the ministry's fears about moral panic were partially true. Several econometric studies recorded a reduction in beef consumption by 8 per cent over the following 5 years with a relative substitution of poultry and pork in the daily European diet. But perhaps more importantly, by spotlighting the relationship between ecological issues and food products, BSE helped dramatize the growing anxieties underwriting industrial food production generally. In doing so BSE also gave a platform for environmental lobby groups mobilizing around food distribution, nutrition and health issues. The mad cow panic alerted the public to be suspicious of what went on behind the abattoir wall. As the doubts about food safety rose, the belief in an impartial and disinterested risk science was called into question. It also cast a harsh spotlight on 'big food'. Vegetarians and organic foodies gloated about their healthy lifestyles, while the representatives of big agriculture defended their investments by increasing the sale of organic beef.

Marianne Lien (2004) has therefore suggested that mad cow marks a transition in environmentalism. Food – both its production and consumption – became the contested zone of the new environmental movement because it fused the health of humans and environmental devastation into a seamless threat. The BSE epidemic in particular, she argues, exemplified this 'historical watershed' in the risk society because it showed that 'many of our most common food stuffs can no longer be taken for granted' (Lein 2004: 3). As cow carcasses smouldered on the TV screen, eating was revealed as the key link between environmental contamination and human health making epidemiology the advocacy science that could best galvanize environmental awareness. Dramatizing the dread factor, environmental advocates attacked the food establishment for its lack of vigilance in identifying and preventing new threats to our well-being. Pesticides and GMOs not only damage the environment but are clearly linked to the daily health and well-being of consumers. Moreover, the state's mandated scientists required constant vigilance. In this sense the fallout from mad cow anxiety was deeply political. Tony Blair, whose government replaced the Tories in 1997, immediately dismantled the Ministry of Agriculture and launched the Food Standards Agency (FSA) with a clear mandate to conduct policy research in a transparent way as the diet watchdog for the nation. The political scene was set, at least in the UK, for the discovery of a new 'unseen' epidemic associated with the industrial food chain. And it was kids not cows that were manifesting the symptoms.

Outline of the book

The following case study of the discursive politics of lifestyle risks associated with weight gain is reported in three parts, each presenting its own review of the scientific literature and original empirical analysis. In Part I, I report a discourse analysis of obesity stories in Britain's leading quality newspaper the *Guardian*, and the *New York Times*, to explore the dynamic relationship between advocacy science (epidemiology), public perceptions of lifestyle risks and the policy debates that arise as moral panic galvanizes the public sphere.[1] The frame analysis of the risk agenda setting process notes that as health advocates mobilized awareness, their epidemic labelling and risk analysis added a sense of urgency to the news coverage which both reported and accentuated the risk factors and costs associated with population weight gain. But as child obesity became the poster-child of the epidemic, the issue of responsibility provoked opposition from the food and media industries, transforming risk analysis into a risk mitigation controversy. We should not be surprised therefore that children's uncertain status as vulnerable consumers resulted in the blaming of advertising for children's risky food choices. The press also reported on the PR efforts mustered by the food industry to defend their reputations as 'responsible marketers'. Contending in the media, in the courts and backstage in the policymaking process, the blame for children's unhealthy lifestyles gradually exposed deeper questions about the systemic biases in mediated markets, as well as the degree to which food marketing was influencing children's consumption in a negative way.

In the process the risks associated with the modern diet have received considerable press attention. In the throes of panic, the public was reminded that underlying market democracy is the quandary of 'free choice' that enables individuals to make informed decisions about their health and happiness, yet burdens the welfare state with the responsibility for the consequences of their bad ones. This quandary is most clearly expressed in the figure of the child who, as a consumer in training, is neither ready to make informed choices about their healthy consumption nor to take full responsibility for the consequences of their exposure to risks. For this reason children become the canaries in the supermarket triggering anxious reflection on the convergent cultural vectors patterning imbalanced lifestyles. Ultimately, the moral panic galvanized by the obesity epidemic both communicated about lifestyle risks and torqued the public policy debate around TV marketing.

In Part II I examine the application of risk analysis in the governmental panels assigned to evaluate children's vulnerability in the market economy. This involves a review of the vast literature on the promotional TV diet and its impact on children's consumption. In a comparative content analysis of food marketing on UK and North American TV, I provide a novel comparative analysis of the biased system of promotion and its potential to communicate about healthy lifestyles to children. I also review the evidence explaining why, despite the bias of food marketing, advertising has been shown to have limited effects on children's diet. Based on a survey of Canadian children I argue that it is their discretionary power to choose snacks and rewards themselves which best illustrates the double vulnerability of children – to the health risks associated with the TV diet and to the persuasion risks associated with the branded food promotion. Although moral panic galvanized policy reviews of TV advertising in both the US and the UK, the outcome depended on the circumstances of market regulation of risk: in Britain a ban was enacted while in the US self-regulation was urged.

In Part III I review the epidemiological evidence that demonstrates that there are multiple lifestyle risks associated with heavy TV viewing – of which exposure to advertising is one. Although the advertising industry attributed obesity to bad parenting, a study of Canadian children's diet and exercise suggests that consumer socialization is perhaps the most important protective risk factor. Indeed, I found that the majority of children are of normal weight because parents have become extremely mindful of the lifestyle risks associated with the media-saturated household. My research on the parenting strategies employed by a sample of Canadian parents indicates the diverse ways Canadian parents negotiate, restrict and allow children to make lifestyle choices. The moral panic about child obesity not only intensified their anxieties about children's health but alerted many to the dangers associated with excessive TV watching, snacking and sedentary living.

I believe that this triangulated analysis of the discursive interplay between the advocacy health sciences, marketplace regulation and domestic consumption helps explain the circuitry of panic escalation in the risk society. Moral panic is a risk communication dynamic which is politicized by law and ideology, so despite the lively debates in both the UK and US I also seek to explain the different ways these two market democracies meet the cultural challenges of lifestyle risk mitigation. Ultimately this case study is meant to remind both policymakers and parents that commercial TV is a risk factor in children's well-being, which if not worthy of pandemic warnings, is telling us something very important about children's imbalanced lifestyles. I conclude that the precautionary policy for children's health developed in Britain can be justified in the consumer society where neoliberal principles warrant freedom of speech to marketers, but the welfare economy socializes the costs of risky lifestyles to all.

Part I
Bad News: Lifestyle Risk Agenda Setting

'Invent writing and democracy follows', wrote Carlyle thinking about the ways that the press began to play a very special historical role as the 'fourth estate' during the eighteenth century through promoting free speech. The belief in the free press as a bulwark against state secrecy, as the prosecutors of public malfeasance and corruption and as the reliable commentators on world events became foundational in modern political theory. Over the years, journalists cultivated the public's trust, not only by providing a reliable public record of legislative debates and government policy but also by offering an independent account of events impacting public life. Journalists perform their public duty by ensuring a free flow of information, consulting diverse points of view about the events of the day and providing balanced commentary.

Communication theorists agree that media coverage not only reflects reality but constitutes it by informing and framing public awareness and policy debate (Tuchman 1978). In most democracies, the rituals of reading the news, hearing it on the radio, watching it on TV and googling it on the web are important parts of the daily life of citizens. People watch news in order to make informed choices about the things they buy, the things they do and ultimately the kind of world they want to live in. For example, news of the daily traffic jams can lead individuals to alter their route to work. The weather forecasts can assist in planning weekend skiing. Similarly, stories about medical discoveries can influence corporate investment or political decisions about health care. Coverage of air crashes can impact travel plans and lead to changing industry regulation. Statements about interest rates by central bankers can deflate house prices, propel bonds up or change gold prices with important economic ramifications for all. Life in the modern world demands a steady diet of information about topics from economics, science and political affairs to fashion styles and entertainment gossip. Opinion polls show that journalists score higher than politicians and scientists on the credibility scales. They are trusted sources whose surveillance of issues is depended upon by the vast majority of citizens.

The agenda-setting model, developed by McCombs and Shaw (1972) during the 1970s, was intended to explain the consequences of a cumulative relationship between the press 'coverage of events' and political outcomes such as voting or attitude change. This model proposes a directional relationship between cumulative journalistic coverage across media channels and public opinion based on the power of the media to select and emphasize particular issues and perspectives in routine reporting. Their studies showed that the press agenda impacted public awareness and values more than it did specific political opinions and candidate judgements. McCombs and Shaw related cumulative coverage of issues, measured by the frequency, length and placement of a particular theme within a variety of prominent news sources over a period of time, to the political priorities expressed in surveys. 'We judge as important what the media judge as important', they concluded.

The press's claim to independent and unbiased coverage of current affairs hinges on two factors, namely their commitment to journalistic ideals and the competitive market system among news sources. Like scientists, journalists apply professional standards which privilege 'facticity' (Tuchman 1972). Informed sources and cross-validated evidence are the professional badges of journalism. For highly controversial or political issues, a journalist's sense of integrity demands the balancing of opposing viewpoints. Their version of objectivity rests upon a style of evidence-based storytelling that seeks to eschew passions and avoid ideological bullying in favour of providing readers with the information they need to decide for themselves. But even if publishers do not spike controversial and investigative stories, daily news reporting provides only a partial and, some argue, biased view of the world's events and traumas. News organizations must compete for audiences, and the pressures of time and resources makes it hard for all stories to gain adequate coverage (Schudson 1989). Although journalists are sometime cowed by publishers, these professional standards are meant to ensure that events will still be interpreted from differing points of view – and ultimately get the truth out into the public.

Taken together, journalistic ideals and a competitive news marketplace driven by readers are mustered to explain how a *free press system* safeguards democracy and promotes reflexive modernization. Yet studies of news flow find that journalistic gatekeeping and organizational protocols structure the flow of news through the media system. There are limits on time, space and labour imposed by the economics of diffusion. Moreover, the hierarchy of stories and the size of the news hole are generally allocated by assignments editors who follow predetermined priorities called news values. Content analysis has found that front pages stories are more or less the same across news media. Critics explain the similarity in mainstream news coverage as the product of common fundamental news values and working practices of journalists (Tuchman 1978;

Schudson 1989). Conventions of journalistic research and storytelling establish criteria for source selection, visuals and framing of commentary. In journalistic traditions political news, foreign events, human interest, business and sports news have long held pride of place within the front pages of the press. So too, coverage of natural disasters, brutal crime and social unrest have always been part of the media's biased surveillance of the world. The phrase 'if it bleeds it leads' has been invoked by critics of news values arguing that sensationalism biases the public policy debates of market democracy.

Sensationalism and environmental risks

Defenders of the liberal media argued that the rise of environmental issues on the news agenda confirmed the press's watchdog role in democracy. Journalistic coverage of environmental risks helped to break down political complacency and challenged the conservative bias of modern industrial states by revealing the unseen consequences of industrialization, by circulating more scientific information to the public and by challenging the mandated complacency of a neoliberal ideology. Yet those that evaluated the news coverage of successive environmental 'crises' found that environmental stories were often overstated in an attempt to sell newspapers (Altheide 2002). The intensified reporting of disasters and health dramatized tragedy without providing background to the problems that caused it. Thus sensationalistic news values could deflect mitigation efforts while leaving the public ignorant of the systemic forces behind the hazards. Sensationalism distorted the public perceptions of risks while skewing policy discussion.

  Since the Vietnam War, the analysis of news agenda setting has been the preferred method for demonstrating the discursive politics of environmentalism. In 1973, extensive press coverage of the Arab-Israeli war precipitated the first 'energy crisis' and propelled environmentalism into the public eye. According to Kepplinger, who deconstructed the journalists' escalating predictions of doom, this crisis cycle is consequential because it reveals the way sensational journalism contributes to risk misperception. The controversy about energy shortages was in fact stimulated by corporate reports released by oil executives who warned that energy costs would rise as the war played out: what followed was an escalating wave of anxious reporting, followed by mayhem at the pumps. In this case, actual shortages increased not because shipments were halted but because individuals began filling their cars up with gas completely because of their 'fear of shortages'. The threat of declining resources propelled by the line-ups at the pumps drew attention to the oil-dependent economy of the western world, and its multiple social, political and environmental consequences. In this sense the public's risk-avoidant behaviour depleted available stocks of gasoline, which in turn further enflamed the angry perception that the 'energy crisis' was manufactured by the oil companies' risk projections. Not only did the credibility of oil giants plummet in the wake of the energy crisis but environmental awareness resulted in growing purchase of small cars for several years.

The energy shortage foreshadowed the role that news media play not only in distributing risk knowledge but in framing the discursive politics of environmental and health 'crises' (Hayes et al. 2005). Brosius and Kepplinger (1990) have argued for a dynamic model of agenda setting based on the temporal interactions of journalists, the public and the policymakers in framing public values within a contested media agenda. The environmental movement gained legitimacy during the 1980s as pollution, resource depletion and nature contamination conjured the growing spectre of the natural world tortured by out-of-control industrialization. Whether it be natural disasters such as earthquakes and hurricanes, or human-made ones, the rise and fall cadence of 'crisis journalism' drew more attention to the specific issues from geological radon (Sandman et al. 1987) to crime (Sorenson et al. 1998). News stories gain salience within the media's crisis agenda according to their impact and drama – not according to the evidence, interests or solutions that explain the risk. Regular reporting of industrial hazards, natural disasters and criminal negligence resulted in hallmark cases of catastrophic risk stories – Chernobyl disaster, Bhopal gas tragedy, Exxon Valdez oil spill, Three Mile Island accident – all of which seemed to elicit a 'dread risk' angle. Content analyses found that the crisis frame impacts daily coverage of both natural and man-made disasters (Greenberg 1989). Besides giving early impetus to the environmental movement, environmentalism forced newspapers to include 'environmental beat reporters', whose role it was to dig up more environmental news. The agenda therefore shifted to include these new priorities.

Competing in the market for advertising revenues, 'dread risk stories' seem to have their own paradoxical biases. If it bleeds it leads is a lamentable truism that ensures coverage of potentially catastrophic environmental risks. Sensationalism narrows the event horizon to the most telegenic disaster stories while it accentuates the dramatic impact of the risk on humans (Muschert 2007). Content analysis has shown that journalists can both overstate and understate the risks. So disasters and contagion cover the front pages for a week, but then disappear without proper resolve or follow-up because the camera must provide new images of death and destruction. Kline (1984) found that the rise and fall of attention to specific risks was typical of crisis coverage as each new revelation about hazards moved public opinion through alarmist discovery to normalized acceptance. That doesn't mean the risks have diminished, only that the story has lost its journalistic priority. In a competitive market for news, the media's actual coverage fails to dig into the underlying risk science and rarely provides political or historical background that explains the systemic causes or long-term prognosis (Hackett and Zhao 2005).

So while the risk agenda highlights spectacular deaths, devastation and crime, it is often at the expense of explanations of the underlying systemic factors that cause them. Although journalists report celebrity visits to AIDS victims, many important aspects of local environmental politics and labour issues simply do not pass through the commercial gate-keeping process, leaving the public blind to many important systemic stories that don't have dramatic force. Conservative journalists often labelled environmentalists 'doom and gloomers' for their apocalyptic pronouncements about risks and their refusal to recognize the human benefits of industrialization. But it also had another consequence: it made 'setting the risk agenda' a key means by which corporate and advocacy groups could put pressure on policymakers.

Media agenda setting and advocacy politics

In the light of the PR competences among environmental and health organizations, I have argued that a journalist's greatest challenge is to report responsibly on the competing scientific, moral and political discourses surrounding threats to society. Their remit in a risk society is an especially hard one, because behind the coverage of news lies a backstage battle between corporate PR flaks, scientific whistle-blowers, advocacy scientists and well-funded public interest groups vying for control of the risk agenda. Garbed in the mantle of free speech, journalists espouse a commitment to 'truth' that leads them to challenge the powerful forces in our society – both political and corporate – that attempt to gull the helpless public with 'statistical lies'. As storytellers and gatekeepers, journalists must adjudicate competing scientific claims and interests. Their challenge is to explain the facts, opinions and arguments behind the science fairly. But they are dependent on their biased sources to do so. This contradiction underscores the risk agenda setting process.

The sensational coverage of hazards is often blamed on journalists. Obviously journalists do not fabricate disasters, but they do select coverage according to a story's news values and perceived relevance to the public. Since they are writers rather than scientists, journalists are not qualified to provide expert commentary about many aspects of public health. To get the story, journalists must find outside sources – insiders, experts and participants in those controversial industries who can provide background information, fair interpretation or insider perspectives. They rely on these independent sources to provide background, scientific assessment and commentary (McCombs and Ghanem 2001). In this respect, journalists do not 'frame' the story angle on their own but do so through the gatekeeping of expert sources. An 'arms-length' relationship with their science sources persists as a central assumption of journalism, which is increasingly honoured in the breach in a democratic market where press coverage is increasingly managed by PR professionals. To the degree that press relations is acknowledged as one of the legitimate ways various interests shape favourable news coverage, journalists also depend on these sources for insider information that helps them write their story.

But it wasn't just the environmental movement which adjusted to the new risk communication environment. Increasingly, health policy and promotion personnel were urged to make 'risk communication' and public advocacy a priority (Chapman 2001). Recognizing the changes taking place within the promotion of public health, most health organizations have redefined their mission at least in part, as scientific advocacy. Forced to take a stand in public debates, researchers and their professional organizations also became proactive communicators competing to set and respond to the ever-changing risk agenda. As Kozel at al. (2006) note:

> To make an issue more salient, known, or important to a population, health promotion stakeholders must systematically and strategically intervene on the perspectives in all three agenda domains; media, public, and policy. To advance health policy formulation and adoption, the issue must become one of the most important or most unacceptable shared problem in the eyes and hearts of the community to effectively influence the media, public, and policy agendas.
>
> (Kozel et al. 2006: 36)

Public health advocates and charities adopted social marketing tactics too. They targeted journalists with press releases, backgrounders and launched research reports with publicity stunts to win public attention. Released to the press with celebrity appearances at carefully orchestrated press conferences, health promotion became the justification and method of risk communication – especially for epidemics (Berry et al. 2007).

Indeed, it is precisely because scientific controversy is such a powerful force in reflexive modernization that those studying risk communication have begun to pay attention to science advocacy as the backstage of risk agenda setting. Observing the under-reporting of many controversial environmental problems, some progressive news analysts argue that a corporatist bias tames environmental coverage, making journalists into the lapdogs, rather than watchdogs, of capitalism. Which is why some critics argue that in the concentrated hands of the press barons, the public response to environmentalism has often been filtered ideologically through marketplace values.

Discourse analysis of the mad cow epidemic illustrated how the setting of the risk agenda involves an admixture of scientific advocacy and political spin doctoring. A British study comparing the coverage of diverse health issues showed that the scientific calculation of mortality risks and the extent of that disease's coverage in the press, are often at odds (Harabin et al. 2003). The researchers note that in 2002 the media vastly over-reported the risks from eating meat while ignoring more important health stories like obesity, driving accidents and alcoholism that resulted in far more deaths. This distortion was largely due to the fact that a foot and mouth 'epidemic' had brought smouldering carcasses and BSE back into the news. The case of vCJD dramatized the disparity between the risk agenda and risk assessment: the story-to-deaths ratio was 3000 times higher than that of smoking. Although it took the death of .33 people from vCJD to merit a news mention on TV, it took 8571 smoking deaths to get a story onto the media's risk agenda. It was only after the announcement of two celebrity cancer cases that this leading dread risk was returned to the number one disease at 10.1 per cent followed by diabetes/obesity at 5.2 per cent, heart disease at 3.9 per cent, and HIV/AIDS at 2.2 per cent of total health coverage.

Worried that advocacy science unwittingly skews and distorts public understanding of health risks, Kimberly Kline (2006) asks whether the popular media accurately and appropriately represents health challenges that Americans face? Summing up research on health advocacy in the American media, Kline claims that the success for many public health issues 'depends on the advocate's ability to articulate a socially and scientifically credible threat to the general public's health' (Kline 2006: 60). Reviewing the limited research on media coverage of health in popular media, her answer is that media generally provides a very partial and limited view of health issues, including the risks we encounter and the reasons why we encounter them. Unless groups can make viable claims about sociocultural causes of public health problems, the promotional bias of 'popular media is likely to perpetuate social and political power differentials with regard to health related issues' (Kline 2006: 44).

A recent study of health coverage during the 18-month period (January 2007–June 2008) in the US media found that health news constitutes about 3.6 per cent of coverage – three times more than education but much less than crime or natural disasters. Yet health priorities fluctuate dramatically as this modest news hole expands during an unexpected 'epidemic' (BSE, Bird Flu, SARS, Swine Flu). For example, 8.3 per cent of all health news in America was devoted to a single tuberculosis-carrying traveller in this 18-month period. The rise and fall reporting of HIV/AIDS provides a similar object lesson in the importance of the epidemic label for garnering positive media coverage to impact health policy (Treichler et al. 1998). The success of their risk communication can be measured not only by the inclusion of advocacy sources, alarming statistics and favourable reports in the press coverage of its victims, but in the persistence of this health issue over a 30-year period.

In a historical study of the coverage of obesity in US newspapers and TV news from 1985 to 2003, Lawrence (2004) shows that after a decade of very limited coverage, in 1997 there is a marked increase in news about obesity in the US, which peaks in the years 2002 and 2003. Lawrence claims that the reporting of obesity increases after the WHO's 1997 first report. In a follow-up study of newspaper coverage of obesity in the US, Kim and Willis (2007) noted that front-page coverage of obesity increased slowly from 157 stories in 1995 to 225 in 1997, peaking in 2003 at 664 unique stories but falling off to 320 in 2004. A German study of media coverage of diseases during 2004–6 confirmed the rise of obesity in the health agenda. Obesity edged out cancer and alcoholism, falling close behind other epidemics like Avian Flu and HIV in 2004, as seen in Figure PI.1, based on content analysis by Media Tenor (2007).

Number of news stories

Asian bird flu	1442
HIV/AIDS	111
Obesity	79
Cancer	62
Alcoholism	38
Mental diseases	25
Allergies	25
Malnutrition	16
BSE	11
Heart diseases	11
Diabetes	10
Cholera	6
Malaria	5
Alzheimer	5
Influenza	5

Figure PI.1   Coverage of diseases in the German press (2004–6)
Source: Media Tenor.

As a Canadian study of health agenda setting (McMaster University 2008) found, contagious diseases that repeatedly show up in the print media – like HIV and bird flu – are considered by the public as more serious than similar diseases that do not receive the same kind of coverage, such as yellow fever. Studying the active role that official and advocacy medical sources play in setting the health risk agenda, Roy et al. (2007) comment on the 'socially constructed nature of news health messages' about obesity. Adopting a natural history approach they examined the inception and mediation of stories following one scientific study reporting on a successful schools-oriented programme to reduce obesity through education. Their work examines not only the stories but also press releases and contacts with the health experts, researchers and journalists to expose the influence of public relations professionals in the journalists' writing of corporate and science advocacy stories. The authors discovered that advocacy science is ingrained in health research because funding agencies supported the press releases and additional expert sources to help get the story out. Indeed, the press officers from the medical research councils established a positive and novel spin to the story that ensured it was picked up by the wire services because it contributed to 'child-obesity'.

Assessing stories about obesity and activity, Roy et al. (2007) found that journalists also respond to these risk communication efforts: stories were found reporting on 98 unique obesity research reports. Most contained basic risk information, with 30 per cent focusing on incidence data and population health issues (epidemiology), while 25 per cent mentioned the risk factors (causes) associated with obesity. Research on the negative health outcomes associated with obesity was the focus of 20.4 per cent of these stories. Of all stories which framed obesity as a risk, 69.7 per cent conformed to what researchers called a negative orientation. Only 11.7 per cent mentioned successful preventive or reduction measures. They conclude by noting that health advocacy uses PR approaches, which assimilate knowledge of news values into the initiatives of garnering coverage. In this light, these researchers claim that news values like novelty, celebrity, controversy, locality, human interest, community relevance and timeliness factor into the journalists' framing of stories to help spin the globesity epidemic into a leading science story – rising above smoking.

Based on her content analysis of obesity news in the US, Lawrence (2004) notes that in the assignment of blame for increasing child obesity, many stories articulated what she calls the 'junk food frame'. Noting that in 2003 stories about restaurant eating and fast food marketing accounted for one-third of all attributions of blame for child obesity (see Figure PI.2), she concludes that ' this question of whether the body politic bears some responsibility for the shape of individual American bodies' was now driving this public health debate (Lawrence 2003: 57). In this sense the moral panic about child obesity was instrumental in highlighting obesity as a public health, as well as medical issue.

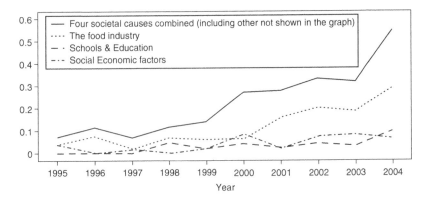

Figure PI.2   Societal causes as mean percentage of news reports in the US
Source: Lawrence 2004.

In their study of US news media reporting of obesity, Kim and Willis (2007) also found that the US food industry was singled out as the dominant societal cause of obesity (mentioned in 15 per cent of stories). The authors suggest three cultural factors might have accounted for this historical trend – the rise of the food politics lead by authors like Schlosser and Nestle; the emergence of health advocacy campaigns launched by public medical bodies like the CDC; and the McDonald's lawsuit story, which mobilized the industry's response. Yet when it came to solving the obesity problem they found that personal solutions like healthy diet, physical activities and medical treatments were mentioned very often, appearing 191 (38.2 per cent), 160 (32.0 per cent) and 153 (30.6 per cent) times, respectively. In the US, socio-economic factors explaining obesity rarely appeared in television news and were mentioned in only three newspaper articles. Yet regulating the food industry and schools' food were mentioned as a public health policy in 18.20 per cent of the total stories.

Panic politics and risk communication

Moral panic is the word that some writers apply to the disproportionate attention given in the press to threats to children's well-being. Thinking about the way mass media accentuated the perception of youth out of control, sociologist Stanley Cohen (1972) observed that news coverage of youth appears to be subject to a phenomenon which he called 'moral panic'. His book *Folk Devils and Moral Panic* offered a critical perspective on the generational divide rending the fabric of post-war Britain and America by arguing that the public's growing concerns about youth culture was the result of moral panic. Comparing the public outcry about the Mods and Rockers to public reactions to natural 'hazards', Cohen coined the term moral panic to highlight the 'sudden and overwhelming fear or anxiety' which seemed to seize the public discourses on youth culture generally. The word panic itself derives from the god Pan who the Greeks imagined unleashed the powers of irrational fear. Cohen felt that these public reactions often amount to a hysterical over-reaction because it crystallized anxiety about 'much of the social change taking place in Britain over the last twenty years' (Cohen 1972: 11). He intended it as a general theory that could be applied to the discursive politics in the media that made 'youth' the ideological centre of struggles over generational change. Cohen's analysis set the study of the media's coverage within a broader dynamic of social control.

Through his detailed study of the media coverage of youth movements, Cohen identified the underlying processes associated with moral panic: 'A condition, episode, person or group of persons emerges to become defined as a threat to societal values and interests; its nature is presented in a stylized and stereotypical fashion …; the moral barricades are manned …; socially accredited experts pronounce their diagnoses and solutions; ways of coping are evolved or (more often) resorted to; the condition then disappears, submerges or deteriorates and becomes more visible' (Cohen 1972: 9). The journalists did not create panic per se, but Cohen believed that media coverage did contribute to what he called *panic amplification*. This is because journalists gave the microphone to a parade of advocates mobilizing around the issues – the health experts, psychologists and sociologists– whose condemnation, prognosis or recommendations further channelled the initial apprehension of 'youth out of control'. Cohen called these advocates 'moral entrepreneurs' and their attempts to use the media to forward their own interests and perspective 'panic exploitation'. Since 'experts' were mostly critical of youth cultures, they framed youth behaviour as deviant labelling it as a symptomatic challenge to the social order. In doing so they morally supercharged the public apprehension of the immanent threat. His theory intentionally drew parallels to witch hunts, inquisitions and public hangings to emphasize how the journalistic coverage of generational change and youth freedom defined the discursive politics of risk. Subsequent studies of youth violence, drugs, lifestyles and even paedophilia have all revealed the same discursive politics as media report the growing anxieties about children's changing lifestyles in the media-saturated family.

Although his case study involved youth culture, Stanley Cohen believed that the same dynamics distorted the public struggles over a wide variety of child and youth 'dangers', from Strontium 90 in milk to asbestos in school walls. Cohen's method was a precursor to the critical discourse analysis which is currently practised in the field of sociology and communication studies (Smith and Best 2007). The term moral panic has gained considerable currency in the accounts of public controversies about risks to children from smoking, drug taking and binge drinking to AIDS and paedophilia (Thompson 1998). Mostly scholars lay emphasis on how protectionist 'moral entrepreneurs' generate distorted rhetorics of 'danger' in the process of demanding more social control of youth freedom (Barker and Petley 1997). Worried about policymakers' reaction to overstated anxieties in the press Critcher (2006) argues that there is a case for seeing moral panics as expressions of a general 'risk consciousness'. Rather than seeing panic as distortions of the facts and distractions in a public policy process, Critcher suggests that the role that media plays in risk controversies is 'the real political purchase of moral panics' (p. 141). For him, the issue is not whether moral panic exists, or how much the anxiety exaggerates the issue, but how useful is it in elucidating the underlying *discursive politics* of our mediated marketplace.

Building on recent developments in discourse analysis of news, Critcher therefore blends Cohen's five-stage description of panic with an agenda-setting model which notes, journalism acts both as 'constitutive and constituent part' of the problem definition and solution process (p. 131). His method implies reading the discursive politics of threats to children in their social context by undertaking independent historical analysis of the agenda-setting process. Rather than a set of linear stages, he characterizes panics as 'circular and amplifying' resulting from the 'continuous interaction between the media, moral entrepreneurs and the control culture' (p. 13). The common elements unifying moral panic and risk controversy, he argues, reveal specific discursive motifs that drive the public policy agenda of risk mitigation:

- child and youth victims identified as 'at risk';
- source of threat to them is identified either in terms of a societal, environmental, physical or psychological causes;
- blame for the threat to moral order is identified;
- pressure groups form and advocacy and spin politics emerge amid rising controversy;
- remedy is called for, regulation or other forms of sanctioning to reduce risks;
- state action achieves some kind of political resolution or containment of the risk.

Critcher suggests this general model of moral panic can be used an ideal type for case studies of risk communication in the public sphere. My own work obviously adopts the same approach to moral panic as a subset of the discursive politics of the risk society. In the following three chapters I provide an historical account of the moral panic about the risks associated with adiposity by examining the obesity pandemic in the quality media in the US and the UK. The study sets out to provide an account not only of the journalistic coverage of this public health issue in the leading British and

US quality newspapers – the *Guardian* and the *New York Times* – during the ten-year period after the WHO's first report in 1997 but also to unravel the discursive struggle between journalism, science advocacy and policymaking within the patterns of risk agenda setting. I undertake both a quantitative and qualitative assessment of these newspapers' communication about lifestyle risks to explain why the news sensationalized children's obesity – and prioritized its mitigation through regulations of fast food and snack advertising. The quantitative analysis is based on Lexis/Nexis searches plotted by year, revealing the number of stories that featured various key words indicating the articulation of scientific evidence, analysis and arguments about lifestyle risks associated with adiposity.

Figure PI.3 summarizes the cumulative press coverage of 'obesity' in the two newspapers during the ten years following WHO's first report in 1997. A threefold increase in stories is evident between 2000 and 2004, when at the height of the controversy both newspapers averaged over a story a day. Not only does this figure reveal the impressive coverage dedicated to this emerging 'lifestyle risk' but also the way medical professionals established their legitimacy in speaking about lifestyle risk taking associated with consumer culture. But my critique seeks to go beyond the questioning of discursive rhetorics of science to the 'political structures, purposes and strategies' that dynamize risk communication. (Philo 2007: 119). As Philo states, to study the political dynamics of the public sphere demands an account of the 'social and political system and conflicting interests within it' – that is the context of the text. My intent in undertaking this frame analysis of this coverage is to reveal the risk communication dynamics, which underwrote the journalistic attention to epidemiological sciences which have made young consumers the poster-child of our 'obesogenic' environment.

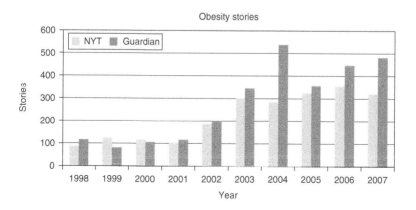

Figure PI.3   News coverage of obesity in the *Guardian* and the *New York Times*

Recognizing that journalists alone are not responsible for setting the risk agenda, in Chapter 2 I go on to show how advocacy scientists and research reports contributed to the framing of obesity as an epidemic. In the process, obesity (a medical term associated with Body Mass Index) was discursively transformed into a population health pandemic focused on the risk factors associated with children's lifestyles. But I note that the WHO's epidemic labelling of child adiposity, however inaccurate, was an excellent risk communication strategy because it helped move 'obesity' up the risk agenda. Medical researchers employed epidemiological risk analysis to identify the promotion of unhealthy food and sedentary lifestyles as risk factors in the obesogenic family. The data suggests that 2004 marks the nadir of the obesity pandemic because press attention gradually shifted from general weight gain and the costs of treating it to the question of blame for overweight children.

Chapter 3 therefore notes that as the press focused attention on millennial children, coalitions of interest formed to contest who was responsible for children's unhealthy diet – marketers or parents. This chapter traces the intensifying moral panic into the policy debates about how to reduce the lifestyle risks associated with children's weight gain by regulating food advertising in both the US and the UK. In both countries anxieties about children's health, compounded by concerns about their vulnerability to marketing persuasion, intensified the sense of urgency. But the struggle over the marketers' role in lifestyle risk communication was waged in the courts in the US and in parliamentary committees in Britain. Through a frame analysis of the coverage of these policy debates I show how the arguments about lifestyle risks contributed significantly to a ban on food advertising in the UK while in the US it resulted only in frustrated calls for the food industry's self-regulation.

Based on this news analysis, I set out to show that the public debates about the obesity epidemic were politicized by two important news agenda setting dynamics: the first was the formation of risk advocacy coalitions around the anxieties about children's health, which contested the blame for children's weight gain; the second was the way children's special status as vulnerable food consumers emerged as the key issue in the discursive politics engendered by their obesogenic lifestyles.

2
Framing the Body Politic: Advocacy Science and Setting the Risk Agenda

Epidemics are defined by the rapid spread of disease through a population. Since John Snow first traced London's typhoid outbreaks of the 1840s to the Broad Street pump, stopping epidemics has been one major achievement of medical sciences. In one of the most notable wins for public health, Snow convinced the Board of Guardians of St. James Parish to remove the typhoid-transmitting pump handle at the local well. The rates of typhoid infection declined rapidly slowing the spread of disease became the basis of much public health policy. Epidemics could be prevented, scientists discovered, as long as the cause of the outbreak could be identified, and the population inoculated against the pathogen. Epidemiology launched the public health movement, and its unique way of improving health, not only through individual treatments but through environmental intervention. Public water, agriculture, nutrition, sanitation, air quality and toxic materials were now all health issues. Over the years medical researchers have become highly accomplished in discovering how viral, bacterial or toxic materials are being communicated through our environment. As with smallpox, diphtheria, flu and polio, epidemiologists have saved millions of lives. They have also made epidemic into the code red word that signals escalating and out-of-control health risks.

Epidemiology and lifestyle risks

The physiological mechanisms and chemical processes associated with weight gain are fairly well described by medical science. Depending on metabolism, normal body weight is maintained when energy intake and expenditure are roughly equivalent over time. Energy intake can be measured in kilocalories, which is a knowable property of foods. Energy expenditure is measured using the same energy units burnt in different kinds of activities. When energy intake exceeds energy expended in daily activities, it will be stored in fat tissue for later use. This mechanism is a biological safeguard against periods of food scarcity. Put simply, individuals gain weight (stored energy) when their energy intake is greater than their energy expenditure.

What researchers look for in risk analysis is a measure that provides diagnostic leverage in population studies of weight gain. In the US, the rising incidence of adiposity (a word that medical professionals use to talk discreetly about people who become excessively fat) has been known for many years. The Body Mass Index (BMI) involves a simple calculation based on the ratio of weight-to-height (mass in kilograms over height in metres squared). Over the last 40 years there has been an 18 per cent decline in the percentage of the adult population that was of healthy body weight. Moreover, after 20 years (1960–80) of relative stability at 13 per cent of men and 17 per cent of women, the percentage of adults who were classified as obese (30 + BMI) began increasing in the 1980s to 21 per cent of men and 27 per cent of women by 1991, and to 28 per cent and 34 per cent by the millennium (NHANES I, II, III).

In 1995 the WHO re-invigorated the epidemiological study of weight gain by adopting BMI as the standard diagnostic measure which could be used to assess adiposity around the world. Because risk factors require a yardstick for comparing rates of weight gain among people of different stature, BMI was a crucial innovation in the assessment of overweight as a health risk. Defining overweight as a BMI greater that 25, and obesity as BMI over 30, the WHO proclaimed the medical establishments' growing interest in diagnosing and treating 'weight gain'. In America, researchers applied these new standards to the NHANES studies and found shockingly visible evidence of caloric imbalance. Using these new classifications, 1 in 3 US adults can now be classified as obese and a similar portion overweight (Flegal et al. 2001). The increases in the BMI were dramatized by the American Obesity Association and the CDC on their websites which provided the public with up to date evidence of the changing weight status of the population (see Figure 2.1).

Once standardized, BMI provided a universal tool for risk assessment because it enabled scientists to easily estimate, graph and compare the incidence of adiposity in different populations. Most developed countries have also been mapping height and weight for years providing an historical record which shows that not only are successive generations getting taller but heavier as well. Reported in the press, the publication of these population health studies shocked the British into recognizing that their bodies were changing too (Bundred et al. 2001; Chinn and Rona 2001).

The relationship between journalists and their scientific sources is the crux of my critical analysis of risk agenda setting. My study found that health researchers were a major source of risk analysis in the public policy debates about weight gain: there is a three-fold increase in the mention of research in the news coverage of the obesity epidemic, peaking in the UK in 2004

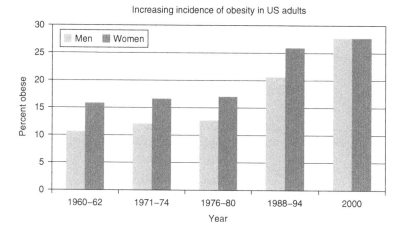

Figure 2.1 Increasing percentage of the US population that is obese according to BMI standardization
Source: Flegal 2001.

and the US in 2005. This discussion of the changes taking place in body morphology began raising alarm bells beyond scientific circles through their repeated mention in the press. The citation of BMI research in particular is charted in Figure 2.2. Journalists obviously found the statistical evidence of weight gain convincing and important enough to include in their stories. BMI increases confirmed that the crisis was getting progressively worse but implicitly also established the legitimacy of a medical lexicon of pathological weight gain in talking about changing lifestyles.

A close reading of the stories about 'obesity' indicated that the growing medical apprehension of weight gain was rarely challenged and disconfirming opinion or scientific analysis rarely reported in the press. For example, the NHANES 1 data used cut-offs that were higher than the WHO's 25 and 30 meaning that the percentage considered at risk was historically overblown. Moreover human body shapes have been naturally changing as nutrition and migration have influenced the physical stature of populations. Additionally, our bodies change through the life course as muscle density and body morphology changes with maturation. Overweight people, especially those who live active lifestyles, are healthy because muscle tissue is 'heavier than fat'. Athletes often find themselves classified as overweight although studies show that they are far less at risk. But these concerns were rarely acknowledged in press stories that focused disproportionately on the health risks associated with children's widening girth at the expense of a population based account of the way class, gender and

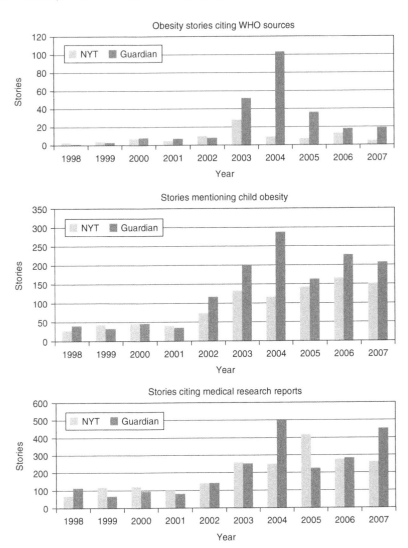

Figure 2.2 Science advocacy and medicalization of weight gain

ethnicity were also determinants of weight gain. But the appropriateness of the term obese to describe abnormal body shapes often got reduced in the reporting to simple discussions of the causes, costs and cures for weight gain in ways that dramatized and focalized on the extremes – the abnormal individuals.

From risk to risk factor

Despite its limitations, because height and weight data can be gathered easily, the BMI > 30 is the risk factor preferred by most medical researchers when comparing the health status of those diagnosed as obese from those considered normal. Because it was accepted by the WHO, there was a growing body of science that used BMI diagnostics to study the relationship between health status and adiposity. Accumulated over the years, medical research indicated that having a BMI > 30 (obese) was associated with a number of health conditions including cardiovascular diseases, diabetes, hypertension, high cholesterol, cancer, stroke, sleep apnea and respiratory problems, pain, gall stones, gout and heart attack. Research into obesity as a 'risk factor' composed an increasing percentage of the health news.

The common statistic used in these clinical risk assessments is an odds ratio (OR), which compares the incidence of a health status indicator in populations with different BMIs. For example, Figure 2.3 (American Obesity Association/NHANES III) shows that 10.10 per cent of obese males have diabetes 2 whereas 2.03 of normal weight males are diagnosed with diabetes 2. This suggests that obese males are over four times as likely to get the disease as normal bodied individuals (OR = 4). Yet it is important to notice that diabetes is not that pervasive in either group – compared, for example, with high blood pressure which 23 per cent of normal individuals have. Almost half of obese males have high blood pressure, even though it is only twice as

	Health indicator	Normal	Overweight	Obese
Male	Diabetes 2	2.03	4.93	10.10
	Heart disease	8.84	9.60	16.01
	Blood pressure	23.47	34.16	48.95
	Osteoarthritis	2.59	4.55	4.66
Female	Diabetes 2	2.38	7.12	7.24
	Heart disease	6.87	11.13	12.56
	Blood pressure	23.26	38.77	47.95
	Osteoarthritis	5.22	8.51	9.94

Recent increases in US overweight and obesity in teens		
Year	2005	2007
Obese	13.1	14.6
Overweight	15.7	16.6

Figure 2.3 Risk factors related to weight status: Comparing normal, overweight and obese US adults

prevalent in obese populations. The significance of any risk factor depends on both the prevalence of the health condition as well as the size of the OR. Yet the prevalence of the disease and the risks associated with it are often confused in their citation in the press.

Another issue skewing the reporting of risk analysis is the competition for research funding within the health sciences. It must be remembered that journalists do not report on every scientific study that is released to news agencies. It is also wise to remember that the health sector is characterized by scientific communities who compete for research funding and public legitimacy. Competition and controversy are inherent to the inner discourses of risk science. Figure 2.4 shows the reporting of the health consequences most frequently associated with the obesity epidemic.

By tracing the relative reporting of risk factors research we can see that risk agenda setting results from successful risk communication as much as accurate reporting of assessed risk. The term epidemic therefore obscured the profound differences within the health community organized around competing 'risk factors' and their appropriate treatment. Although this idea is controversial, one example serves to make the point. Evidence showed growing press interest in diabetes in the UK after 2002 and in the US more recently when a single study in 2006 provoked 400 stories about the link between obesity and diabetes 2.

Although Cardio Vascular Disease (CVD) is a far more common affliction in adult populations in the UK and US, its relationship to excessive weight gain is rarely mentioned in stories about the epidemic. Diabetes's mounting coverage provides some indication of the research investment in that subfield as well as their PR acumen in setting the risk agenda. Even though far more obese adults suffer from CVD, the OR associated with diabetes 2 is highest among the younger population. Moreover, when it comes to questions of treatments, medical interests argue with each other over their approach and results: some recommending surgery, others drugs and some others diet.

The limits of epidemiological risk analysis

BMI provided the gold standard for health advocates' press releases. Yet medical researchers have long known why diagnostic categories 'overweight' and 'obese' based on normalized height-to-weight ratios may not be the most useful indicator of health risks to adults, let alone children. But in the scientific community the uncertainties surrounding using BMI, which had long circulated, were illustrated by a finding from the Interheart study (Yusuf et al. 2004; Rosengren et al. 2004) which undertook an extensive case-controlled examination of Acute Myocardial Infarction (AMI) in 50 countries around the world. AMI, or heart attack, is rated as the number one killer of men and women around the world, so this study provides an important test case for BMI as a risk factor. The statistical analysis compared the OR for 12,461 first MI attacks with that of a matched control sample of 9459 individuals

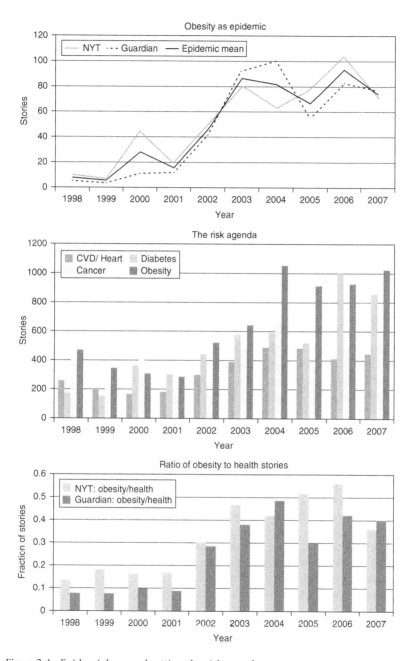

Figure 2.4 Epidemiology and setting the risk agenda

on 9 known risk factors including obesity measured in two ways – by BMI and waist-to-hip size ratio. The results were fairly indicative concerning the factors contributing to heart disease: the two top risk factors were cholesterol levels (lipoprotein ratio OR=3.25) (50 per cent) and smoking (OR=2.87) (36 per cent) which together accounted for 66.4 per cent of AMIs world-wide. Psychosocial stress, diabetes and hypertension were also significant independent predictors of heart attacks adding to the predictive model independently. Daily consumption of fruits and vegetables, moderate exercise and moderate alcohol consumption were all found in the Yusuf study to be protective factors, meaning they counteracted other risk factors.

Obesity was found to be an independent risk factor with an adjusted OR of 1.62 which means it was a moderate predictor of heart attack in the model. But when compared through subsequent regression analysis, abdominal obesity measured by waist-to-hip ratio proved superior to the standard BMI measure in accounting for heart attacks. The study found that body shape measured by hip-to-waist ratio is a far better predictor of the health outcomes associated with energy imbalance. The authors of this study conclude that the apple-shaped body rather than the height-to-weight ratio of BMI provides the superior estimate of risks because subjects with a muscular body type can be heavier than the norms for their height. Since muscle tissue is denser than fat, the active rugby or football player may find themselves statistically overweight but at no additional risk because of body morphology. Other studies of overweight individuals who exercise regularly show few of the health consequences associated with sedentary individuals of similar body mass suggesting that it is less the adiposity than the factors impacting the distribution of weight that contributes to disease.

Of course the medical professionals are aware of the problematic nature of the gross statistical abstractions necessary for population health studies of changing weight status. Epidemiologists caution their report readers to understand that BMI is only a rough measure of risk given variations in body morphology, levels of fitness (muscle mass is greater than fat mass) and especially for children who go through growth spurts where their bodies change dramatically. Stating the limits of research is standard practice in scientific circles and can be found on public health websites. Journalists faithfully reported the health risks associated with obesity, now citing the medical terminology and statistical evidence that legitimized the health advocates' concerns about excessive weight gain. Yet they dropped the researchers' statistical provisos (as too complex) and ignored the scientific disputes that exist in all fields preferring to emphasize the overall trends in BMI rather than the nuance of interpreting risk probabilities.

The Yusuf study cautioned epidemiologists not to rely on the 'BMI classifications' for projecting the risks and costs associated with this epidemic. Firstly because adult BMI is perhaps not the best way to estimate the health outcomes and morbidity associated with obesity. Secondly, obesity itself proves only a modest predictor of AMI in adults whereas other factors – especially high cholesterol levels and smoking – provide far better indications of impending heart attack. And thirdly, as this study indicates, there are many interacting variables, which in combination explain why excessive weight contributes to illness and death. This study provided a cautionary tale, against predictions of a looming health crisis based upon the rapid increase in BMI as a 'risk factor' – but one which was largely ignored by journalists. Its finding did little to bracket the gathering storm of public attention given to overweight children.

Epidemic obesity: Setting the risk agenda

It would appear that by labelling obesity as a global health 'epidemic' the WHO successfully baited the hook for a bad news story. In view of the impending health crisis, journalists now called weight gain an epidemic. Using a comparative analysis of the stories that mention 'epidemic' in tandem with obesity there is a clear rise with each major WHO report – in 1997, 2000, and especially in 2002 when obesity was named 'the leading science story of 2002' by the American Association for the Advancement of Science. Journalists, especially in the *NYT*, accepted the term epidemic as a viable index of this looming health crisis: The term is used in one in four stories after 2000. As noted earlier, the epidemic label gives priority by making a malady into a dread risk. Discourse analysis of these stories revealed that the language of flab and puppy fat is gradually dropped in favour of the medical terms 'overweight' and 'obese'. By branding changing body morphology an epidemic, the public health authorities were able to get the epidemiological perspective on weight gain out despite the absence of a pathogen and rather modest rates of contagion measured in years, not weeks.

Graphics illustrating weight gain in the US population were prepared by the Center for Disease Control (CDC) and issued in press packages which were used by journalists as supporting evidence of an impending public health crisis. We generally think of epidemics as sudden 'outbreaks' in which pathogens are transmitted rapidly through populations. Did this rise in BMI really constitute an epidemic? A careful review of the BMI statistics they provide however reveals that the incidence of overweight has increased relatively slowly over the last 40 years with obesity rising in the adult population only during the last decade before the millennium. Between 2000 and 2004 the percentage of American women who were obese actually remained constant at 33 per cent while the incidence in men rose 3.6 per cent to 31.1 per cent of the male population (CDC 2004). Similarly, evidence in Canada shows a relatively stable picture, with only the young adult age group (18–35) showing any significant increase in BMI recently. Rather than the typical outbreak pattern of SARS or swine flu, obesity's contagion is actually characterized by a slow and steady transmission through populations – more like a seepage than a pandemic (Hopman et al. 2007). Not only has the spread through the population slowed but also the trends suggest that weight gain is greatest among the already overweight who become obese or hyper-obese (BMI > 40). Although this is worrisome, it is not evidence of contagion.

Escalating costs of treating obesity

Once health risks are established clinically, health policy analysts can use them to calculate the costs associated with increases in obesity and over-weight. There are many ways of costing the health problems associated with an increasingly obese population (Zaninotto et al. 2006). One of the most obvious is by tallying the amount that is already spent on treating it. In February 2001 the UK's National Audit Office was among the first to publish estimates of the costs of obesity based on their increased hospital visits and incidence of CVD. These projections were seized on by *Guardian* journalists as evidence of a future threat to the British health care. In America, similar projection were reported. Finklestein et al. (2003), for example, used the 1998 Medical Expenditure Panel Survey to provide similar estimates of the rising costs of obesity in the US. They found that by 1998, obesity accounted for approximately 78.5 billion dollars or about 9.1 per cent of the total annual US medical expenditure. This marked an increase in medical costs of 3.7 per cent for overweight individuals and a 5.3 per cent increase in average expenses for obese adults. This study also drew considerable press attention because it implied that public health resources would soon be stretched. But the authors note that projections based on average expen-ditures are somewhat misleading, as the elderly obese – a relatively small demographic – account for 25 per cent of all health care expenditures.

Unfortunately, the interpretation of risk cost analysis projections requires statistical expertise that journalists rarely possess when reporting on these cost models. For example, considering only cases diagnosed morbidly obese (BMI > 35), Milliman (Fitch et al. 2004) published a study which found that their health care claims are as much as three times higher. Given ris-ing hospital admission rates of the morbidly obese, the press seized on this story by noting that the cost of replacing the standard toilets in hospitals, whose 300 pound rating is now considered inadequate, could be as much as 3 billion dollars. Another story that received press attention was the costs encountered for ambulance equipment that can bring morbidly obese patients to the hospital for treatment (Monheit et al. 2006). The projections of the cost of obesity were published widely, sometimes accompanied by dramatic graphics or pictures of overweight individuals. Yet the prevalence statistics for morbid obesity were never mentioned.

Despite the usual scientific precautions, public health advocates contin-ued to issue dire warnings about the future costs of health care associated with children's obesity. They conjured what would happen when these kids grow up. But this advocacy strategy proved counterproductive when a study reported by the CDC in March 2004 used rising BMI prevalence data to estimate the deaths associated with the obesity epidemic. In it the CDC claimed that deaths due to obesity were up 33 per cent from 1990, and predicted things getting worse due to accelerating child obesity rates projected forward. They warned that the number of premature deaths in the US due to obesity would reach 400,000, a mortality rate comparable to those associated with tobacco. Journalists published these predictions with bold headlines, although this study was clearly part of the CDC's efforts to beat the drum about child obesity (Snider 2004). Industry scientists criticized these predictions, pointing out problems with the methodology and forcing the CDC to modify their mortality rates and lower their estimates of the future expenditure associated with child obesity dramatically.

In keeping with the bad news angle, most journalists reported on the rising costs of various treatments and cures for obesity. Figure 2.5 shows that the costs of obesity are mentioned throughout the 10-year study. Yet discussion of the treatments differs. In the US, surgery has been used frequently to treat obesity with hospital costs climbing to $25,000 per operation

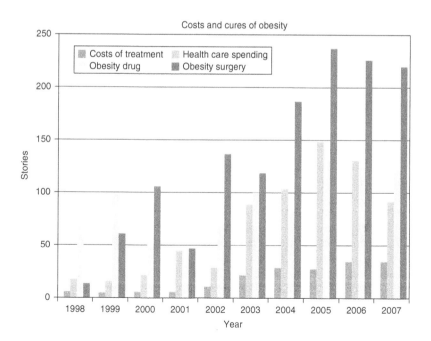

Figure 2.5 Reporting on medical cures and health care spending

(Fitch et al. 2004). Perhaps it is with good reason then that the *NYT* wrote often about individual medical treatments such as obesity drugs and bariatric surgery. Given its public health tradition, in the UK these drug and surgery solutions received very little press coverage, while the reporting of mounting costs to the public health system constituted a permanent threat, given evidence of increases in BMI in the youngest citizens (Jolliffe 2004).

Children at risk

The WHO's leadership in setting the 'health risk agenda' is not only evidenced by journalists' acceptance of overweight as a costly epidemic but in the frequency with which this organization is cited as an expert source on weight-related issues (see Figure 2.6). Receiving extensive coverage in both countries, the year 2002 seems to be the tipping point in the moral panic about overweight. In 2002 the WHO published a series of studies which highlighted the risks associated with children's excessive consumption of soft drinks (Chopra et al. 2002; Bellisle and Rolland-Cachera 2001). Citing evidence that children who watched four or more hours of television a day had significantly higher BMIs, the medical community had become more confirmed in its view that although the science was equivocal, 'the heavy marketing of these food and beverages to young children causes obesity ... there is sufficient indirect evidence to warrant this practice being placed in the "probably" category and thus becoming a potential target for interventions' (FAO/WHO 2002: 67). The WHO obviously played to a well-known news frame. A cascade of reports were launched after 2002, all with carefully managed press conferences, demanding that something urgent needs to be done about children's nutrition before it is too late. Journalists cited the statistics the health authorities fed them, but it was rarely acknowledged that both the rate of increase and incidence of child obesity were lower than that of adults. Today, one in three adults is obese, when only one in 12 children are.

Epidemic child obesity was a phrase that came to dominate the discussion of children's health in the press. The words child and epidemic were constantly paired. In story after story the rising incidence of overweight among the young was emphasized; yet the labelling of child obesity an epidemic seemed scientifically at odds with the fact that overweight only rose from 4 per cent to 9 per cent in the under-11 population over the last 40 years in the US. In the UK too, longitudinal studies were cited indicating that overweight was out of control in the young. Yet it only increased modestly in the under-10 age group for boys, rising from 9.6 per cent in 1995 to 14.9 per cent in 2003, and for girls from 10.3 per cent to 12.5 per cent. Moreover, the rates for pre-teens were also stabilizing: data for 2005–6 are broadly similar to 2004–5 (21.5 per cent overweight), including 9.0 per cent obese and 4.3 per cent severely obese. This shows little change from 2003–4 (21.8 per cent, 9.0 per cent, 4.6 per cent

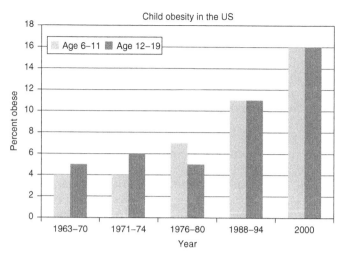

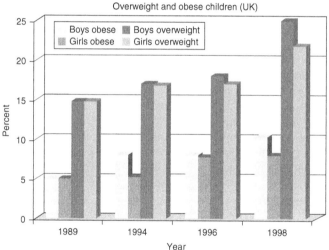

Figure 2.6 Increasing child obesity in the UK (1989–98) and US
Source: Bundred 2001 (UK) and CDC (US).

respectively). Change is however noted in a large sample of American teens; between 2005 and 2007 there was 1.5 per cent increase in the incidence of obese adolescents and a 0.9 per cent increase in those classified as overweight. Trends in youth populations seem to have slowed and the fact remains that whereas 31.2 per cent of American teens are outside the range of normal weight, more than 67 per cent of adults are classified as obese or overweight.

Moral panic framing therefore meant that the health risks to younger children were often overstated in the press, which voiced an oft-repeated refrain that obesity was rising fastest among paediatric populations without the usual scientific qualifications. An occasional journalist cautioned that 'Concern about childhood obesity is shading into hysteria, fomented by well-meaning government committees such as the one that claimed last week that today's children may live shorter lives than their parents' (*Globe and Mail* 2007).

Despite the provisos, as Figure 2.5 indicates, child obesity came to dominate the reporting of health risks factors associated with obesity. Over 45 per cent of all obesity stories in 2004 in the *Guardian* focused on this topic and 55 per cent in 2006 in the *NYT*. But these 'obese' and 'at risk' diagnostics are regarded by medical science as especially limited predictors of children's health status because their bodies are subject to growth spurts. These classifications are particularly suspect before age 5 and at the moment of puberty when hormonal and growth effects create huge variability in youthful populations. Although the norms for 'obesity' can be corrected statistically, the classifications have sizeable error that limits their use in the prediction of the health status of children – a subtlety the journalists more or less ignored. But it did set alarm bells ringing. No doubt the medical world's intention was to raise public awareness by focusing on the growing risks to children. After all, part of the function of the public health agencies is to generate support for public policy (WHO 1997). Fat kids were the poster-child of the health-promotion campaign. If trends continued, health officials argued, the child obesity epidemic threatened to smother public health under an avalanche of costs stemming from future heart attacks and diabetes 2. What mattered to epidemiologists and policymakers was perhaps not the extent of these risks but the prospect that in children they were more preventable.

The new tobacco

The medical establishments' success in establishing childhood obesity as a significant public health problem is indicated in Figure 2.7 by the triumph of obesity against smoking stories. In 2003 obesity jumped ahead on the risk agenda, leading observers to declare correctly that obesity had become the 'the new tobacco'. Having raised awareness about children's changing health status, what the health community needed to do was to focus on the risk factors associated with children's weight gain. It is in this respect that the WHO's report on soft drinks (WHO 2003) became the rally point for the public health advocates' quest for a way of slowing the epidemic's spread. Risk analysis after all can be performed on any factors that are measurable. Associations between BMI and drinking soft drinks, eating fast food, not participating in sports and watching lots TV indicate possible risk factors linked to excessive weight gain. The WHO's reports helped mobilize the

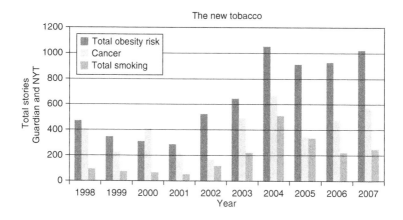

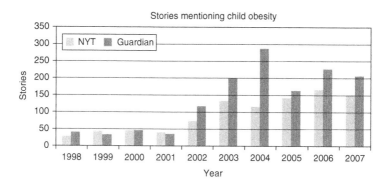

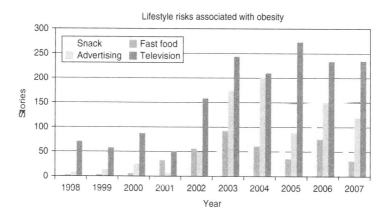

Figure 2.7 The new tobacco: Children and their lifestyle risks associated with TV

medical research community around the part played by poor nutrition in the child obesity epidemic. Studies of the changing diet of Americans suggested that excessive consumption of energy dense foods was implicated in the imbalance between some children's energy intake and expenditure (Nicklas et al. 2001; Neilson and Popkin 2003, 2004; Bauer et al. 2009). Their consumption of fast food, snacks and soft drinks provided an easy explanation of the obesity epidemic in children and the best way to stop its spread (Apovian 2004). Obviously epidemiologists believe that both individual and environmental factors are impacting weight gain (Swinburn et al. 1999). Yet medical advocacy began to inverse the environmental logic of risk analysis.

A detailed analysis of the scientific sources used after 2002 indicated it was an array of public and mandated health organizations – the CDC, the American Pediatrics Association, nutritionists and the AMA – who became the 'moral entrepreneurs' of child obesity. In the US, mandated scientists at the CDC, the WHO, and the International Obesity Task force were repeatedly cited as the expert source of epidemiological data. Governmental scientists at the FSA and Ministry of Health in the UK also were quoted in the debates as costs and mitigation policies were discussed. Government reports were issued and subjected to criticism by various advocacy groups whose job it is to question public policy and offer their own solutions about what can be done to prevent a crisis. The result was a lively public controversy about both the causes and how to stop the 'epidemic of obesity' in children. But what also gets lost in the public reporting of epidemiological risk factors is that 'obesity' has gone from signalling the changes in children's lifestyle to being a risk factor in children's obesity. The diversity and systemic interactions assumed in epidemiology became conflated with the failure to differentiate between symptoms and causes. Rising BMI in child populations was no longer a symptom of our obesogenic lifestyles but a disease in its own right that had to be stopped. So health advocates issued precautionary warnings about risk factors associated with children's fast food diets and sedentary lifestyles based on small changes in the OR and knowledge that few treatments were successful (Campbell et al. 2001). And journalists found it difficult to assess the significance of the changing patterns of energy imbalance preferring to isolate and simplify by reporting on a single cause – such as fast food, school lunches or sweets.

To nutritional scientists it seemed self-evident that the increased availability and TV promotion of a wide variety of good tasting, inexpensive, energy dense foods were implicated in child obesity. In the West, where household spending on food was actually decreasing, nutritional research showed that the average caloric intake had increased by 15 per cent. Britons, long reputed to have the worst diet in Europe, learnt that their health was at risk because how much, what and where they ate was changing (UK National

Nutrition and Diet Study 2000). Nutritionist argued that changing dietary practices were putting children at risk. They were getting fatter because the average family ate out more, drank more soft drinks, devoured larger portions and did not eat sufficient fruits and vegetables. In the US too, the majority of adults consume more than the 35 per cent recommended calories from fat and eat far fewer than the five recommended portions of fruit and vegetables a day (Neilson and Popkin, 2003). Nutritional studies showed that the changing diet was related to both environmental and life-style changes including food availability, parental modeling, meal structure, parenting style and food socialization practices (Nicklas et al. 2001; Wardle et al. 2001). Fast food was one of the most significant of them: between 1970 and 1995, fast food consumption in the US rose from 3 per cent to 9 per cent of all eating occasions so that the average family was acquiring 12 per cent of calories from fast foods (Lin et al. 1999). Children especially were at risk because larger portions of energy dense foods, drinks and snacks had become standard family fare (Smiciklas-Wright et al. 2002).

Many of these studies were duly reported by the press assigning greater priority to food-related health issues and television as can be seen in Figure 2.8. Especially after 2002, caloric intake moved to the centre of the debate about child obesity. As a lifestyle risk, weight gain can indicate the consumption of too much of the wrong foods. It can also indicate too little exercise. This drift towards sedentary lifestyles has been compounded by the fact that physical education, once an important part of every child's school day, has been cut back at many schools. And children are driven to school rather than walking or riding their bikes. This means that dietary change alone is unlikely to account for population weight gain. And studies had documented the gradual reduction of vigorous exertion across the popula-tion, but especially in children, whose love of play and sports long kept them active (Wardle et al. 2001; Eisenmann et al. 2002; Fang et al. 2003). But content analysis of newspapers indicated that coverage of physical activity research was lower in priority (Faulkner et al. 2007). It seems that the activ-ity advocates were less effective in their spinning of their risk analysis of sedentary lives. It was mostly in relationship to food ads that the unhealthy lifestyles of school-aged children received disproportionate press coverage.

There was another important bias underlining the journalistic take on lifestyle risk analysis. Population health analysis shows that not everyone is equally at risk to changes in lifestyle. Prevalence statistics show that the incidence of obesity was highest among the poor of the developed world and the rich of the developing one (*Economist* 2003). There is also evidence of regional differences in climate, policy and lifestyle which lead some groups to be more prone to overweight than others – for example the South in the US and Scotland in the UK. But it was hard to isolate the risk factors underwriting these distributional patterns of weight gain. The data showed that both diet and lack of physical activity were socially distributed risk

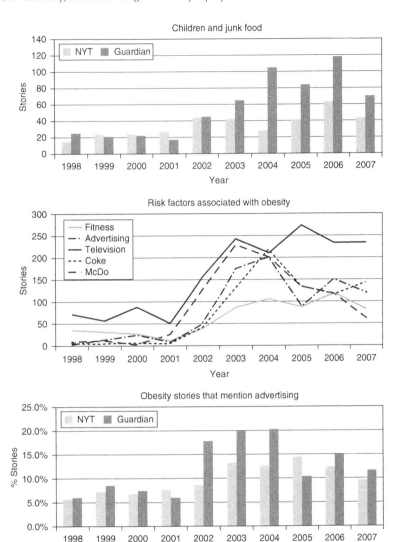

Figure 2.8 The fast food frame: Focusing stories on lifestyle risks associated with children

factors too. Less than half of US schoolchildren for example, have access to daily physical education classes. So too, the frequency of eating fast food and increasing portion size were associated with social economic status and region (Phipps et al. 2006).

Although it is prudent to focus attention on the most vulnerable segments for health advocacy, in fact not all children were equally at risk. Especially in the US, the highest incidence of child obesity is among the poor, southern and ethnic populations – many of whom are more than twice at risk. Around the world, the sociocultural roots of obesity are found among the most disadvantaged ethnic groups, who are clearly 'at risk' because of their social circumstances and lifestyles (Morgenstern et al. 2009). In the US, whereas 45 per cent of black adults and 36.8 per cent of Mexican Americans were at risk due to obesity, only 30.6 per cent of white adult Americans were (NHANES III). Based on my own analysis of Youth Risk Behaviour Survey (YRBS) data (Figure 2.9), the incidence of obesity was dramatically increasing in the Afro-Hispanic teen demographics while it was decreasing in white teens between 2005 and 2007.

So too, gender differences are found within teen population trends, which reveal that males are at more risk than females and the rate of change is greater. Male teens classified obese increased from 16 per cent in 2005 to 19.2 per cent in 2007 whereas females increased from 10 to 11.2 per cent in the same period. But little of this was analysed in the press. Poverty, climate, culture, sedentary lifestyles, public policy and regional dietary practices were clearly factors in a general upward trend in BMI. But arguments about the bad diets of poor people, southerners and blacks are not going to draw press attention or win research dollars for that matter.

This overview of the press coverage of epidemiological science suggests that the WHO's campaign to promote awareness of child globesity was a PR success. The campaign gained momentum as the research community mobilized around three controversial health communication strategies. The first was to make the public aware of the risks of obesity by highlighting the increase in BMI in child populations. The second was to estimate the soaring costs associated with projected population weight trends. And the third was to raise questions about the lifestyle risks that contributed to children being overweight. In this way, not only did overweight children become the focal point of the scientific discussion of our obesogenic lifestyles but of its politicization as well.

Scientists who study population health are well aware of the problems associated with declaring children's expanding body morphology a global epidemic. In the first place there was no single toxin and no substantiation that weight gain was being transmitted suddenly through the global population. Instead, the population health evidence indicates that the change was both slow and clearly selective. Weight gain seemed to be an idiosyncratic affliction of our 'obesogenic environment' (Hill et al. 2003) rather than an epidemic with an identifiable toxin. Journalists however seemed uncomfortable with communicating about the complexity of their analysis of obesogenic lifestyles. Was it sedentary leisure, poverty, ethnicity or fast food advertising that caused the rise in obesity? The multiple and interacting

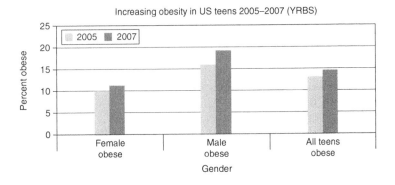

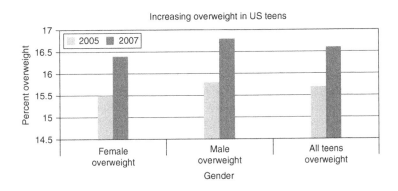

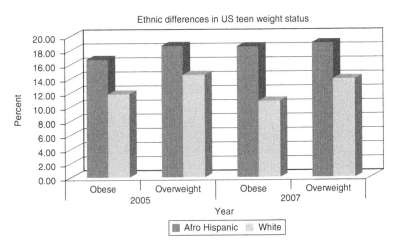

Figure 2.9 The distribution of obesogenic lifestyles in US teen populations

lifestyle changes taking place in our affluent media-saturated market culture just did not make a good story. More importantly, the distributional issues associated with obesity seemed beyond the pale for the liberal press. Though lifestyle risks are unequally distributed in a market society, the systemic risk factors remained largely under reported – except for one – namely, those associated with commercialized TV (Boyce 2007). But TV viewing was related to both diet and physical activity levels as well as ethnic and gender differences (Robinson and Killen 1995; Boumtje et al. 2005) – a part of the risk analysis that got swamped in the ensuing debate about the causes of weight gain.

3
Putting the Pan in the Pandemic

Although epidemiology was the spark for expanding press coverage of child obesity, attention quickly turned to the mitigation of children's obesogenic lifestyles. By 2002 scientific studies had shown that children breakfasted regularly on oversweet cereals and snacked on super-saturated chips and drank hyper-sweetened soft drinks during the day. The knowledge of life-style risks therefore neatly dovetailed with growing parental anxieties about 'couch potato' kids and their fast food diets. The geographical march of adiposity across middle America was famously immortalized in the popular film *Super Size Me* which opened with a group of overweight campers singing the McDonalds skipping song. And why were they overweight? Their school meals were unhealthy because they refused to taste anything but burgers and fries. Vegging out in front of the screen had become the national sport. Few children rode bikes or even walked to school. The 'fast food' frame identified by Lawrence (2004) in her study of American news grew into a full-blown moral panic in both countries which started with the growing anxiety about children's weight gain, which mounted with the evidence that fast food and sedentary lifestyles put them at risk and which ascribed great urgency to protecting children from the 'obesogenic' cultural environment.

The politicization of lifestyle choice: A comparison of US and British moral panics 2000–5

The study of the discursive politics of lifestyle risks sees risk analysis as both constitutive of public perception and provocative of risk controversy as the public assimilates, interprets, reacts and contests solutions to the threat. Calls for a ban on fast food marketing on children's TV became the focal point of this mitigation debate (although in the US the hope for a drug treatment continued). I have already noted that long-held anxieties about children's vulnerability to advertising inflamed the political strug-gle over who is responsible for childhood obesity – bad parents or big food. Children's uncertain status in the consumer marketplace became the fulcrum of this risk mitigation controversy, which put parenting, food and health advocates on one side and food corporations, advertising and media on the other. As the threat to children filled the front pages, the risks associated with the fast food diets and sedentary lifestyles of children were reinterpreted as a morality play about spoilt children, pester power, deregulated markets and irresponsible corporations. 'Moral entrepreneurs' armed with epidemiological analysis of the risks to children stepped forward proposing draconian measures – as if turning off TV advertising would improve children's diet. References to the regulation of food marketing (see Figure 3.1) increased in the press in tandem with the perception of the threat to children (see Figure 3.2). The calls for regulation peaked in Britain in 2003 and by 2007 Britain had legislated a ban on food advertising on TV. In the US, a lawsuit launched in 2002 preoccupied the press but vindicated the

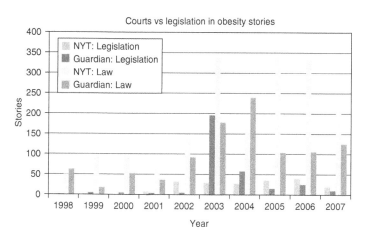

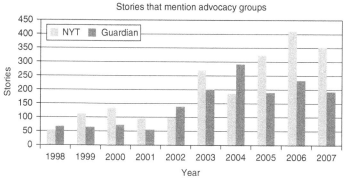

Figure 3.1   The discursive politics of food marketing: Stories focusing on court cases and advertising legislation

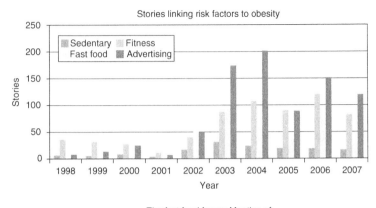

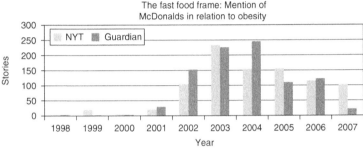

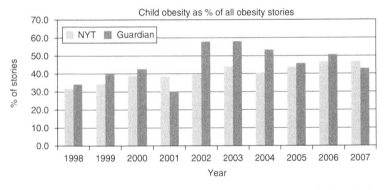

Figure 3.2   Moral panic: Focusing on lifestyle risks associated with children's obesity

fast food industry, resulting in legislated calls for advertising regulation in 2005 and 2006.

In this chapter, I provide a historical analysis of the discursive politics of blame for fat kids unfolding on the pages of the *New York Times* and the *Guardian*.[1] Tracing the expert sources used in this debate provides a clue to the shift that takes place as risk science slips into the background and mitigation comes to the fore. After 2002, the mandated scientists of the CDC and the FSA gradually lost ground to a list of over 50 public interest and corporate advocacy groups, from the Physicians for a Responsible Medicine and the Clinton Foundation to Kelloggs and Coke in the US, from Sustain and the Consumers Association and the Royal College of Pediatrics to the Sugar Bureau, the Institute of Practitioners of Advertising (IPA) and McDonalds in Britain (Cozens 2002). Overall there is a five-fold increase of non-governmental organizations within this debate about risk mitigation indicating the strength of their lobbying and PR efforts. In Britain, in fact, the voice of public interest groups is both strong and varied. Their pronouncements on advertising even outnumber those of corporate spokespersons whereas in the US it is the other way around. Public interest advocacy played a crucial role in the formation of the British response, whereas in the US the corporate lobby successfully defended its self-regulatory ideology.

Moral panic in the US

When the globesity pandemic hit the front pages of the newspapers in America, the health and parenting advocates were waiting in the wings. Brandishing the statistics, they rallied against big food. The renewed struggle began in 2000, when Stop Commercial Exploitation of Children (SCEC) went to the Golden Arches Awards for advertising to children with the following message:

> Intensive marketing harms children. It harms their health and sense of well being. It compromises their safety and undermines their family life. In this era of unprecedented and rampant exploitation of children as a consumer group, it's time for people who care about kids to take a stand against an industry that seeks to manipulate for profit our most vulnerable citizens.
>
> (CCFC 2000)[2]

With constitutional guarantees of commercial free speech, with the FTC backing down from strictly enforcing the mandated food labelling laid down in the *Nutrition Labeling and Education Act of 1990* and with no national health system, the battle over fast food quickly moved from the media to the courts in the US where public policy is often laid down in supreme court rulings (Richards 2004).

The first salvo was a case brought by Caesar Barber, as lead plaintiff in a class action suit heard in the Supreme Court of New York in July of 2002. The case was against McDonald's, Burger King Corp., KFC Corp. and Wendy's International, blaming the chains for making him and others overweight and raising his risk of illness related to being overweight. Mr. Barber, a 56-year-old, single, 272-pound maintenance worker from the Bronx was a poor cook and therefore ate out at fast food restaurants four to five times a week for as long as he could remember. He testified in court 'I always thought it was good for you. I never thought there was anything wrong with it.' After two heart attacks and other medical complications he was surprised to learn from his doctor in 1996 that his penchant for the Big Mac and Super Sized fries wasn't as good for him as he thought.

In court, his lawyer Samuel Hirsch, argued that not only are the fast food merchandisers to blame for Mr Barber's poor health but for the obesity epidemic plaguing the nation that have made more than half of all Americans overweight. The suit cited companies for irresponsibly and deceptively selling foods that are high in salt, fat, cholesterol content and sugar, which ostensibly cause a myriad of health-related problems, including obesity, diabetes, coronary heart disease, strokes, high blood pressure, cancers and other detrimental and adverse health effects and diseases. The intense marketing effort of the fast food corporations not only persuaded people like Mr Barber that the food was good to eat but also had made him addicted to burgers and fries.

Against these seemingly frivolous accusations, the fast food industry defended itself successfully by arguing that eating a burger does not constitute a 'health risk'. It is a legal product sold in the market which many consume without getting fat. Moreover any normally informed consumer should know that a steady diet of fried foods and sugary desserts would cause one to become overweight. Finding no evidence that fast food is an addiction, the judge emphasized the personal agency of the consumer in this suit arguing that health risks associated with eating are voluntary acts taken by consumers and that nobody is forced to eat at McDonald's. Corporations that sell these legal products therefore cannot be held liable for the lifestyle choices made by their consumers.

This ruling sent a ripple through the legal community because so much was at stake in this decision about the corporate liabilities for lifestyle health risks (Colb 2003). Widely reported in the media, the case had legal wags anticipating that fast food was becoming the new tobacco – a litigious gold mine for class action lawyers seeking blood money from corporations who promote their risky products to innocent children while denying the unhealthy side effects of the evil hamburger. The website, Lawyers Stink, criticized this class action suit as a 'shameless money grab', claiming the addiction claim was frivolous and it seemed beyond credulity that anyone in this day and age could be ignorant of the lifestyle risks associated with a steady diet of fast food. The Centre for Consumer Freedoms produced an ad campaign that featured an exploitative lawyer seeking damages from a Girl Scout for selling cookies.

But that didn't deter crusading lawyer Hirsch, who then played 'the child' card in a second suit on behalf of the parents of two overweight teenagers – Jazlyn Bradley, 19, who was 5-feet-6 and weighed 270 pounds and Ashley

Pelman, 14, who was 4-feet-10 and 170 pounds – whom he claimed had serious health problems related to their penchant for McDonald's. *Pelman* vs. *McDonald's Corporation* was filed in August, 2002. The suit claimed that McDonald's and two of its restaurants in the Bronx failed to clearly and conspicuously disclose the ingredients and effects of its food, including high levels of fat, salt, sugar and cholesterol to the girls. Hirsch argued that McDonald's franchises are therefore negligently selling risky products and should be held accountable for the girls' obesity, heart disease, diabetes, high blood pressure and elevated cholesterol. US District Court judge, Robert Sweet however dismissed this case too on 22 January because he felt the plaintiffs failed to show that McDonald's food was 'dangerous in any way other than that which was open and obvious to a reasonable consumer'. But he gave the plaintiffs 30 days to amend the complaint to try to establish that there were dangers that were 'not commonly well known'. In short, the case hinged on the consumers' knowledge of the risks.

In February Hirsch filed a revised complaint accusing the fast food giant of making misleading nutritional claims, citing McDonald's for 'deceptive practices in the advertising, processing and sale of foods, including Chicken McNuggets, Filet-O-Fish, Chicken Sandwich, French fries and hamburgers'. The revised complaint not only included the two original girls but was a class action suit filed on behalf of 'hundreds of thousands of New York state residents under the age of 18' who suffer health problems as a result of eating McDonald's food. Hirsch claimed that the legal principle – caveat emptor – was not without limits in the consumer marketplace, for a countervailing principle governing sales transactions of risky products was the need for informed consent. The corporation's responsibilities for the plaintiffs' obesity extended beyond the lifestyle risks associated with their products to McDonald's' failure to communicate them adequately.

A reasonable person under the law can only accept personal responsibility for what he or she consumes when he or she is not misled or deceived about both risks and benefits. So if there is a known risk associated with the use of the product, the vendor must communicate that risk to the potential consumer or potentially be held liable for health and safety consequences of its sale. In his 46-page complaint, Hirsch alleged that McDonald's does not make its nutritional information 'adequately available' and said numerous claims made by the fast-food chain are misleading and untrue. Reviewing a variety of McDonald's promotional material such as a booklet that claims the fish in a Filet-O-Fish is '100 percent cod with a pinch of salt to taste after cooking', Hirsch alleged that the information was deceptive. He also criticized an advertisement in which McDonald's claimed that its beef is nutritious and leaner than beef purchased in a supermarket, but the levels of saturated fat and cholesterol would not make the beef nutritious.

McDonald's quickly responded, calling the lawsuit 'senseless' (Cloud 2002). Their lawyers accused the plaintiffs of wrongly 'focusing on only one food organization' which 'serves quality food and ingredients from quality suppliers and continues to be a leader in providing customers with nutritional information about our food'. McDonald's' lawyers also contended that it would be impossible to establish whether eating at McDonald's was a major cause of ailments because genetics, medical conditions and sedentary lifestyles could also be factors. Moreover, they maintained that 'every responsible person understands what is in products such as hamburgers and fries, as well as the consequence to one's waistline, and potentially to one's health, of excessively eating those foods over a prolonged period of time'. So it is parents, not the fast food industry's fault if kids are eating too many hamburgers.

News value aside, the McDonald's case reveals why it is so difficult to do anything about lifestyle risks legally distributed in the marketplace such as those associated with tobacco, pharmaceuticals or fast food in the US. These behaviours are voluntary actions assumed to be undertaken legally in the marketplace by informed consumers. Without a way of showing that consumers are deceived, the courts concluded that merchants have no obligation to communicate the risks in their marketing because every reasonable person already knows that consuming fast food regularly can have unhealthy consequences. The judge determined that reasonable adults are informed consumers of fast food products so the lifestyle risks they take must be understood as voluntary.

This judge determined that McDonald's was only responsible for disclosing the risks when requested at the point of sale. This means that under current regulations, food advertisers are not held responsible for communicating about known risks in their marketing, and are only required to ensure that their claims (low fat, Atkins friendly) are substantiated with evidence when challenged at the FTC. Moreover, current regulatory frameworks can only deal with specific ads in relationship to the deceptive health claims they make. In short there is no regulatory mechanism mandating lifestyle risk disclosure or for stalling the promotional bias in the US mediated market system. After all, even the successful ban on tobacco advertising was 'voluntary'. This case therefore highlighted the underlying legal issues confronting the regulation of lifestyle risks distributed in the US marketplace. The first concerns responsibility for distributing accurate information to all consumers about risky products. The second concerns whether young consumers are sufficiently informed to perform the cost-benefit-risk analysis necessary for legally informed consent in a risk society. Although the ruling addressed the former, what legal commentator Sherry Colb, on 29 January 2003, noted was that the judge didn't determine whether children under 12 years of age could also be expected to understand the risks they were facing when they chose hamburger and fries as part of their regular consumption. As Eberstadt (2003) also argued, if markets were only about free choosing adults, 'we could perhaps rest content in the knowledge that the fat problem, like smoking, will ultimately right or at least ameliorate itself in the long run' but child fat is, for a variety of reasons, 'a different order of problem' from a policy perspective.

In the US, this predictable legal ruling mobilized the child advocacy movement, re-igniting the long simmering struggle over de-regulation of children's commercial television. With overweight children at the centre of public health, the American Psychological Association's (APA) Task Force on Advertising to Children reviewed the research on the impact of marketing on children under the age of eight, concluding 'that all advertising to children is, by its very nature, exploitive. Long-standing public policy holds that all commercial content must be clearly identifiable as such to its intended audience, in order to allow the consumer to consider the source of the message in evaluating its claims. Advertising that violates this standard is deemed deceptive, and a violation of federal law' (Kunkel et al. 2004). Their precautionary position was widely circulated and echoed when independent authorities at the Kaiser Foundation (2003) published its own review of the causes of 'supersized children' in America. These reports were brandished by anti-commercialization advocacy groups calling for federal restrictions on food advertising aimed at children who were under eight years old (CCFC 2004). Children needed to be protected in the marketplace because of their developmental inadequacies which became the rally cry of this new generation of anti-commercialization advocates such as Susan Linn (2004) and Juliet Schor (2004).

Disputing the child advocates' interpretation of the APA's findings, industry spokespersons argued that they were the ones being victimized. Children's advertising, they claimed, was already heavily regulated and now bans threatened to violate their corporate rights of commercial free speech. After all, advertisers were following guidelines and marketing legal products, children were savvy consumers entitled to make up their own minds and there were many things besides advertising contributing to the increase in child obesity. Certainly complacent parents who bought the snacks and let children watch TV all day must accept some blame for increasingly overweight children, they retorted. Was it not the parents' responsibility to monitor how much their kids watched, to provide healthy food and foster healthy eating practices (Groom 2004). As one advertising executive responded in an Advertising Age survey, 'It's simple. Parents should be held liable. Kids do not have the purchasing power to make themselves fat' (Advertising Age 2006). And was it not the state schools' responsibility to feed students properly at lunch, to provide sports and PE, and to educate them about healthy lifestyles? If they all did their job better, the kids would be fine. So why blame advertising (Cebrzynski 2007)?

At the same time, the implications of the public sentiments did not go unremarked by the food marketers. Coke found its share of the US market slipping to less than one fifth as more and more youngsters drank juice and water (Walsh 2004). McDonald's too, found its menu increasingly out of step with the health-conscious ideals of today's young people (Sanders 2005). As the health risks associated with fast food worked their way through the market, the industry decided on a repositioning strategy (Botterill and Kline 2007). Although a voluntary ban on advertising was vigorously resisted, the fast food and soft drink sector responded by putting orange juice in their dispensing machines, salads on their menus and advisories on their packaging and ads announcing 'low fat' options. Coke decided to withdraw its advertising spends from children's time TV programmes and put water and juice in its soft drink dispensers in schools. Kellogg's launched healthier brands of cereal while Danone brandished its latest no-fat fruit yoghurts for kids. Even KFC announced it was taking the hydrogenated fat out of its 50-year old recipe. Disney banished junk food from its theme parks. Ex-president Bill Clinton's revival was linked to a campaign to crackdown on junk food in schools by securing agreements with food industry leaders to limit content by weight of sugar to 35 per cent and saturated fats to 10 per cent.

Leading this charge to corporate responsibility, McDonald's declared that media literacy and dynamic advertising could be an active force in countering the sedentary lifestyles of children. At Times Square, McDonald's CEO Jim Skinner launched their corporate responsibility campaign noting that considerable resources world wide would be devoted to TV commercials, sponsorships with various media and non-profit organizations, websites, in-restaurant promotions and endorsements from celebrities and athletes, all aimed at families and children to focus attention on the message, 'People should pay attention to the foods they eat and their level of activity to find the right balance.' Head of global marketing campaign Dean Barrett said, 'We have a job to do in communicating this message. We are not going to back away; we are not going to stop talking to kids in ways that are relevant.' It is well known, 'chief happiness officer' Ronald McDonald will go on a new lifestyle mission. He will appear in a variety of creative executions from ads to website health education lessons, all of which show him in some form of physical activity or as a spokesperson for healthy eating. In the contemporary marketplace, the corporate world announced, responsible food advertisers not only helped to fund children's television programmes but proved an educational force for healthy lifestyles (Sanders 2005).

Despite changes to food marketing targeting children, under intense pressure from health advocates, legislators began to rethink the laws governing children's consumer socialization. In 2005, a report championed by US senator Tom Harkin cited the APA review, comparing the food marketers to big tobacco, he called on them to take responsibility for the rising incidence of child obesity. This report argued that the billions of marketing dollars only serve to woo children away from good dietary choices. It threatened the return of the FTC's authority in regulating children's marketing unless they stopped (Advertising Age 2005). Responding to this congressional report, Dick O'Brien, executive VP of the Association of American Advertising

Agencies called the report 'a breathless overreaction' and a 'flawed study' based on no new data. Industry executives contended that the report fails to take into account recent changes in food marketing; Wally S. Snyder, president-CEO of the American Advertising Federation, said the proposed recommendations are inappropriate and unconstitutional. 'It would come down to stopping truthful advertising to children. That is not the standard we are following', he said. 'They want us to choose good products and bad products, when advertising of all products that is truthful is appropriate' (AEF 2005).

The issue received further public attention (Teinowitz 2005) due to the publication of an Institute of Medicine report (Koplan et al. 2006) into food marketing to children and youth. The FTC started to reconsider its 'self-regulatory' framework for food advertising to children. It joined with the Department of Health and Human Services to organize a joint workshop on marketing, self-regulation and childhood obesity in June 2005. Research was undertaken for the FTC to determine the extent of children's exposure to food advertising on television. It reported that not much had changed since the 1970s (McGinnis et al. 2006). Using longitudinal data from NYSTC survey in the US, Chou et al. (2005) estimated that a ban on these advertisements would reduce the number of overweight children aged 3–11 in a fixed population by 10 per cent and would reduce the number of overweight adolescents aged 12–18 by 12 per cent.

In the face of mounting evidence about the effects of children's exposure to food advertising, a lawsuit was launched against Viacom and Kellogg for unfair and deceptive practices related to the marketing and sale of foods of poor nutritional quality to children under the age of eight (Center for Science in the Public Interest 2006). The Federal Communications Commission then established a task force to study the relationship between the media and childhood obesity which received considerable mention in the business press (WARC 2007). Yet by 2010 all of this policy research had resulted in no changes in US policy – no legislation, no new guidelines and no advisories to industry. Meanwhile estimates of the potential benefits of reducing advertising to children were in the 15 per cent range (Veerman et al. 2009). Although advocacy groups like CCFC continue to lobby for precautionary legislation of children's food marketing, the neoliberal principles governing children's status as consumers remain unchanged from the Reagan era.

In the US therefore, the health advocates continue their campaign against child obesity (American Obesity Society, 2008). Yet the constitutional issue established in the courts has been enough to scare off potential legislation – at least so far (Mello 2010). After all, advertisers were marketing legal products, promoting healthy lifestyle. Children were savvy consumers entitled to make up their own minds and there were many lifestyle risk factors besides advertising contributing to the increase in child obesity. Until evidence of harm done by food marketers is proven definitively, following tobacco and violent video game precedents, commercial free speech continues to narrow the US public health response to mitigating lifestyle risks to Public Service Announcements (PSA) and health education.

Precautionary politics: Moral panic with a British accent

From the start in Britain, the globesity epidemic was treated as a societal scourge rather than a personal choice. Public health policy and communication rather than lawsuits tend to be the way political change takes place in the British market. A nation that was once chided for its mediocre palate and overcooked foods, was growing increasingly anguished about its food supplies. Stories on the food industry, about restaurants and the history of haute cuisine, were also an important facet of the swelling interest in food. Organics were in, health food stores abounded and the nation's diet was changing – if not everywhere for the better. Popular food writers, from sexy Nigella to devilish ones like Gordon Ramsey, were part of the new food culturati. They testified to the cultural centrality of food as part of middle-class cultural capital. The dinner party, dining out and eating healthy had become very acceptable.

In the wake of scientific revelations about cloned sheep, BSE and genetically modified 'frankenfoods', lifestyle risks associated with food had clearly moved high up on the risk agenda. Not only was the nation's diet changing but also, under pressure, the New Labour government decided to establish the Food Standards Agency in 2000 with a broad remit spanning from the production of food to the dietary health of the nation. Brandishing the National Diet and Nutrition Survey (2000) which showed that children breakfasted regularly on oversweet cereals, snacked on super-saturated chips and guzzled fizzy drinks, foodies now turned their attention to children's unhealthy diets.

One of the first stories to tilt directly at the obesity epidemic in Britain, and away from fat camps and diet pills, was a book review titled 'Fat or Thin, Rich or Poor, the Politics of Food Eats at us All'. This thoughtful book review reflects upon the growing interest in food as both a cultural and economic factor of globalization. 'Forget bacteria and viruses', the Guardian reviewer writes, 'half of the ill health that dogs the world is related to the 'excessive or inadequate consumption of food'. Although globesity was seen as a levelling force, the writer did point out that medical opinion now held that the millennial generation had become indulged, dependent on cars, and spent too much time watching TV or playing video games while energy supply has increased due to their energy dense 'junk food' diets.

This perception was augmented when the health minister released a national nutritional survey on 1 June 2000, which revealed that young people were eating far too little fruit and vegetables. James Meikle, the *Guardian* food writer, wrote the next day that the government was planning to do something about the problem. Ministers were expected to lay down nutritional guidelines in schools amid mounting fears that some children find it easier to get drugs than cheap, good food. The guidelines will not tell parents what they must put in children's lunchboxes, but school canteens must ensure a proper choice of four main categories of food: fruit and vegetables, meat and protein, starchy foods, and milk and dairy products. Moreover the food industry executives will be asked to tone down the way they advertise fizzy drinks, crisps and snacks popular with children and help to promote healthy lifestyles instead.

In a story 15 February 2001 titled 'Action Urged to Cut the Fat of the Land', James Meikle was one of the first to claim that 'obesity in England is nearing epidemic proportions'. He notes that according to figures just released, 'obesity is costing Britain £1.7bn a year for which poor diet and lack of exercise are to be blamed'. 6 per cent of all deaths, he notes, alarmingly can be attributed to 'a lifestyle of fatty diets, over-reliance on the car and energy-saving devices such as lifts and escalators'. Citing research in the *British Medical Journal* he predicts that things are getting worse because not only have adult rates tripled over the last 10 years but also one in 10 children aged four or under is already obese, while one in four is overweight. The article concludes quoting Philip James who now chairs the International Obesity Taskforce: 'We need to focus on transforming the diet of children and adults, even if the initiatives threaten some components of the food and soft drinks industries.' The forming coalition of health, parenting and children's advocacy groups was taken a step further when Sustain published research on the TV diet (Dibb and Gordon 2001) connecting the dots between diet and advertising. TV Dinners documented the relationship between children's diet and the foods advertised on television. Its release was accompanied by calls to Minister Tessa Jowell to ban advertising as a preventative health measure.

This alarmist rhetoric was gradually assimilated by the medical community. At conferences and in papers, the obesity epidemic was becoming a fact. And in spite of the fact that children were one-third as likely to be suffering from obesity as male adults, and that by adulthood almost half of these would have adjusted their weight, children were pictured as the prime victims of the obesity epidemic. For example, in a story on 17 September 2002 titled 'Childhood Obesity at Epidemic Levels' university obesity researchers were quoted as saying that although the problem has been around for two decades it is only being recognized now, predicting 'we will get a lot more long standing childhood obesity than we have ever had previously and that is a lot more dangerous'. The unfolding coverage of the politics of childhood obesity in Britain over the next few years unleashed a moral panic increasingly centred on food advertising to children. In a story in the *Observer* (the Guardian's Sunday cousin) sometime in January 2001 for example, Mark Gould notes with alarm that 'more than a million under-16s in the UK' are classed as overweight or obese – double the number in the mid-80s as 'junk food and couch-potato lifestyle is speeding their bodies into a disease of middle age'. On 23 April 2002 James Meikle writes animatedly that 'Britain is suffering an epidemic of obesity, but the government is powerless to change the behaviour of food manufacturers or consumers.' The costs of obesity on the work force are soaring and 'concern is also mounting over the content of children's diet, and the role of fizzy drink companies and food manufacturers in promoting high-fat, high-salt and high-sugar foods'. Noting the formation of an all-party group forming to push obesity up the political agenda, he claims that 'Perhaps it is time for the state, which picks up the bill for the mounting health toll through our taxes, to behave more like a nanny.'

Behind the scenes, a new coalition was forming in Britain, bringing together food, environmentalism, family values and health. Since Britain's Labour government was in the throes of overhauling the health care system it remained responsive to the vocal food and organic agricultural advocacy sector (Sustain, The Soil Association, and The Worldwatch Institute) which were engaged in long-running battles with the big food industries over GMO. Driven by groups like Sustain, the pressure was growing to regulate children's junk food advertising. In 17 June 2002 a story announced that the 'government's food standards agency is to commission research into whether advertising of foods high in fat, sugar and salt to children is undermining healthy eating programmes and contributing to the rapid rise in obesity. Naturally the food advertising industry was incredulous, asking 'Why are they targeting advertising and promotional activity when most decent quality research suggests that at most it is a minor influence on dietary choice?'

Yet as the panic mounted, the *Guardian* documented the parade of medical researchers who championed fruit in schools, cutting back on fizzy drinks, sending kids to fat camps, increased physical education in schools and active leisure holidays for the family. For example, Dr Pauline Emmett reported on research into children's diets that suggested that obesity was related to the mother's lack of nutritional risk knowledge. Her contribution maintained, 'It is important that health professionals have a role encouraging the less educated mothers to follow best nutritional practices'. Yet these single factor solutions to systemic problems often encountered opposition from other scientists who pointed out the limitations of such approaches. Fast foods were cheaper, easier to prepare and nutritionally acceptable in the context of a normal diet. Why shouldn't the less well off be granted a break today as well.

Other stories discuss parents attempting to cope with the daily pressures of fast food marketing. Indeed, by 2002 the *Observer* began to turn obesity into a crusade. In an article titled 'The Kids aren't Alright' writer Dave Hill laments that 69 per cent of 3-year-olds know the golden arches of McDonald's but not their own name. His article expressed the underlying media panic frame. It focuses on his personal experiences of pester power: 'Another Saturday, another full-on engagement with kiddie consumer world. First, to the supermarket where my second youngest Boy, five, sits in the trolley as we roll down the heaving aisles and familiar faces beam at him from all sides. Boy, five, keeps his counsel but when we reach the breakfast cereals, he sweetly makes his pitch. 'Daddy, can we have Golden Grahams?' 'No, my lovely, we cannot.' 'Can we have Cheerios?' 'Sorry, pal ...' 'Can we have Coco Pops?' Such experiences provoke him to wonder about ' the effect of my children's daily immersion in a swarming consumer culture?'

Another oft-voiced concern was that children's excessive consumption of fizzy drinks, which add approximately 160 calories to a typical McDonald's Happy Meal and are available in schools from Coke dispensers, was a major health problem. Parents' groups insisted that Coke machines be removed from schools and that children be given fruit juices instead. But as dental experts point out, if the child drinks orange juice instead, they have neither reduced the calories nor lessened the risk of cavities. In short, there is growing wariness of simplistic solutions to this lifestyle problem as it becomes evident that dieting, fitness regimes, sending kids to fat camps or handing out apples at lunchtime are not very effective. The Labour Party's stance on food advertising came under scrutiny after the publication in December 2002 of the Government Chief Medical Officer's annual report, which highlighted the continuing upward trend in the proportion of obese and overweight children.

Amid growing frustration among parents' groups, the *Guardian* gave rather extensive coverage to the World Health Organization's second report in March 2003. As noted previously, this report launched a major assault on the food industry with a scientific report blaming sugar in soft drinks and fast food advertising to children for the global rise in obesity. It notes how many foods marketed around the globe are at variance with the nutritional guidelines offered by the WHO. The report's special focus was on sugar in the diet claiming, 'Children with a high consumption of soft drinks rich in free sugars are more likely to be overweight and to gain excess weight. ... It has been estimated that each additional can or glass of sugar-sweetened drink that they consume every day increases the risk of becoming obese by 60 per cent.' It goes on to suggest that television advertising is one of the main driving forces behind the excessive consumption of sugar and energy dense foods. 'Part of the consistent and strong relationships between television viewing and obesity in children may relate to the food advertising to which they are exposed', the WHO committee concludes (WHO 2003). Young children are targeted because they will pester their parents for the foods advertised, it claims, calling for action by governments around the world to counteract this threat to children's health.

In Britain, where the controversies about BSE and GM foods seemed to have laid the foundation of food advocacy, the Labour government responded to the public pressure by setting up a task force on obesity and commissioning both OFCOM and the FSA to consider whether advertising contributed to lifestyle risks. In March 2003, the Hastings Committee report provided a thorough review of the extant literature on the systemic effects of food promotion to children. Commissioned by the FSA, Hastings et al. (2003) reviewed the international evidence about the extent of direct to child food marketing. Although current advertising standards can ensure that no advertiser deceives or misleads consumers with false claims, they wrote, 'there is no regulatory mechanism in place that deters heavy investment in targeting children, using sophisticated branding strategies or ensures that health risk information is communicated to young consumers'. The review concluded that there was a 'systemic bias' in marketing: across countries 'a clear pattern emerged that the advertised diet was too high in fats, sugars and salt and also that it was lacking in meats, fruit and vegetables (especially fresh, non-processed meat, fruit and vegetables)' (Hastings et al. 2003: 84). The reports qualified scientific findings were generally reduced in the press to its main bullet point conclusions in its executive summary: (1) There is a lot of food advertising to children; (2) The advertised diet is less healthy than the recommended one; (3) Food promotion is having an effect, particularly on children's preferences, purchase behaviour and consumption. As the National Parenting Institute (Boseley 2003) argued, given this evidence of marketing's influence on children's health, it was clear that the current advertising standards were failing to stop the targeting of very young kids. To curtail this, it was necessary to create an outright ban on TV marketing directed at children under five who were simply incapable of critically evaluating the health claims.

The journalists smelt a good story. On Wednesday, 8 October 2003 a story titled 'Parents Told to Play Role in Tackling Child Obesity' reported on a position paper on the management of obesity and overweight issued by the Health Development Agency (HDA). The journalists cited the latest figures on childhood obesity from 2001which indicated that 8.5 per cent of British six-year-olds are obese, rising to 15 per cent of 15-year-olds. This governmental body worried about the nation's future health. The journalists picked up on this analysis: About 30,000 people die every year as a result of being obese, costing the NHS around £2.6bn per year – and this figure is expected to rise to £3.6bn by 2010, they reported. Professor Mike Kelly, the HDA's Director of Evidence was also cited as blaming the country's expanding waistlines on the proliferation of fast food outlets and junk food advertising, as well as unhealthy lifestyles. 'We live in an "obesogenic" environment – a plethora of fast food outlets, reliance on cars, and offers enticing us to eat larger portion sizes all contribute to the problem', he said. Since by adulthood this figure rose to over 30 per cent, it concludes the 'myriad of child-focused food advertising is a real challenge' to the British health care system (Campos 2004).

Opposing blame being cast on their marketing efforts, the food industry remained dubious about the scientific evidence linking fast food advertising to rising obesity rates (Brook 2004; Ashton 2004). Citing the same scientific literature reviewed by the critics, they argued research suggested that if there is any influence of advertising at all, it is only on their brand preferences and requests for the specific product – not on taste or the calories consumed. If the affluent world had an obesity epidemic it was because bad parents, sedentary lifestyles and failed schools fitness programmes were to blame (Pringle 2004; Clarke 2003). The industry spokespersons Dominic Lyle's (2004) strident defence of food marketing was reported in the press too. Their stance was that advertising effects were unproven:

1. There is no demonstrable empirical relationship between advertising expenditure and market growth;
2. Advertising regulation alone does not achieve public health objectives;
3. Advertising can play a useful role in helping to promote a sensible and balanced approach to healthier lifestyles.

Advertising spokespersons ridiculed these protectionist anxieties with their own ideology of the empowered child consumer. They cited arguments that young people were media literate and not influenced by advertising nearly as much as the food nannies insisted. Moreover, an occasional hamburger or chocolate bar will certainly not make a child fat. Besides which it was a parent's responsibility to provision children with healthy food.

These arguments about the effectiveness of advertising ban clearly registered with the policymakers. Journalists in the *Guardian* reported that although the government has come under 'mounting pressure to do something to stop children gorging on junk food and fizzy drinks after research showed that 15 per cent of children in the UK are clinically obese', the culture secretary, Tessa Jowell, was willing to rethink the 'inadequate code', but stated she would prefer to work with the food industry to promote healthier eating. 'The fact is that 70 per cent of the cost of children's programmes comes from advertising and that of that about 40 per cent comes from food ads. There are no simple answers. I remain to be convinced that a ban on advertising would have any significant impact. ... We want the industry, with the enormous resources it invests in advertising on television, to join with government in promoting healthy eating'.

Judging by the number and tone of the stories on children's obesity, the argument of the food, health and parental advocates was gaining ground. On 7 March, editorial writer Nick Cohen lambasted Jowell's equivocating stand on children's advertising as a 'capitulation before the capitalist ideology that any constraint on the market is pernicious'. Exposing the market ideology behind this decision, he argues forcefully, 'As children get fatter and more stupid, what neither side of the non-debate can admit is that propaganda works and that the young need to be protected from advertising for the same reason they need to be protected from sex – they are not old enough to handle it yet.' Later that month Sustain issued a report which notes that 'having acknowledged children's natural credulity, the current advertising code 'does not recognize any potential for cumulative effect of advertising on children and thus fails to protect children from the current state of imbalanced food advertising on television' (Sustain 2004). This system argument could not be addressed by regulatory tinkering of codes.

In a political story on 25 April, Gaby Hinsliff notes the government's focus on the obesity issue, citing the Chief Medical Officer's report warning against a 'couch potato culture' and urging parents to ensure that children are active for more than 45 minutes five days a week. Also noted were attempts to provide health vending machines in schools, fitness classes of up to 2 hours per week and the FSA's proposed nutrition guidelines for schools. Mocking these play-your-way-to-fitness initiatives in the *Observer* (2 May 2004), Nick Cohen chided that it would take the average child 45 minutes to run off a bag of crisps and a child who had a burger and fries needed to run a marathon. Drawing parallels to tobacco, he points out that not only does the industry deny the influence of their marketing on kids but 'the need for health warnings, let alone advertising bans, is denied with an incredulous fervour'. There could be no half measures, at least for these campaigning *Guardian* journalists.

As we have seen, in the UK the public health advocates were particularly effective in seizing the risk agenda by focusing attention on 'big food'. Reports from Sustain (2005), the WHO, FSA and the Parliamentary Health Committee all put the pressure on Tessa Jowell, whose ministry was responsible for regulating media under the auspices of its new agency Ofcom. Ofcom commissioned scientific panels and launched consultations with the industry to gather evidence about the effects of food marketing on children and on the industry. A scientific review by Livingstone and Helsper released in 2004 supported the idea that advertising's impact on children's food consumption was not adequately understood. Not only did the scientific record confirm advertising's limited impact on children's diet but showed that media literacy, scepticism about advertising and parental guidance could all mitigate its influence on their preferences. The policy implications were clear. Although a precautionary approach was advisable, a ban on children's advertising was unlikely to dramatically reduce obesity. Given the multiple interacting lifestyle choices that impact children's weight gain they recommended 'a multi-stranded intervention, in which the media form one strand' (Livingstone and Helsper 2004).

The pressure for restrictions on advertising of foods high in salt, sugar or fat during children's viewing times gained momentum as the coalition of food, parenting and health advocates used this policy research to pressure for regulation. Late in 2004 a Private Member's Bill addressed the failure of market democracies to allocate responsibility for educating young consumers about the long-term health risks and exposing them to a barrage of unhealthy food ads. 160 national and 129 local organizations in the UK rallied behind this idea of a watershed on all advertising of foods high in salt, sugar or fat during children's viewing times. Parliamentary debate on the *The Children's Food Bill* began in October 2005, which Reid (2004) refers to as the 'watershed moment'. The group that supported it argued that however complex the data, the only viable response was to ban unhealthy food and drink ads to children under five. It obtained support from 100 MPs. Building on the Department of Health's 2004 White Paper, *Choosing Health*, Tony Blair's government threatened that 'if there was not a change in the nature and balance of food promotion by early 2007, the Government would take action to implement a clearly defined framework for regulating the promotion of food to children'.

The industry's response was short and sharp. On 15 November the *Guardian* reported the derisive response of Jeremy Preston, director of the Advertising Association's food advertising unit: 'A ban on pre-watershed television advertising for certain foods would be a short-term, populist and disproportionate response which is unlikely to have much impact on the problem of obesity'. Agreeing that there were multiple lifestyle changes that account for the rise in obesity food marketers denied that they were to blame. However as a gesture of good will, they accepted Ofcom's designation of some foods as high in saturated fat, salt or sugar (developed by the Food Standards Agency 2005) and agreed to voluntarily avoid advertising these products in children's day parts. They argued that self-regulation was the preferred response to the obesity epidemic: 'With regulators, we can deliver a code that will change the way food is promoted, but we cannot deliver changes in food preferences simply through restrictions in advertising'. They also announced their willingness to promote fitness and health education in their campaign material (FAU, 2006).

The obesity coalitions campaign climaxed with a report by the parliamentary health select committee on the ramifications of the globesity epidemic. The *Sun* headlined its story on this report: 'Fat & Dead ... at 3'; the *Express*: 'Child 3 Dies from Being Fat: The Terrifying Truth Behind Britain's Obesity Epidemic'; and the *Telegraph* shouted 'Now Obesity Kills Child Aged Three'. Their stories hinged on a letter written by Dr McKenzie to the committee claiming that 'one child at the age of three has died of heart failure due to extreme obesity'. The committee decided to include this claim no doubt for dramatic effect, even though, as was later discovered, the child actually died of a congenital heart condition. An independent MP and member of the committee, Richard Taylor, explained: 'We had had a lot of evidence throughout the inquiry that obesity in children is a huge, huge increasing problem. ... It was felt that this was a way of emphasizing the danger for children.'

The report was immediately rubbished by the food scientist Tom Sanders who called the report 'flawed, ill-researched and ... factually wrong'. In the *Daily Telegraph*, he attacked the report's authors for 'tarting it up' to attract headlines and please 'anti-food lobbyists' claiming that 'that most published studies do not show that overweight children report eating more "junk food" than their lean peers'. David Hinchliffe, the Health Committee's chairman, responded by counterclaiming that the aggressive media assaults on his committee were a result of behind-the-scenes manipulation by the food industry in a battle for public opinion. 'Sanders acts as a consultant to the food industry, and was obviously wheeled out to do a hatchet job on its behalf. ... We didn't mention the three-year-old in our media summary, or even at our news conference', he claimed. 'But she was used by those who wished to divert attention from the substance of the report. It was co-ordinated and used to discredit the report. It was a disgrace.' On Thursday, 3 June 2004, Vivienne Parry (2004) summarized the problem in the *Guardian*: 'And where was science in all of this? Both muted and strident. ... The reason is that we all think we know about obesity; it's a simple energy equation – intake v output. The reality is that weight regulation is incredibly complex science. It also has more attendant confounding baggage – psychological and cultural – than any other health issue.'

Clearly the backstage interests on both sides were now fully on the table. But the risks were undeniable, even if they were being distorted by the press. So despite the PR gaff, the coalition of food, parent and health interests had clearly made their point. In November 2004, the Labour government tabled their plans for dealing with obesity: 'Junk food adverts during children's programmes will be banned and unhealthy foods issued with warning labels under a "traffic light" scheme to help tackle Britain's obesity crisis. The moves will be the centrepiece of the government's long-awaited report on public health, to be published on Tuesday, which will cover the nation's slide into unhealthy habits, including eating, smoking and drinking to excess', reported the *Guardian*.

Still policymaking is a drawn out affair in Britain, especially given the high stakes. A subsequent Ofcom (2006) committee reviewing the findings of the literature review again declaring:

- The evidence indicates that promotional activity influences children's eating habits.
- That parents and children needed help to reduce the proportion of children's diets which are made up of foods, snacks or meals high in fat, sugar or salt in favour of healthier options.
- It is time to move from debating the issue to determining solutions – and these must involve parents, children and young people, government, regulators, schools and industry.

Given the excess of HFSS (High in Fat, Salt or Sugar) foods and the continued targeting of children by the food industries, it was important to change the way that foods are promoted on TV. A watershed ban on unhealthy food marketing on programmes with 50 per cent child audiences was one way of achieving this, they concluded. So the battle was essentially over. The industry knew that a point of 'no return' had been passed and admitted that they must adapt to a new reality. After three years of deliberation the New Labour government announced legislation in 2007, banning TV advertising on children's time television targeting young people under 16 years of age. The food advertising ban came into force in 2007 and has been monitored and strengthened since. Yet a report in 2009 found that although the food ads targeting children were much healthier, and millions had been spend on 'anti-obesity' advertising, young people's overall exposure to food ads was increasing (Advertising Standards Association 2009).

Media culture as an obesogenic environment

In the light of the dynamics of advocacy, it is hard to blame only journalists for the trajectory that moral panic took. TV advertising was a familiar villain. And public interest groups were primed for the public struggle because of the ambiguous legal standing of child consumers. In both countries, law courts, legislators and policy wonks had to weigh up the different arguments about the causes of obesity. In their dependence on expert sources, they had to interpret the complexities of risk analysis that indicated that TV was the intersection between the obesogenic environment and the obesogenic family. Although these policy debates unfolded very differently in the UK and the US, it is clear that the market's communication of consumption risks was now a public health issue.

Moral panic is a volatile political force in the risk society. When the obesity pandemic intensified anxiety about children's lifestyles, the political pressure mounted in both the US and the UK to do something to alter fast food culture. Driving this discursive politics was the question of blame for increasingly sedentary overweight children. But the epidemiological analysis of the 'environmental' risk factors highlighted the systemic dietary bias in the mediated marketplace and its potential impact on children's brand preferences and food choices. The policy reviews focused on two contested empirical questions: first, the extent to which children were exposed to a biased diet on TV and second, whether children are 'unduly influenced' by the food marketing they see. In Britain, Tony Blair's government passed legislation banning advertising of food on children's TV as a precautionary measure which was part of its comprehensive policy to fight child obesity. In America, where the debate was stymied in the courts and frustrated by laws that granted commercial speech to marketers, the government could only encourage corporate responsibility in the vain hope that industry would turn the rising tide of child obesity.

In the above account I have shown how the press discourses on child obesity differed considerably in the US and the UK largely because the laws, traditions, advocacy groups and ideologies differed. In the US three histori-cal issues framed the policy response to the controversy. The first was an established coalition of anti-commercial interests formed by the battles over commercial TV. The second is American constitutional law and litigious policymaking process that has established commercial free speech as a foun-dational right of corporations. And the third is what Regina Lawrence calls the strong individualism that characterizes American neoliberal ideology which puts the responsibility for health on the individual, not the govern-ment. In her study of the news coverage of obesity she notes how a 'vigorous frame contest' was underway 'which opposed the arguments emphasizing personal responsibility for health with arguments emphasizing the social environment, including corporate and public policy' (Lawrence 2004: 56). This seems an apt account of this political controversy where lifestyle choices of children were being called a public health concern.

In Britain, the situation was different. First there was a powerful 'foodie lobby' mobilized in the aftermath of BSE and GMO campaigns. Second there were strong public health traditions that had prioritized children's health and mandated the FSA to undertake research that protected it. And third, with Labour in power, the minister responsible for media regulation was trapped in the contradictions implied by Ofcom's neoliberal mandate to empower child consumers. As I write Michele Obama has put the weight of the Oval Office behind the campaign against child obesity while in Britain the issue has disappeared from the front pages – panic over.

Part II
The Policy Nexus: Assessing Children's Vulnerability to the TV Diet

Epidemiology had revealed that obesity was a health risk, and TV viewing a risk factor associated with both children's sedentary lifestyles and fast food diets. Interpreting the research into obesogenic lifestyles through the 'fast food frame', journalists in both America and Britain demanded to know how to stop the trend towards overweight children. Health advocates brandishing scientific studies of media exposure risks commandeered the news in an attempt to shift public policy priorities in both countries. Galvanized by anxieties about children's choices, the debates about their obesogenic lifestyles became politically charged. On one side stood the health advocates demanding a ban on ads targeting 'vulnerable' children and on the other stood the food marketers arguing that parents should do a better job. Caught between the health lobby and the big food corporations, legislators faced a Solomonesque problem: were corporations, schools or parents to blame for children's increasingly unhealthy diet and sedentary lifestyles?

The discursive politics of globesity, I believe, helped to crystallize the realization that the mediated marketplace is a system both of risk distribution and risk communication. The application of risk analysis to children's weight gain reminded everyone that the marketplace promotes risk taking through its food advertising. In both countries, long-held concerns about children's lifestyles dovetailed neatly with the legal uncertainties surrounding children's status as consumers. In the battle of spin that was transacted in the press, the only way for the state to reduce the soaring public health costs was to regulate food marketing or to encroach on parenting prerogatives – neither option could be easily achieved. In both countries public bodies considered the question. Hearings were held, reports commissioned and the evidence about the market's promotion of lifestyle risks to children reviewed exhaustively. The Hastings Report and Federal Trade Commission studies had established that children in both countries are regularly exposed to a TV diet which is far from balanced and void of fruits and vegetables. And the Ofcom (2006) and Institute of Medicine (Koplan et al. 2006) reviews had supported the idea that because children's preferences and requests could be shaped by food advertising, something should be done. Yet despite looking at the same evidence of the contribution of marketing communication to children's unhealthy diets, in the UK a ban was legislated whereas in the US policy remained the same.

Acknowledging the part played by medical research in framing the discussion of obesogenic lifestyles, Kline (2006) has suggested that neoliberalism is implicit in the 'medicalization of health care' in the US because Americans ascribe responsibility for ill health to the individual, rather than to the public health system. This ideological factor was in evidence in the greater reporting of both the obesity drug and bariatric surgery in the US news, compared with the *Guardian*. The limit of the medical perspective on the obesogenic environment, Kline implies, is that it potentially obfuscates other ways of thinking about who is responsible for causing and curing lifestyle risks. Noting the inability of US policymakers to do anything about the obesogenic lifestyles of children, Lawrence (2004) argues that the failure can be attributed to the neoliberal ideology: 'as with many other social problems, in the United States public health issues face cultural and political resistance to claims of systemic causation and governmental responsibility for solutions'. Lifestyle risks, whether smoking, obesity or eating hormone-enhanced meat, remain consumer choices and therefore a matter that individuals must take responsibility for. But as we saw, they also augured rising health costs.

This may be true, but I don't think the restraint of American legislators is simply attitudinal. Although health care is clearly framed as an individual responsibility in the US, the health advocates also ran up against the constitutional laws circumscribing risk communication in the neoliberal marketplace. The precedent of tobacco had established that the state can mandate warnings and nutritional labelling on the packages, set standards for truthful claims in ads and fund PSAs to inform the public about the risks. The courts decided that these principles applied to hamburgers too. Granted commercial free speech, manufacturers of hazardous goods (especially food and drugs) must disclose all 'known' risks so that consumers can exercise informed consent in their purchases. It was with these legal constraints in mind that the US judiciary imposed no additional burdens on McDonald's to warn customers about the lifestyle risks associated with a lifelong diet of burgers and chips. Indeed the judge felt that most consumers were already well informed of these.

But as the McFat case also pointed out, even if normal adults understand lifestyle risks and corporations duly make risk information available, two unresolved issues were highlighted by pandemic obesity: the first concerned the 'unknown' and largely unintended systemic risks posed by the skewed targeting of children by marketers of energy-dense foods. The second concerned those individuals who were incapable of informed consent in market transactions – namely children, who were neither sufficiently informed or sufficiently rational to make informed choices about risky products like cigarettes or foods. In their review of the literature on marketing to children, the APA committee found that 'given that young children inherently lack the cognitive capability to effectively recognize and defend against televised commercial persuasion in this manner, we recommend that policymakers pursue efforts to constrain advertising specifically directed to this particular age group' (Wilcox et al. 2004: 1). The obesity pandemic thus posed a twin challenge to neoliberal market ideology in the risk society because unless children are both fully informed and rational, they must be protected from harm. The first was to conceive of the marketplace itself as a system of risk communication. The second was to acknowledge the exceptional circumstances of child consumers who were deemed insufficiently capable of informed consent to lifestyle risk taking. Although US legislators have ducked the question, in the UK these issues were confronted with a radically different result: a legislated ban on food advertising targeting children under 16.

I have noted that when the obesity epidemic spilt onto the front pages in the UK, the public health system was already reformulating its strategy for managing food risks. As a pioneer in public health and welfare state medicine, Britain also has an established tradition of protecting children's health. Arguing that in the UK the moral panic about food marketing distorted the policymaking process, David Buckingham reviews Ofcom's decision-making process to explore 'the way the figure of the child consumer was conceptualised both in the research and the policy debates' (Buckingham 2009a: 217). In a series of articles Buckingham (2009a, 2009b) critiques Ofcom's precautionary regulation of food advertising because he thinks political expediency and parental anxiety resulted in a policy that 'was not ultimately justified by the evidence' and which reflected the 'continuing incoherence about the very definition of childhood' by confirming their status as 'vulnerable' consumers.

Buckingham rightly notes that Ofcom was initially launched by the Labour Government in 2003 with a neoliberal mandate (adapted from the US) with the intent of shifting responsibilities for children's cultural choice from producers to consumers. Ofcom at first championed media literacy because it 'can be seen as a kind of antidote to harmful media effects' based on its assumption of children's competence (Buckingham 2009a: 223). For this reason media literacy was included in Ofcom's mandate under the rewritten Broadcast Act (2003). But he goes on to note that as Ofcom reviewed the evidence gathered by scientific reviews of children's systematic exposure to HFSS food advertising (products high in fat, sugars and salts) and the possibility that marketing was impacting their diet, it qualified this principle. These regulators concluded that research revealed a sufficient threat to children's health that a precautionary policy was a 'proportionate response' given their mandate to protect children under the age of 18 from ads 'that may be misleading, harmful or offensive'. Buckingham declares with distain, 'While "responsibilisation" may be a characteristic strategy of modern forms of (media) governance, it is clearly seen to have its limits when it comes to the regulation of children' in the UK.

He is critical of Ofcom's approach for a number of reasons, some practical, some ideological and some empirical. Of the practical ones he rightly notes that the policy did not go as far as some advocates demanded, leaving children exposed to skewed diet of prime time TV advertising. In fact a ban was likely to reduce exposure to the prime time diet very little. Secondly he notes the regulations imposed an 'exceptionally rigid' definition of healthy foods which makes it impossible to promote full fat milk, nuts and cheese, for example, to children. That may be so, but it was the FSA and not Ofcom that developed those guidelines based on nutritional science. Thirdly he claims that a ban weakens the economic base for the production of children's TV, and therefore threatens the quality of children's programming. It also might redirect ad funds to other media such as online and stealth media that were not included in the act. But the shift would not cut gross revenue if food advertisers simply redirect their children's spends to prime time. And finally, Buckingham argues the cut-off at age 16 cannot be justified on the research evidence which shows that children over 8 are generally media literate (i.e. they understand the intent to sell and are sceptical and informed consumers). But the Broadcast Act of 2003 mandated Ofcom with protecting children up to age 18 with an eye to 'the vulnerability of children and to the degree of harm and offence likely to be caused'. Age 18 is defined by the UN Convention on the Rights of the Child which Britain signed and the US did not.

Precautionary policymaking and the weight of evidence

Policy analysis involves a complex weighing up a complex system of multiple interacting risk factors as they influence different populations under different circumstances. It applies a 'balance of probabilities' rather than a 'proof of harm' criteria to evaluate the evidence gathered about the interrelationships between these variables. A relationship between a determinant (exposure to food ads) and dependent variable (requests to parents) can be significant, but only in the absence of other factors (such as advertising scepticism), which can also enhance or counteract it. This relationship could also be moderated by intervening variables (brand affect) that are known only if measured. This means that researchers must conceive of these complex interrelationships in order to account for the variation caused by intervening and mitigating factors. Policy analysis therefore demands a weighing up of complex evidence undertaken in different circumstances, at different times, and on different populations in which no one finding is definitive nor are findings necessarily of equal explanatory power. In reviewing a body of evidence, therefore, the different constructs measured, the qualitative differences in research design, the known limitations of each methodology and the unaccounted for variables must be acknowledged. For this reason, scientific reviewers qualify their judgements by reading the studies critically and proposing evaluative criteria which can be applied to the body of research.

Buckingham implies that Ofcom's protectionist approach is informed by a biased reading of the research evaluating the exposure risks to children. He particularly accuses Ofcom of relying on the Livingstone and Helsper and the Institute of Medicine reviews which recommended precautionary principles, although both found evidence of only 'limited effects' of children's advertising and inconsistencies in the evidence of consumer competence. Ofcom commissioned and consulted a number of independent researchers before it came to its conclusions. As in all empirical research, there are diverse interpretations of findings depending on when the research was done and the sample and the methods used. Many studies were undertaken in the US and might not reflect the situation in Britain. Research results depend on the marketing practices deployed, the populations studied, the variables operationalized and the explanations being evaluated. But the evidence of limited effects was consistent. As Livingstone and Helsper noted, both correlational and experimental studies tend to reveal fairly consistent but fairly modest effects, 'accounting for some 5% of the variance in the dependent variable'. They conclude therefore that TV advertising has a modest direct effect on children's food choices and an indirect one on children's patterns of eating independent of their media literacy. The persuasion effect is modest, they note, because the influence of brand advertising on product preferences and requests is moderated by the family context and therefore varies depending on the age, gender and social background of the child.

I believe that Ofcom was mindful of these limitations and fully aware that multiple factors account for child obesity and TV advertising is one among many influences on food choices. But given the controversial implications of research on the TV diet and its influences on children, I set out in Part II of this book to revisit this literature and review current evidence about the communication of health risks in TV food advertising targeting children. In particular, I want to explain why a precautionary policy can be justified by a 'strong finding of a weak effect' of the TV diet on brand preferences and requests.

Chapter 4 starts with the Food Standards Commission's review of food advertising which argued that there is a systematic bias in the marketing of foods on children's TV (Hastings et al. 2003). Assessing 44 studies from around the world, they found the food ads that children were exposed to provided a skewed and unhealthy representation of the daily diet – greatly at odds with recommended caloric intake. Even where ostensibly 'healthy' rather than snack foods were promoted, these tended to be in their least healthy form, such as sweetened 'wholegrain' breakfast cereal or deep-fried vegetables. Hastings et al. concluded that 'a clear pattern emerged that the advertised diet was too high in fats, sugars and salt' (Hastings et al. 2003: 84). My own review of studies undertaken since 2003 notes that despite repeated calls for responsible marketing, not much was changing in American food advertising. Reporting a comparative content analysis I go on to report the differences between the food advertising messages directed at children in the UK and North America. Assessing the changes taking place in food advertising directed at children I note that some advertisers repositioned themselves around the banner of 'corporate responsibility'. The discursive politics of obesity not only provoked but reinforced the state's efforts to responsibilize the food industry. Yet the evidence suggests that the threat of a regulatory ban was impacting advertising strategies of British food marketers considerably more than North American.

Confusing the meaning of market regulation with the 'regulation of children' turns out to be an important ideological torquing of the policy reflecting Buckingham's conviction that older children should be considered competent rather than vulnerable consumers because of their media literacy. The threat of regulation is part of the welfare state's means of market regulation and in the UK it resulted in a modest shift in 'responsible marketing of foods'. But I must point out that the policy directed at HFSS food advertising in children's programming is not strictly a regulation of children, and only indirectly children's media choices. Ofcom's mandate after all is the regulation of mediated markets, specifically the promotional communication to young consumers about products associated with lifestyle risks. Ofcom's policy imposes restrictions on those who are targeting children with 'risky' foods – not on all advertising of food. It seeks to protect children until they can be deemed fully cognizant of the lifestyle risks associated with HFSS foods. At the same time it encouraged producers to advertise healthy foods. In short, this precautionary policy recognizes the role of the state in regulating risk communication in mediated markets. It does so by balancing the *responsibilization of producers* with the *responsibilization of consumers*. Given its regulatory mandate, Ofcom's 'precautionary' ban on advertising of foods on children's time TV appears to me to be a pioneering attempt to make risk communication in the marketplace part of a broader strategy for promoting children's health and well-being.

Although I disagree with Buckingham's assessment of the merits of this precautionary policy, I believe he is right in noting the salience of scientific evidence in these deliberations about children's exposure to risks in mediated markets. Parallelling the role that the science of epidemiology played in framing the public debates about lifestyle risks associated with weight gain, the science of media effects played a crucial role in the policy determination of marketplace risk factors. Since the 1970s the issue of direct-to-child advertising has been the subject of considerable research which provided the evidentiary basis for making these policy decisions about the impact of food advertising on children's food consumption. Like all fields of empirical research the science of risk communication uses diverse methods and offers different, and sometimes competing, explanations of complex processes. To adjudicate these empirical questions, policymakers commission systematic reviews of the existent scientific literature on food marketing as a risk factor in children's obesity. Researchers were most interested in three key ways that TV advertisers influence children's diet negatively. The first question concerned the extent of advertising's persuasive influence on children's product knowledge, brand preferences and actual consumption choices. The second concerned their media literacy – the age when children can be assumed to be sceptical about marketing and understand that advertising on TV is intended to persuade them. The third concerned children's growing power within the family – known as pester power, it involved the success of their requests for unhealthy foods.

In Chapter 5 I review the advertising effects literature noting the diversity of approaches that have been used to study the processes through which advertising can influence children's choices. The evidence is clear: children are neither 'manipulated' by advertisers or 'hopeless dupes'. But that does not mean they are competent or fully empowered as consumers either. The evidence consistently shows that young children cannot be assumed to meet the criteria of informed choice so critical to the neoliberal model of consumer responsibilization. The evidence is strong that along with other factors, food marketing influences some children's consumption knowledge, preferences, requests and choices, both directly and indirectly.

Yet in Chapter 6 I examine the reasons why advertisers' influence on children's weight status is so limited. Although advertising literacy proves a modest buffer, other mitigating circumstances such as an early taste for healthy foods, family control of diet and nutritional knowledge can mitigate the impacts of a biased mediated marketplace too. In a cross-sectional diary study of Vancouver students aged 8–12, I examine a model of the patterns of children's food consumption, preferences and discretionary choices which shows that taste, media literacy and parental control of diet interact with TV exposure. Noting the importance of brand knowledge, parental provisioning and children's own taste and nutritional knowledge, I argue that the lifestyle risks associated with their exposure to advertising are most related to children's *discretionary snacking choices* sanctioned by their consumer empowerment in the 'obesogenic' family. Moreover despite their scepticism and understanding of the advertisers' intent to sell, older children are not immune to the influences of branded campaigns either their growing empowerment is accompanied by a willingness to take lifestyle risks.

4
The TV Diet: Advertising as a Biased System of Risk Communication

Because of their uncertain status as consumers, the globesity controversy focused public attention on the degree to which children are exposed to food advertising targeting them. A penetrating spotlight was cast on the magnitude of marketing resources devoted to selling energy-dense foods on television. A quick glance at the adspends reminds us that food products are prominent in global advertising spends. Harris et al. (2002) documented more than 20 per cent increases in total US food advertising spending from 1995 to 1999. The magazine *Advertising Age* attempted to estimate advertisement spending in terms of measured media purchase in 2005. It placed the spending of global food advertising at US$8129 million, soft drink advertising at US$3971 million, restaurant advertising at US$3349 million and candy advertising at US$1109 million (Endicott 2005). Overall, these food-related categories accounted for 16.8 per cent of the total amount spent on advertising in 2005 (Advertising Age 2006: 7). Of this approximately 65–70 per cent of all food spending was devoted to television (Warren et al. 2008).

In 2006, the FTC subpoenaed adspends from 44 food and beverage companies for its inquiry, estimating that $1,618,600, 000 was spent to promote food and beverages to children and adolescents in the US (Holt et al. 2007). This represents all spending on promotion. But television remains the preferred venue for branded products, which disproportionately feature the so-called bad five 'core' product categories – soft drinks, fast food, confections, snacks and sweetened cereals. Although meat, milk, fruit and vegetables are also advertised sometimes, it is to a lesser degree and mostly in supermarket ads that use local print media.

The chart in Figure 4.1 uses Advertising Age figures to estimate the spends on five core products among the top 200 TV brands, which account for 85 per cent of the US TV spends. Food accounts for approximately 8 per cent of TV time, ranking as the third most advertised product sector. Moreover it is also evident that fast food, cereals and soft drinks contribute the lion's share of the revenues to media. In 2006, fast food accounted for almost

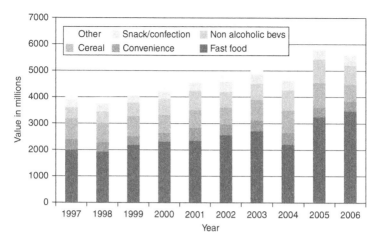

Figure 4.1 Ad spending by food types in the US (top 200 advertisers)

60 per cent of the food sectors media buy. The 'other' food category rarely constitutes more than 8 per cent of the food industry's TV marketing in the US. It is immediately evident that with the exception of 1998, 2004 and 2006 the total spends of fast food companies and restaurants has increased over the last few years, whereas other food categories have remained relatively stable. Even if advertising were banned in children's programmes, children would still be exposed to a skewed representation of the range of food products, to the degree that they watch prime time TV.

It has long been argued that TV offers a biased representation of eating as a cultural practice. Story and Faulkner (1990) undertook a study of what they called the 'prime time diet' by coding the appearance of food in the 15 top ranked television programmes on US networks. Almost five mentions were made to food in each half hour of TV programming, and closer analysis revealed that over 60 per cent of all foods shown were for low-nutrient beverages and sweets. Of the foods represented 75 per cent were shown being eaten 'between' meals and on the run and snacking occurred 2.2 times each half hour. Naturally, snacks tend to be biased towards sweet or energy-dense treats while less than 10 per cent of eating occasions include fruit or vegetables. The study noted that there was remarkably little difference between the food culture of prime time programmes and that of the advertising. Most studies of children's advertising similarly report the 'unhealthy' bias of the recent advertised diet, which tends to emphasize sweet, salty and energy-dense food brands in their children's time marketing campaigns. The 'Saturday Morning Pyramid' described by Kotz and Story (1994) is the complete antithesis of the Food Guide Pyramid set forth by the US Department of Agriculture. The Hastings et al. (2003) review summarized what 30 years of research into the

TV diet had shown. The review noted that whether the studies were conducted in the UK, New Zealand, Australia or the US, most of the advertised foods were high in fat, sugar, and/or salt with very low nutritional value (Hill and Radimer 1997; Lewis and Hill 1998; Byrd-Bredbenner and Grasso 1999; Østbye et al. 1993; Hammond et al. 1999; Wilson et al. 1999.

Studies in the US, UK and especially Australia (Hill and Radimer 1997; Kuribayashi 2001) confirmed that television does not represent the range of the foods necessary for a balanced diet. Not only is there a preponderance of poor nutritional items but also 'healthier' food options are rarely shown at all. Hill and Radimer (1997), for example, argue that 'the overall picture portrayed to children was poorly balanced and involved a narrow range of foods, particularly snack and "extra" foods, and thus was far from that recommended for health eating' (Hill and Radimer 1997). They noted that fruits or vegetables were mostly shown to imply (incorrectly) that the product was healthy when the actual content of these core foods in the advertised product was negligible (Hill and Radimer 1997). Kuribayashi (2001) found that 'the average number of calories from advertised products is over 400 per serving for children' (Kuribayashi 2001: 317).

Byrd-Bredbenner and Grasso (2001) also considered the potential effect of food advertising policy changes and found in a prime time sample that regulation can have a potentially negative impact on health communication in advertising. Overall, there is a decline in nutrient quality of the foods advertised whereas the general health claims remain about the same and are made in approximately 25 per cent of all ads. Advertising policy restricting nutrition claims, they argue, is not an inducement to making healthy foods. Reflecting on the impact of policy and self-regulation on advertising time in the US, Carol Byrd-Bredbenner (2002) reports on the changes taking place in Saturday morning food advertising since 1971. Although total commercial time has decreased to 9.5 minutes per hour, the composition of non-programme time has been filled with network promos and PSAs, resulting in an average exposure rate of 37 spots per hour. This leads to an increase from 12.4 to 17.2 food ads per hour over the period 1971–99. She also notes that breads and cereals decreased from 40 per cent to 16 per cent by 1999 and sweetened breakfast cereals steadily declined from 33 per cent in 1975 to 14 per cent in 1999 of all food ads. Meanwhile beverages and soft drinks decline from 30 per cent in 1970 to 6 per cent in 1999 of all food ads shown on Saturday morning. On the other hand Fast Food ads increase from 8 per cent in 1971 to 28 per cent of all food ads in 1999.

Hastings et al. (2003) add that it is not just what is advertised excessively but what is missing that matters. They found that the advertising targeting children 'was lacking in meats, fruit and vegetables (especially fresh, non-processed meat, fruit and vegetables)' (Hastings et al. 2003: 84). Healthier products were often shown in their most unhealthy form – 'pre-sugared breakfast cereals, sweetened dairy products, processed meat (burgers), breaded fish, canned fruit and deep-fried vegetables' (Hastings et al. 2003: 85). Healthier products were also used to boost the perceived nutritional value of food products with low levels of nutrition. Hastings et al. therefore concluded that 'creative appeals in children's food advertising concentrated on "fun" and "taste", rather than on health or nutrition' (Hastings et al. 2003: 100).

The Hastings report also examined the various creative strategies employed in children's food advertising. Animation was found to be a frequently utilized device and was 'particularly strongly associated with children's food advertisements compared with non-food. … Breakfast cereal advertisements were identified as particularly likely to involve a mixed animation/live action format in which children encounter fantasy cartoon characters' (Hastings et al. 2003: 95). These findings are consistent with a study by Reece et al. which found that 'cartoon characters appeared, alone or with real people, in nearly half of the ads. … Celebrities were rarely used, and they were as likely to be fictional characters … as they were to be well-known stars' (Reece et al. 1999: 203). Thus animation is a commonly used device in the attempts to attract and hold the attention of children. This device ties in with the notion of fun, which runs through the most frequently appearing general themes employed in the ads themselves. Hill and Radimer (1997: 210) found that 'fun messages' predominated in Australian advertisements for many of the core foods which can be consumed as snacks. This is consistent with Lewis and Hill's (1998) British study which confirmed the greater use of animation, stories, humour and the promotion of fun/happiness/mood alteration in food advertising for children (Lewis and Hill 1998). More recent research also agrees that a great deal of children's advertising associates food and eating with the themes of fun, happiness and play as branding transforms nutrition into 'fun food' (Connor 2006).

Since Hastings

Studies published after the Hastings et al. (2003) report do little to disturb this picture (Cairns et al. 2009). Story and French (2004) report a sample from 52.5 hours of US Saturday morning programming that 57 per cent of all ads were for food products. 44 per cent of these were for foods high in fats and sugar, 11 per cent were for fast food restaurants. The cereals were predominantly pre-sweetened breakfast cereals. In short, not much had changed from their earlier study. Others have found that food ads represent only 20 per cent of children's television advertising in the UK (Ofcom 2005), but between 30 per cent and 34 per cent in the US and Australia (Harrison and Marske 2005; Neville et al. 2005; Folta et al. 2006) and 37 per cent in New Zealand (Wilson et al. 2006). British and Australian food advertising was found to be more intensive in programming for children than for adults (Neville et al. 2005). One Australian study estimated that of the 406 advertisements found on children's programming 252 advertisements were for fast food (including hamburgers, pizza and fried chicken); 84 advertisements were for soft drinks; and 28 were for ice cream products. A child watching four hours of television per day over the six-week holiday period would have seen a total of 649 junk food ads including 404 advertisements for fast food, 135 advertisements for soft beverages and 44 for ice cream products (Australian Division of General Practice 2003).

A content analysis of food promotion on British terrestrial and non-terrestrial channels for March and April of 2005 has been reported (Ofcom 2006). Core category products accounted for 20 per cent of the 12,839 commercials included, but only 13 per cent of commercial airtime, again indicating that advertisers in this category favour shorter ads. Core category products also accounted for 8 per cent of the 3,161 sponsorship credits and 5 per cent of 526 programme promotion credits. There was an average of 3.4 core category ads per hour on the terrestrial channels, rising to 5 per hour on the dedicated children's channels, which accounted for 81 per cent of all core category ads in the sample. Within the core categories, the largest groupings were for prepared convenience foods (26 per cent) and confectionery (20 per cent). Dairy products accounted for 17 per cent, chain restaurants for 12 per cent and soft drinks for 9 per cent. 20 per cent of core category ads on terrestrial children's airtime were for chain restaurants, 20 per cent for cereal and 15 per cent for soft drinks compared with 8 per cent, 14 per cent and 6 per cent respectively on terrestrial adult time, making these the most child-targeted categories.

Chapman et al.'s (2006) recent study in Australia finds that 31 per cent of all ads are for food products (higher than in the US), and of these, 81 per cent are unhealthy (includes fruit juices) whereas 19 per cent are relatively healthy products (breads, unsweetened cereals). They also report that Saturday morning between 7 a.m. and 9 a.m. and G-class programming (for unsupervised child watching) was highest in food ads and the unhealthiest at a rate of 6 per hour. On these children's time shows, fast food constitutes 30 per cent of ads, confection and candy 13 per cent, snacks 8 per cent and sweet breakfast 6 per cent. They argue that the levels of unhealthy food advertising have not decreased, in spite of a national fruit and vegetable month campaign (between 60 and 80 per cent of the foods are in the high-fat–low-nutrition category). They also report violations of the advertising guidelines (mostly misleading information and unacceptable promotional practices) imply that current regulations are ineffective in staunching the most egregious techniques of targeting.

The nutritional value of the advertised diet gave cause for concern too. A study in Australia found that foods high in fat and sugar accounted for 55 per cent of children's food ads. It also found that 83 per cent of American food ads shown during the top rated children's programmes were for candy, sweets, soft drinks, convenience foods, or fast food restaurants (Neville et al. 2005; Harrison and Marske 2005). In New Zealand, Wilson et al. (2006) found 73 per cent of children's food ads were for less healthy food. Fast food advertising in New Zealand became more intense as the weekday afternoon slots progressed, suggesting the targeting of children near meal time, encouraging requests to the parents. Similarly, in a separate analysis of commercials in Sydney, Neville et al. (2005) found nearly three times as many confectionery ads and twice as many fast food restaurant ads per hour during children's programmes than during adults' programmes. Roberts and Pettigrew conclude that 'the foods advertised to children were diametrically opposed to the foods recommended for children' (Roberts and Pettigrew 2007: 360). Overall, there exists a great deal of support for the idea that food marketed on kids TV does not provide a roadmap for healthy eating.

Techniques for targeting and appealing to kids

Most studies also note that the ads targeting children employ marketing techniques such as celebrity testimonials, pester power, animated narratives and overstatement, which in the past have been considered difficult for children to understand. In America, advertisers utilize a wide range of food marketing practices to target children including in-school marketing, product placements, kids' clubs, online media, toys and products with brand logos, and youth-targeted promotions using cross-selling, tie-ins and sweepstake prizes (Story and French 2004; Wootan 2003). Such tactics tend to be subject to less regulation than advertising (Hawkes 2004). This view is echoed by Byrd-Bredbenner (2002) who found that 'The most common misleading image was fresh fruit shown in advertisements for fruit-flavoured candy and beverages. Through visual images of fruits, advertisers conveyed a false impression of the fruit content of foods even though they did not make any false verbal statements' (Byrd-Bredbenner 2002: 394).

In the UK, the Food Commission reports on 41 non-broadcast food marketing techniques aimed at children, observing that

> [m]arketing campaigns aimed at children and young people move smoothly between different formats, perhaps combining product placement in blockbuster films; which in turn feature characters who will appear on food products and in interactive games; backed by websites offering music downloads and movie clips, containing yet more inducements to buy.
>
> (2005: 3)

In these cases, healthy food products are being used to provide 'symbolic health' value to low-health food products. Which?, the leading the Consumers' Association in Britain recently undertook its own study to 'expose the top twelve "dirty" marketing tricks that food companies use and which parents may not even be aware of' (Which? 2006: 2).

Harrison and Marske (2005) found that 90.8 per cent of the American children's time food ads coded as targeting children contained no health-related messages (claims of 'natural ingredients', the most common message in this category, accounted for 5.1 per cent of food ads targeting children). The characters depicted in the children's food ads were more likely to be male (61.3 per cent) and white (73.5 per cent). Over 80 per cent of characters were depicted as of average body size; as Harrison and Marske (2005: 1572) observe, 'The prevalence of average-sized and thin characters in our sample also suggests that anyone can eat a diet low in fiber and high in fat and salt and still remain slender'. Finally, in terms of eating occasions and locations, snack time was the most common eating occasion across the sample, accounting for 58.4 per cent of child ads and 40.3 per cent of general ads. The pattern of eating locations was consistent with this. When characters were shown eating, this happened in locations other than homes or restaurants in 56.2 per cent of the child ads and in 54 per cent of general ads.

In terms of creative strategies, several studies found animation was common in food advertising, sometimes combined with live action to show children interacting with cartoon characters. The most popular appeals were hedonistic, emphasizing taste, humour, fun and action-adventure. There was relatively little evidence of overt attempts to encourage pester power, or of widespread use of celebrity endorsements. Premiums or competition prizes were found in up to 25 per cent of children's food ads, however, particularly for cereals and fast foods. If children use several media simultaneously, the implications of such integrated marketing communications are potentially much more significant.

Page and Brewster (2007) examined the frequency of promotional strategies and attention elements in 147 distinct commercials for foods shown during children's programming blocks on US broadcast networks. Food ads were 43 per cent of all commercials, toy ads were 33 per cent, and other children's entertainment products were 15 per cent of the total non-programming time. Of the food ads, 25 per cent featured sugary cereals and 16 per cent were for fast food restaurants. Snacks and confections accounted for 13 per cent, soft drinks 8 per cent and pizza and other ready foods were 7.5 per cent. Of the food ads the promotional tactics included cross selling 39 per cent, real children shown with food 54 per cent, brand characters 44 per cent, contests and collectables 17 per cent and15 per cent of the ads referred children to a website including cross media promotion and web games. The dominant attention-grabbing techniques are typical of advertising designed to build brand awareness, including humour, animals, lively animation and fast pacing of action and scenes.

Arguing that the cumulative effects of advertising on children are due to the repeated exposure to the thematic and social subtext of messages about eating and meaning of food, Roberts and Pettigrew (2007) undertook a thematic content analysis of Australian children's food advertising. Their study of children's morning television programmes found that 22 per cent of the commercial spots were for food but these consisted of only 30 unique campaigns (some of which were repeated up to 11 times in the sample). Of the unique ads, 72 per cent were for foods that needed to be eaten in moderation whereas 16 per cent were for milk products, 3 per cent for fruit and vegetables, 4 per cent for healthy grains and 4.5 per cent for protein rich meat products. This led the researchers to conclude that foods promoted on TV were overwhelmingly unhealthy and not supportive of healthy eating guidelines. Their study also described four major food-related themes common in Australian children's food advertising – portrayal of grazing (a tendency for snacking to be portrayed as the most frequent method of consuming food rather than a specific meal activity), denigration of raw foods (a tendency for ads to position packaged food as a more desirable option than unprocessed alternatives), exaggerated health claims and enhancement of popularity, performance and mood (consumption of a food product would enhance one of these traits). Overall, it was concluded that these messages 'communicated numerous themes that disregard healthy eating practices' (Roberts and Pettigrew 2007: 365). They go on to note that the various techniques used by marketers to hold the attention of their audience and to 'establish brand loyalty among kids' (Page and Brewster 2007: 900) are a crucial part of the biased representations. Examining the marketing techniques used, they found that the predominant appeal is to children's fantasy (57 per cent), sense of fun (43 per cent), humour (38 per cent) or adventure (33 per cent). Of the ads 35 per cent referred to the taste of the product while 30 per cent had some reference to health appeal. Of the promotional tactics, 33 per cent had a premium or offer, 30 per cent had a brand character and 17 per cent used a celebrity. The study is unique in that it also identified the higher level lifestyle themes associated with food finding, 53 per cent showed snacking rather than meal time eating, 50 per cent showed solitary eating and family meals only occurred in 7 per cent.

In a sample containing 4324 food and beverage advertisements aired during a total of 672 hours of programming Warren et al. (2008) found that the five energy-dense categories comprised 74 per cent of all food advertisements: pizza/fast food (24 per cent), sweets (16 per cent), breakfast foods (13 per cent), family restaurants (12 per cent) and convenience entrees/meals (9 per cent). By contrast, the five healthiest food groups comprised barely more than 12 per cent of the product categories advertised. These categories were dairy (3.6 per cent), pasta/bread (3.5 per cent), juice (3 per cent), meat (1.4 per cent) and fruits/vegetables (0.4 per cent). Carbonated or artificially flavoured beverages and fats/condiments each accounted for 4 per cent of the advertisements collected. The data showed that 73 per cent of the ads with animation were child-targeted, as were 60 per cent of ads with SFX, 59 per cent of the ads with musical jingles and 51 per cent of the ads with VFX.

By contrast, 60 per cent of the ads that did not use any of these production techniques were targeted at general audiences. Of the eight appeals appearing more in child-targeted ads, seven were emotional (mood alteration, speed/strength, action/adventure, magic/fantasy, peer acceptance, adult approval, trickery/deceit) and one was a product appeal (premium offers). Of the four appearing more in general audience ads, two were emotional (health/well-being, appearance) and two were product appeals (taste/flavour, novelty).

Exposure issues

One problem with studies of content on their own is that the audience advertisers target by buying particular day-parts does not necessarily reflect what children actually watch. Many studies of children's viewing have noted that even young children view a lot of adult and prime time television in the course of their average 2+ hours' viewing. With this in mind, several recent studies have attempted to combine audience-viewing statistics with content analysis to estimate what ads children actually see while watching TV. A 2007 report compiled for the Federal Trade Commission titled 'Children's Exposure to TV Advertising' in 1977 and 2004 (Holt et al. 2007) combined audience statistics and content analysis to estimate children's exposure to food ads on US cable and broadcast networks. In 2004, children aged 2–11 saw about 25,600 television advertisements of which approximately 18,300 were paid ads or about 10,700 minutes of TV advertising. Compared with the FTC's Children's Advertising Rulemaking Study of 1977, it was estimated that for children aged 2–11 exposure to paid advertising fell by about 9 per cent, and yet exposure to all advertising rose by about 17 per cent since 1977. This difference reflects the substantial increase in children's exposure to promotional ads for television programming and PSAs over this time period and a relative increase in ads for toys and sedentary leisure products. Estimates for adult exposure were five times greater, with the average adult viewing 52,500 ads and 22,300 minutes of advertising.

Gantz et al. (2007) also estimate children aged 2–7 see up to 12 food ads on TV each day and those aged 8–12 see 21 food ads each day (given their different viewing and the industry's media buying practices). 8–12-year olds watch more TV but less kids TV implying greater exposure to ads in prime time. This study also found that Saturday morning viewing contributed only 4.3 percent of the total exposure to ads whereas prime time constituted nearly 29 per cent of children's total ad exposure and the after school slot 26 per cent. Children aged 2–11 saw approximately 5,500 food ads in 2004, which are about 22 per cent of all ads viewed. Ads for sedentary entertainment products outnumber food ads by 2 to 1. Of the food ads they see, the most prominent are fast food restaurants (23 per cent), cereals (17 per cent) and desserts (16 per cent), which together compose 56 per cent of all food advertisements. Soft beverages comprise about 7 per cent of all food ads but only 1.6 per cent of all ads seen. The Kaiser Study also notes that children aged 8–12 are exposed to the most food ads. Interestingly, although the study concluded that at this age 'children see more ads overall', there was actually a decline in the amount of paid advertising being shown on US television. From 1977 to 2004, paid non-food ads experienced a 6 per cent decrease and paid food ads experienced a 9 per cent decrease in total airtime. This shift was more than offset by a giant growth of 234 per cent in the amount of promos and PSAs being aired. Overall, this implies that children are being exposed to more advertising, but it is advertising that focuses on station and programming promotions rather than paid advertising from various products. However, their exposure to PSAs for healthy lifestyles is outweighed by food ads at a rate of 45:1.

The proportion of food advertising increases from 22 per cent on all shows to 32 per cent on children's shows (children > 50 per cent share of the audience). The report concludes that while the foods advertised on children's programming in 2004 do not constitute a balanced diet, this was the case in 1977 as well, before the rise in obesity. The researchers note that half of the food advertising children watch is during shows specifically targeting them, which is considerably larger than in 1977 because of specialized programming and cable. Successful children's programming is now largely on children's cable networks. Broadcast networks had very few programmes where children were more than 50 per cent of the audience. In fact, over 97 per cent of food advertisements children see on children's shows are from cable programming. These channels have considerable food advertising targeting children. As a result children get nearly 80 per cent of their cereal ad exposure on children's shows and about one-third of their sweetened drink, restaurant and fast food advertising there. This means that any restriction on advertising on children's programming would have its greatest impact on specialty children's programming.

Exposure to advertising in Britain

A 2004 study by Ofcom in Britain attempted to explore the impact of policy options for childhood obesity and food advertising by estimating children's exposure risks (Ofcom 2005). Part of the study examined children's exposure to food advertising on different day parts. It found that children's (>12 years) total viewing of television had remained consistent over the previous three years – the average child was watching approximately 17 hours of television per week. However, only 5 hours per week was spent watching children's airtime. In terms of advertising, the majority (71%) seen by children was from outside children's airtime. 'Core Category' products (defined in the study as food, soft drinks and chain restaurants) accounted for approximately 1 in 5 of all TV commercials seen by children. The analysis also covered a range of creative techniques. Overall, 14 per cent of core category ads included some form of product tie-in. Tie-ins were predominantly in the form of collectibles, with cereal and chain restaurants dominating this activity: 22 per cent of cereal ads and 52 per cent of chain restaurant ads used collectibles. In this context, a separate analysis of the core category ads most watched by children in 2003 and 2004 noted two changes in relation to tie-ins. First, McDonald's Happy Meal ads were a little more restrained in 2004; they still displayed the range of collectibles but no longer used a voice-over stating the number available to collect. Second, four out of ten of the top cereal ads in 2004 offered free gifts linked to active pursuits such as football or swimming. Given the distribution of cereal and chain restaurant advertising across the channels, it is not surprising that tie-ins were much more common on children's airtime (25 per cent) and dedicated children's channels (14 per cent) than on adult terrestrial airtime (7 per cent).

Only 6 per cent of core category ads were found to use celebrities, but characters were used by 27 per cent overall, rising to 36 per cent of chain restaurant and 59 per cent of cereal ads. This is not surprising in light of these advertisers' development of brand characters such as Tony the Tiger and Ronald McDonald. In the McDonald's ads characters linked to product tie-ins (such as Sonic the Hedgehog) displaced Ronald McDonald. Only 5 per cent of confectionery ads used either celebrities or characters, whereas 31 per cent of savoury snack ads did, with the latter figure strongly influenced by Walker's Crisps' long association with football celebrity Gary Lineker. Overall, 56 per cent of core category ads used live action, 27 per cent used animation, 3 per cent used stills, none used music videos exclusively, and 15 per cent used some combination of these techniques. Cereal ads favoured animation (47 per cent used this technique), while confectionery and savoury snacks tended to use live action (94 per cent and 83 per cent respectively) and chain restaurants relied on a combination of techniques (68 per cent). Not surprisingly, animation was used in 25 per cent of core category ads in children's terrestrial airtime but only 10 per cent of adult airtime.

Turning to settings, 32 per cent of core category ads were set outdoors, 20 per cent in domestic surroundings, only 1 per cent in school, 7 per cent in fantasy locations and 40 per cent in other surroundings. Chain restaurants used other settings 91 per cent of the time, reflecting McDonald's use of locations such as Disneyland in Paris. Half of all confectionery and savoury snack ads were also set in other locations. Outdoor settings were relatively common for cereal (47 per cent), savoury snack (35 per cent) and soft drink (34 per cent) ads; they were twice as common in children's terrestrial airtime than adult airtime. Domestic settings were used for 27 per cent of confectionery ads, 14 per cent of cereal ads and 10 per cent of savoury snack ads. This report also offers some analysis of the 'health claims' used, with these subdivided into scientific claims, causal claims, quality claims and other claims. Overall, 15 per cent made scientific claims, while causal and quality claims were each made by 8 per cent and 15 per cent made other claims. Confectionery and savoury snack ads used health claims the least (2 per cent and 20 per cent respectively). Most (93 per cent) cereal ads made some health claim, although 69 per cent made an 'other' health claim, with these often taking the form of disclaimers such as advising children to 'run around, have fun, eat a balanced diet'; only 9 per cent of cereal ads made scientific claims. Soft drinks made greatest use (34 per cent) of scientific claims, reflecting one heavily advertised brand's claim to be 'free from artificial colourings and preservatives'. Chain restaurants made health claims in 30 per cent of ads, almost entirely in terms of quality. Although the proportion of ads making health claims were very similar between children's and adult airtime on terrestrial channels, the balance of claims was different: scientific claims were made in 16 per cent of adult airtime ads, twice that of children's airtime ads, while 'other' claims accounted for 19 per cent of children's airtime ads but only 4 per cent of ads in adult airtime.

Naturally, the question of actual impressions has greatly preoccupied the advertising industry too, whose response to Ofcom attempted to demonstrate how self-regulation could work. In Britain the industry responded to the debate about targeting children with some research of its own, which claimed that food advertisers were voluntarily changing. The FAU (Annual Report 2006) analysis showed that children were seeing less advertising for Core Category products in 2006, partly as a result of food and soft drink advertisers voluntarily scaling back from advertising during children's TV programmes in keeping with their pledge of social responsibility. Even before the ban was enacted, the products advertised on children's TV were getting healthier, the labelling was better and advertisers were promoting healthy lifestyle choices. Their data shows that not only do core category 'impacts' among children aged 5–9 decline but specifically confection advertising declined from 87.5 to 72.9 million pounds and fast food advertising expenditures declined from 70.5 to 57.2 million pounds. Moreover, more of the messages were touting images of active living for kids. As such the ban was unwarranted and would have little effect (FAU 2006). Given that children, even young ones, mostly watch adult television, the industry maintained that a ban was already unnecessary.

Limitations

Although the unhealthy bias of the TV diet is a consistent finding, close examination of the content analysis studies also demonstrate considerable variation in the estimates of children's exposure to 'junk food advertising' in the US, Canada, Australia and the UK. There is considerable variation in the proportion of food products on TV, which ranges in the US from 51 per cent to 21 per cent and in Britain from 49 per cent to 16 per cent depending on when the study was undertaken, how the sample was drawn and how the ads were categorized. Caution is advised because many of these samples are drawn from different day-parts: some drawn from times when children represent a large portion of the audience and some using a spectrum sample of multiple TV stations capturing largely prime time advertising. Moreover there are seasonal fluctuations in the children's marketing cycle. During the pre-Christmas quarter toy and entertainment advertising intensifies to some degree driving out other categories. And finally, many of these studies use different category systems for reporting the product category and the nutrient quality of the food. For example is an ice cream bar reported as a diary product or a confection. What constitutes 'junk' or 'unhealthy' food is of course imprecise and so many opt for the food guide or pyramid which in some ways proves unhelpful in making useful distinctions in 'fun food'. For example, is a sweetened cereal put in the same grain category as porridge oats?

The problems with undertaking cross-national research comparing market environments is well known yet urgent, given the questions raised by child obesity. Given the changing regulatory environment for food ads, one of the few recent cross-national studies compared one week's advertising in the UK and Canada on four channels in each country. Adams et al. (2009) found that of the 2315 food-related ads in Canada 4.5 per cent were targeted at children (<13) and of the 1365 ads in the UK, 10.2 per cent were targeted at children. Using nutritional categories based on caloric content and the FSA's 'less healthy' distinction, the researchers found few significant differences between the types, or nutritional content, of foods that were promoted in prime and child-targeted programming. 'In all cases, more than half of food advertisements were for "less healthy" products. There was no evidence that the proportion of food advertisements that were for "less healthy" products differed between food advertisements that were and were not OPAT children in either country' (2009: 660).

But the limits of this sampling strategy was evident in the small portion of food ads targeting children on the channels sampled which excluded specialty stations in both countries. In the UK sample, for example, they found no restaurant ads and no ads for salty snacks within the whole sample. Moreover by employing food guide criteria to distinguish nutrition rather than consumption criteria they were unable to distinguish between 'core' foods like sweetened cereals from bread or grains. In what follows I report my own comparison of North American and UK food advertising practices which applied a common sample strategy and coding framework to estimate the food types, nutritional qualities, as well as the marketing techniques and the social context of eating over a much longer time frame using a sampling strategy intended to test differences between prime time and kids time TV diets.

Methodology

Although it is often assumed that American children are most 'at risk' from marketers, caution is advised when comparing content analyses across countries where food marketing practices (targeting) and food advertising regulations (health claims, risk disclosures) are different. The following study was undertaken to compare the marketing of foods to children in the UK and North America from 2004 to 2007. There were a number of policy questions I wanted to address in this comparison related to the policy debates raging about the effects of the systematic bias on children. The first concerned the degree to which children are targeted differently as a special category of consumers in each country including the techniques and values used to appeal to them. The second concerned the degree of nutritional risk associated with the quality of snacks, cereals and fast foods advertised. The third concerned the degree to which the moral panic about obesity resulted in food marketers changing their advertising strategies by selling healthier foods, by abandoning the children's day part, by promoting healthy lifestyles and by communicating about the risks associated with HFSS foods. I was also interested in the broader depiction of the 'culture of food' in each market.

For the purposes of this study, a sample of advertising was collected from a variety of networks in Canada, the US and the UK over a 4-year period (2003–7) and submitted to a detailed content analysis.[1] Since targeting involves both the media buy and the design of the ads, the content analysis explores the relationship between the products, brand characters, health claims and marketing tactics that are used to appeal to children as a discreet group of consumers. The analysis also looks at the underlying social communication dimension surrounding food products, generally including who eats, where they eat and the nature and social context of food consumption. A strategy was developed to sample during adult-family television programming, 'prime time TV', and the other child-targeted television programming, 'kids time TV', based on the audience composition figures. Networks were varied to include a full range of commonly watched programming in each country. Kids-time programming sampled children's specialty networks including YTV, Nickelodeon and Toon.

Two time periods were also sampled to balance seasonal fluctuations in advertising spends: the rolling sample reported here included a spring sample in February/March and an autumn sample in October/November/December. The extent of food advertising did vary between the seasons with 17 per cent of all ads in the fall compared to 29 per cent percent of all ads for the spring. This can be explained by the volume of toy advertising, which increases dramatically in the months leading up to Christmas. The increase in toy advertising works to offset all other ads. Since the products and techniques used in different seasons do not vary significantly, these samples were amalgamated for each year.

Ads were drawn from a basket of major networks in each country during prime time and children's time day-parts and coded for product category. The total sample consisted of 11,719 ads shown on cable TV between February 2004 and December 2007 (see Figure 4.2): 609 food ads composed 28 per cent of the sample in the US, , 286 food ads composed 21 per cent of the sample in the UK and 986 food ads composed 49 per cent of the food ad sample in Canada. Ads shown in prime time constituted 42.4 per cent of the sample while ads shown during designated children's programmes (explicitly targeted at the child audience) composed 57 per cent of the sample. In Canada there were slightly more food ads on the kids time programmes (18 per cent) than adult (15 per cent).

Relative to other studies, the proportion of food ads on both children's and prime time day-parts seems relatively low. In Figure 4.3 we see that in the UK, food ads comprise 22 per cent of all prime time ads, but only 8 per cent of all ads on kids time day-parts. Moreover a significant decline from 13 to 7 per cent was noted between the first sample taken in 2004 and the second drawn in 2006. In the US, food ads were equally represented in Prime Time (PT) and Kids Time (KT) samples (19 per cent) whereas in Canada the food

	UK	US	CAN	Total - ALL
Total	2494 (21.3%)	3321 (28.3%)	5823 (49.7%)	11719 (100%)
PT	1289 (51.7%)	1129 (37.0%)	2449 (42.1%)	4974 (42.4%)
KT	1205 (48.3%)	2092 (63.0%)	3303 (56.7%)	6692 (57.2%)
Food	376 (15%)	609 (19%)	986 (16.9%)	1865 (15.9%)
PT	286/1289=22%	213/1129=19%	356/ 2449=15%	
KT	90/ 1205=8%	396/2092=19%	591/ 3303=18%	

Figure 4.2   Number of ads in sample by country expressed as percentage of sample by day part and country

	Prime time	Kids time
US	19%	19%
Canada	15%	18%
UK	22%	8%

Figure 4.3   Food ads as a percentage of total advertising time in the US, Canada and the UK

ads targeted at children were 18 per cent of the ads shown whereas in PT it was 15 per cent. Overall the percentage of food advertising on television is slightly lower than many of the past studies, especially in the UK.

A comparison found that in Canadian kids' day-parts 76 per cent of ads were for unhealthy foods but 62 per cent of prime time were. Canadian kids time is dominated by three categories: confections (22.7 per cent), cereal (21.8 per cent) and fast food (20.6 per cent). A similar distribution is noted in the US food ads with kids day-parts consisting of 84 per cent 'unhealthy' products whereas prime time consists of 68 per cent. Of kids' food ads confection (26.8 per cent), fast food (24.5 per cent) and cereal (15.4 per cent) predominate. In the UK, the less healthy categories are less prevalent but more concentrated, constituting 61 per cent of kids sample core and 57 per cent of the prime time sample. Fast food (27.8 per cent) and cereal (26.7 per cent) are heavily advertised on kids TV although no beverage ads were found. These foods are broadcast relatively less in UK prime time with the exception beverages (14.4 per cent) and fast food (25 per cent). British prime time ads have the least fast food and 40 per cent of all ads are within the 'nutritionally acceptable' categories including dairy (22.2 per cent) and fruit (5.6 per cent). Comparing the prevalence of the 'bad five' on national TV we find that 81 per cent of US ads, 72 per cent of Canadian ads and 59 per cent of UK ads fall into this category. 9.6 per cent of UK ads are for nutritious products (meat, dairy, fruit and vegetables) whereas 1 per cent of US and Canadian ads are for these foods.

Although some minor differences were noted in the distribution by product category on Canadian and US networks (see Figure 4.4), the proportional pattern was remarkably similar and the magnitude of these differences insignificant. Since, in both countries, the same seven categories account for over 80 per cent of all food advertising, for the remainder of the analysis the

| Food | Total | US | | Total | Canada | |
		Prime Time	Kids time		Prime Time	Kids Time
Beverage	10.3	16	7	9.2	10.7	8
Cereal	11	2	16	15	15	22
Confection	21	11	27	21	21	23
Convenience	10	10	10	16	16	15
Fast food	29	37	24	24	28	21
Snacks	10	5	12	3	3	3

Figure 4.4 Detailed Comparison of the 'bad five' in the Canadian and US samples

results are amalgamated into a single North American sample for comparison with the UK as most of the ads shown on Canadian networks are made for the US market as well (Canadian children regularly watch US channels on cable anyway).

A comparison of TV diet on British and North American television

Looking at the sample as a whole there were clear indications that in both countries kids are targeted as consumers of specific food categories. Whereas cereals, snacks, confection and fast food are relatively more advertised on child day-parts, beverages, sit-down restaurants, meats and grocery stores are targeted mainly at adults. Convenience foods, dairy and fruits are more evenly found in both day-parts (see Figure 4.5).

When comparing ads overall (see Figures 4.6 and 4.7), the striking differences concern the greater prevalence of fast food, confection, snacks and sit-down restaurants in the North American ads. The UK ads are distinguished by the pre-eminence of dairy, fruit, grocery stores and meat advertising as well as a slightly greater advertising of convenience and beverages.

When the whole sample is compared across countries we find that in the UK, beverage advertising is concentrated in prime time while fast food

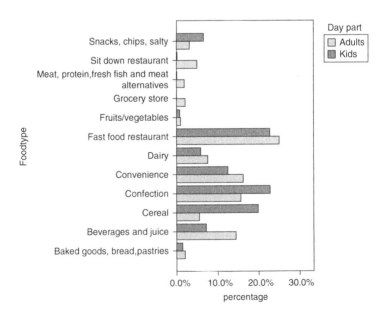

Figure 4.5   Food types as percentage of day part

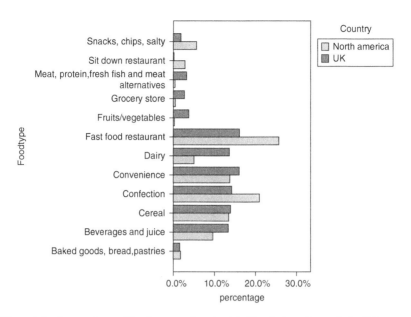

Figure 4.6 Comparison of food types advertised in North America and the UK

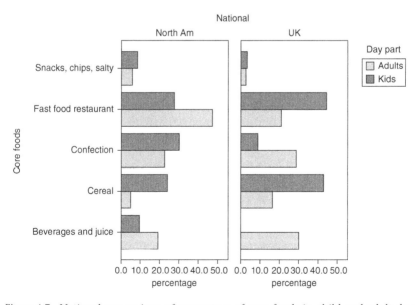

Figure 4.7 National comparison of percentage of core foods in child and adult day parts

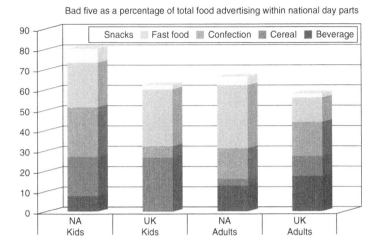

Figure 4.8   Relative weight of 'bad five' food categories as percentage of food advertising in each national day part

and cereal were the remaining two of the bad five food categories in kids time slots (see Figure 4.8). In the North American sample not only were 'unhealthy' food groups more prevalent but also more proportionate. The major difference between prime and kids time North American ads is noted in the increased cereal, confection and snack categories and the decrease in beverages.

Health risks

Two different measures were employed in the evaluation of the lifestyle risks associated with the type of foods advertised on TV: their energic value and their overall nutritional quality. For energy content, the caloric value for a product's recommended serving was used for the serving shown in the ad. For a restaurant meal, this was based on the sum of calories per meal or combo. To evaluate the nutritional quality, a simple categorization scale (1–4) was developed by an independent nutritionist, which takes into account the energy density by factoring in fat and protein. The healthiest foods (such as fruits and vegetables) were rated a one, with the least healthy foods (such as chocolate bars and sugary soda pop) rated a four (see the online appendix for a detailed breakdown of the health categorization). The nutritional quality rating distinguishes between an unsweetened cereal and milk serving (rated a 2) and a sugared cereal and milk serving (rated a 3). During the analysis, those anomalous foods that were technically low in calories such as coffee, tea, gum and diet soda were rated a 0.

The UK ads generally featured healthier products than the North American commercials: 51 per cent of foods advertised in the UK prime time and 38 per cent of kids time ads were for nutritionally acceptable products (rated 0–2). In North America, 42 per cent of prime time and 25 per cent of kids time ads were considered nutritionally unproblematic. Overall the food advertised on British kids TV is healthier: 61 per cent of UK kids ads but three-quarters of North American ads were regarded as foods that needed to be eaten in moderation (3) or 'junk' food (4). This is in keeping with the evidence that UK screens proportionally fewer snack, confection and fast food ads and more beverage, fruit and dairy product ads than North American networks. The intensity of political pressure on the industry obviously

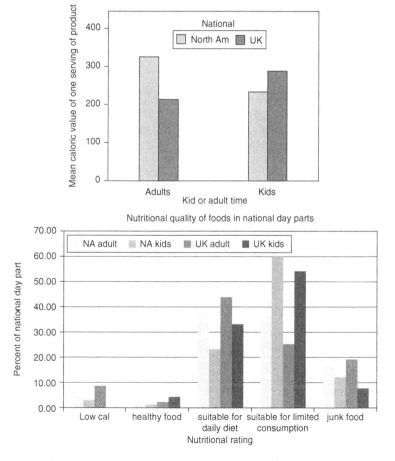

Figure 4.9 Nutritional qualities of foods advertised in North America and the UK

alerted them to the need to change their marketing strategies (Botterill and Kline 2007).

The mean caloric value (by serving) of foods advertised on British prime time was also generally lower than North American ads (212 kcals vs 325 kcals) (see Figure 4.9). However, British children's advertising averaged 287 kcals per serving compared with North American ads, which averaged 234 kcals. The North American mean caloric value was highest, at 280 average calories per serving which can be explained by the prevalence of restaurant and fast food dinner advertising (averaging 600kcals/serving). As will be noted later, a dinner featured at a fast food outlet is generally lower in caloric content than that shown at a sit-down restaurant (698 kcals). Comparisons show that American advertising has higher caloric content, which is largely accounted for by the frequency of restaurants and fast food ads. These categories account for 50 per cent of all foods shown in prime time. Restaurant ads (fast food: 600; sit down: 690) tend to show full meals whereas children's portions such as a Happy Meal tend to be lower in calories (420 kcals) but still considerably more energy dense than a snack (147 kcals) or cereal (136 kcals).

The mention of positive health values associated with eating is significantly higher in the UK prime time ads (33 per cent) compared to kids (24 per cent) (see Figure 4.10). In North America, positive health mentions are found in just under one quarter of all ads on both prime and child oriented day-parts. The advertisements that mention positive health benefits were for products that contained, on average, fewer calories per serving in both countries and day-parts.

Advertisements that explicitly mentioned health benefits were most frequently from the two more acceptable nutrition categories, although in North America 49 per cent of the health mentions were associated with the

	Adult	Kids
Beverage	31	69
Cereal	57	31
Confection	13	14
Fast food	26	12
Snacks	26	27
Total North American	18	24
Total UK	27	21

Figure 4.10 Percentage of 'bad five' food ads which mention health properties of food by day part

	Adult	Kids
Percent of day part that makes a health claim	27	23.4
• Part of healthy lifestyle choice	24	38
• Source of healthy ingredients	22	19
• Helps avoid risky ingredients	17	5
• Wholesome or natural ingredients	21	30
• Low calorie or weight loss	20	2
• Provides energy	3	6

Figure 4.11   Percentage of all claims when ad mentions health by day parts

less healthy categories and in the UK 33 per cent of the health mentions were for foods in the less healthy categories. Fruit, meat, beverages, dairy and cereal products were the most likely to have an explicit mention of positive health benefits (see Figure 4.11). Children's day-parts contain 25 per cent of all mentions of health associated with eating that occur within the fast food and confection categories, however. It is noted that in North America 50 per cent of all health mentions are associated with sweetened cereals, confections and fast food ads – generally considered by nutritionists to be eaten in moderation.

Techniques of targeting

The ways of appealing to children are well known among food advertisers around the world. The prevalence of children, animation, cross marketing and an atmosphere of fun has been noted in previous studies of food advertising on TV. One of the most important differences between children's and adult television ads has to do with the frequency of repetition. Brand saturation strategies not only reduce the cost of campaigns but also achieve the goal of making the product more memorable in a competitive market. For this reason, the mean number of repeats of a unique ad was compared. Children's ads in North America were shown 5.5 times compared with 2.2 on prime time. In the UK, children's ads were repeated 5.5 times compared with 2.66 prime time ads within this sample. Not only are children's ads repeated but also campaigns within the 'core' categories are most repeated, especially on children's day-parts and channels. In North America cereal, confection, fast food and snack ads are much more likely to be repeated on children's time than prime time, indicating the degree of targeting of these campaigns. On British TV too, cereal, dairy and fast food ads are more likely

	North America		UK	
	Prime time	Kid Time	Prime Time	Kid Time
Cross marketing	19	36	13	20
Celebrity	5	1.5	2.8	2.2
Animation	13.2	46.1	20	63.3
Brand character	6.2	32.3	.7	23.3

Figure 4.12   Child-targeting strategies by country and day part

to average 5 or more repetitions on children's time slots. The most repeated in the UK were fast food (8.2) and cereal (6.1) ads which both featured prominently in children's television.

Cross marketing is a technique favoured by North American food advertisers, which occurs in 17 per cent of adult and 34 per cent of children's ads (see Figure 4.12). 36 per cent of North American children's ads use cross marketing compared with 20 per cent of UK ads. Celebrities are used less often, appearing in 4.3 per cent of prime time but 1.6 per cent of kids time ads. Animation is a traditional technique used by food advertisers to appeal to children because this presentation style imbues an ad with lively humour and fun. 47.5 per cent of all children's ads use animation, with UK ads more likely to use this technique in both prime time (20 per cent) and kids time (63.3 per cent) advertising. Brand characters also predominantly mark the child targeting of ads (31.6 per cent) vs (4.3 per cent) prime time ads, but especially in the North American children's ads in which 32.3 per cent feature a brand character. In terms of execution, the UK data showed that animation was used in 42 per cent of 'core category' (food, fast food and soft drink) ads during children's airtime, compared with 16 per cent of children's ads overall. Product tie-ins also emerged as a popular choice of food advertisers targeting children: 28 per cent of core category ads in children's airtime included a product tie-in, compared to 11 per cent of children's ads in general.

Activity levels

As a way of making their ads communicate healthy lifestyles to kids, advertisers promised regulators that they were willing to depict kids engaged in active leisure. Generally speaking, the images of discernable activity were depicted in about 80 per cent of ads on both sides of the Atlantic. Generally speaking British ads depicted scenes with sedentary lifestyles (sitting around, watching TV) in 32.1 per cent of ads whereas North American ads depicted sedentary lifestyles in 53.7 per cent of ads. When activity occurred in British prime time advertising they were more likely to show moderate levels of activity (that is housework, walking, shopping) 40.4 per cent vs 29.6 per cent of North American ads. High levels of activity involving sports or physical exertion occurred in 27.5 per cent of UK food ads but only 16.7 per cent of North American food ads. Kids-targeted advertising was much more likely to show higher activity levels than prime time ads. Sedentary activities were shown in 45.5 per cent of all North American ads but only 17.9 per cent of UK ads. High levels of activity were depicted in 47.6 per cent of kids' time UK ads but only 23.5 per cent of North American ads.

Activity levels also varied across core food categories. In the key areas of confection, fast food and convenience meals, UK ads depicted higher levels of activity than North American ads. Snack foods, which are more prominent on North American TV, are associated with sedentary living (76.9 per cent). Cereal ads in both countries and fast food advertising in Britain both stress images of highly active living in more than 40 per cent of their ads. Healthy foods are less advertised in North America, but when depicted they are more likely to be sanctioned with a positive health mention. Ads for the bad five are also more likely to depict active lifestyles when shown on children's time than when shown on prime time. Overall kids ads for unhealthy foods depict scenes of active living most frequently, revealing that true to their promise the worst food categories are promoting healthy living as compensation for the caloric input.

Children

The use of children in ads is a key aspect of targeting, building a social connection with the brand through association and telling the child that this ad is for them. Overall, humans appear in about 80 per cent of all food ads. Children, however appear in only 21 per cent of prime time ads but in 67.6 per cent of kids ads. Ads on prime time were much more likely to show adult characters only (60 per cent) when compared with those on kids TV (9.6 per cent). Child characters on their own appear on 22 per cent of all food ads, but are more prevalent within children's TV, which feature child-only groups 36 per cent of the time compared with prime time ads (4.3 per cent). Mixed groups of adults and children appear in 32 per cent of all children's time food ads and 17 per cent of prime time ads.

UK and North American food cultures compared

Although the health critics have focused on nutrition and health, eating is not just fuelling the body but is also a pleasurable consumption activity set in the social practices of friendship, family and peers. Critics have long noted that children's food is often associated with fun and play, as part of the appeal and targeting. With fun food in mind, the content analysis also compared the broader ideas and values associated with food and its consumption in North America (NA) and Britain (UK). It has been noted that in the UK, children are much more likely to watch prime time as well as children's time television. Moreover, a portion of their viewing of child day-parts is taken up with non-commercial TV (BBC) and so on average they are exposed to fewer commercials. The following comparison of the TV food cultures must recognize that children are exposed to food advertising differently in North America and the UK. Given the different (and changing) media buys for different sectors, British children are still more likely to see fast food, confection and dairy products during prime time. On the other hand, ads for healthy foods like meat, fruit and dairy have not flooded into children's time and so the range of healthy products young children are exposed to has not increased dramatically. The debate about children's exposure to 'unhealthy' food ads needs to recognize that in both countries, but especially in the UK, children are learning more generally about 'food culture and lifestyle' from their broader exposure to prime time ads as well as those targeting them.

Playfulness has long been a defining characteristic of the promotion of children's foods. Many scenes in children's targeted ads show children playing with their food – spelling words in their soup, skateboarding with their hamburgers, dancing with their fruit roll ups or tossing pizza pops into each other's mouths. Others show them eating before, after or during their leisure activities, whether going to McDonald's after the basketball game or eating snacks while watching a movie. Whereas 65 per cent of all kids ads made some reference to play, under 15 per cent of prime time ads referenced playfulness in its symbolic field. Figure 4.13 shows the types of playful leisure activities that get referenced in food ads. Generally speaking they are absent

	Adult	Kids
No leisure	86	35
Activity, high energy	1.5	11.4
Prizes, rewards, surprise	1.5	11.3
Sports	3.2	7.3
Toy play	1.6	7.8
Jokes/ pranks	1.3	4.7

Figure 4.13   Percentage of ads referencing energetic forms of leisure by day part

in adult ads whereas high-energy activity, sports and toys define the ideas about fun in the child-targeted field of food advertising.

Kids ads feature imaginary eating environments and outdoor eating more, whereas eating in restaurants is more likely on adult ads than kids time ads. In prime time, actors are more likely to be female only, whereas mixed gender groups are more common in kids' time ads. Although 40 per cent of ads don't show anyone actually eating, when actors do eat in kids time ads they are more likely to be males, whereas female characters eat on prime time ads. Characters are shown eating at home in about 30 per cent of ads – mostly the kitchen or dining room, or in the living room, regardless of whom the ad targets. Snacking occasions are more frequent than actual meals (44 per cent vs 32 per cent), especially on kids' ads (47 per cent on kids time vs 40 per cent on prime time). When meals are shown on kids time, however, it is more likely to be breakfast whereas prime time ads are more likely to feature people eating dinner.

Figure 4.14 shows the strong differences between the values implicit in the scenes depicted in ads. Although coder reliability scores are slightly lower for the values category (partly because the protocol made 18 value distinctions) they are well within the range of acceptable levels for inter-coder reliability (reliability > 80 per cent agreement). Fun (38 per cent), fantasy (18 per cent) and independence (8 per cent) clearly dominate the symbolic discourses of children's time ads whereas vitality (14 per cent), value for

	Adult	Kids
Fun / happy	8	38
Fantasy / escape	2	18
Independence/ adventure	1	6
Healthy/vitality	14	6
Family tradition	8.5	3
Value for money	9	1
Luxury/ pamper self	8	0
Romance	5.5	.5
Nature	5.5	1
Taste of food/ quality	3	1

Figure 4.14 Percentage of ads stressing lifestyle values by day part

money (9 per cent) and family (8.5 per cent) and luxury (8 per cent) are more prevalent in the prime time sample. The cluster of values surrounding a healthy lifestyle – active, healthy and wholesome living are found in 24 per cent of prime time ads but only 11 per cent of kids ads although it is noted that of these active living is twice as likely to be emphasized in kids targeted ads (4 per cent vs 2 per cent).

Because the emphasis on high energy fun and active leisure is so important in children's time ads, this protocol also tried to categorize the symbolic field of playfulness – what I have ironically called 'jeu-essence' (active play plus fun food) in reference to the abstract notion of pleasure symbolically expressed in the fun relationship to food that is represented in food ads. The fun–leisure theme appears in 14 per cent of prime time ads but 65 per cent of child-targeted ads. This association of food with fun perhaps constitutes the most striking difference in the representation of eating in the North American sample (44 per cent of all NA ads vs 37 per cent of UK ads) because of its greater concentration in child oriented advertising campaigns.

Fast food culture

Since fast food advertisements accounted for nearly one quarter of all food ads (25 per cent of commercials during prime time, and 23 per cent during children's programming), it becomes necessary to look at this specific group independently. Interestingly, the caloric mean for fast food advertisements was lowest in the US at approximately 560 calories per serving, with Canada following at 600 and the UK surpassing the North American averages at 770. This, however, can be accounted for by the fact that while only 45 per cent of North American fast food ads were aimed at a prime time adult audience, 60 per cent of UK fast food advertisements were directed towards adults, thus skewing the overall caloric value. The 'Fast Food' category within the overall data set significantly affected the overall caloric value for all food advertisements. The difference between the caloric value of the entire data set and the 'Fast Food' category for the UK advertisements was in excess of 500 calories, while the North American difference was a still significant 340 (Canada) and 275 (US) mean calories.

Cereals

The mean caloric value of advertised cereal servings is the same in the UK and NA. Yet prime time cereal advertisements contained approximately 35 more calories than those shown during kids' programming. However, the cereal advertised during kids' time was considerably less healthy in terms of the four-part nutrition table that assesses sugar and fat content. Only 15 per cent of children's cereal ads could be considered healthy, while nearly

70 per cent of cereal advertisements during adult programming fell into the two 'healthy' categories. This is an extremely significant difference that points to the abundance of children's cereal advertisements that promote sweetened products. Another noteworthy trend in the UK data is that cereal ads are considerably healthier than North American commercials. While 76 per cent of UK cereals advertised could be considered healthy, merely 15 per cent of the North American ones could. Again, this is primarily due to the fact that over 90 per cent of North American cereal commercials occur during children's programming, thus tending to promote cereal products that are notably less healthy, while only one-third of UK cereal advertisements are aired during kids' time.

Snacks

A similar, albeit less pronounced pattern is observable for snack and convenience foods. These categories encompass products that are advertised as being consumed as a snack instead of a meal, or are quick to serve, pre-made and processed. Confections, candy and chocolate are also included in this snacking category. As with the cereal advertisements, the caloric mean does not reveal much discrepancy between countries or day-parts. However, once again the nutritional categories reveal that American children's advertised snack foods are markedly less healthy. While 40 per cent of snack/convenience food advertisements during prime time can be categorized as extremely or somewhat healthy, only one quarter of similar advertisements during children's programming could be categorized as such. Again, this is significant as over 40 per cent of food advertisements targeted at children are for either snack or convenience foods in the UK. Canada once again trails the other two countries, with only 28 per cent of snack/convenience foods advertised that can be considered healthy, as compared to 31 per cent of American products and 44 per cent of UK snack/convenience food products.

Conclusion

Given the growing political pressure on the food industry, especially in Britain, this comparative study indicates how food marketers have responded to the globesity pandemic by slightly altering their marketing strategies. In the UK there was evidence of significant reductions in their child-targeted media buys from 12 per cent in 2005 to 8 per cent in a 2006 sample. Compared with Hill and Radimer's study which found food rising from 49 per cent to 63 per cent of all ads between 1994 and 1996, things on UK children's time TV are changing. That study found that cereals accounted for 30 per cent of all food ads, up from 24 per cent in 1994, while fast food advertising had declined from 13 per cent to 6 per cent. 'Convenience' foods however were heading up from 0 per cent to 21.2 per cent of all ads. How different things are now: many companies, in the sensitive soft drinks industry, shifted their advertising entirely into prime time television. Others in the cereal and fast food industries decided to make health claims about their products or to increase the emphasis on active play and lifestyle health. It seems therefore, that in the throes of public controversy and policy battles, the UK food industry responded more dramatically to the threat of a ban on advertising to children by proving that to some degree a ban didn't really matter that much anyway.

In North America, things appear to be slightly different in two respects. Firstly, children who watch specialty networks and made for children programming ghettos in the after-school and Saturday morning day-parts are exposed to more 'unhealthy' child-targeted marketing because they watch more kids-oriented campaigns, which are on the whole for less healthy foods. Secondly, the industry in North America seems not to have shifted their campaigning to the extent that we have seen in the UK. Not only are the types of foods more likely to be in the 'bad five' category but the techniques and appeals used in brand campaigning to children are more likely to be those traditionally used to interest them. In short, the problems articulated by the health community with the bias of the TV food culture is still well in place in North America despite some drift to responsibilization. Targeting of children continues to perpetuate a food culture which diminishes family meals and transforms the concerns for health and nutrition associated with food into a pleasurable experience enlivened by fun and fantasy. But the question remains, in what ways does this skewed promotional food culture impact children?

5
Risks of Exposure: The Influence of Food Advertising on Children's Consumption

As commercial TV grew more controversial during the 1970s, policymakers at the FTC asked marketing researchers to study the impact of TV ads on children's choices. Ward et al. (1977) developed a regression model to study the multiple risk factors determining children's consumerism. They found that the level of exposure to TV advertising was positively correlated with attitudes to advertising, requests for advertised goods and the intensity of family conflict over purchases. Developmental factors were also shown to be involved in the formation of children's product preferences and ability to shop, when cognitive and information-processing skills are controlled in empirical studies. Recognizing the mitigating factors in family life involved in consumer socialization, these researchers suggested that the regulation of advertising to children might be helpful not only in protecting very young children from persuasion they don't fully understand but in reducing family conflicts over lifestyle choices.

Based on a Ward et al.'s (1977) review of the research, the FTC proposed strict guidelines for the marketing of goods on children's TV. Yet this precautionary approach to marketing communication regulation was jettisoned in a wave of 1980's neoliberalism. Provoked by increasing child obesity, the same questions resurfaced 30 years later, and policymakers once again had to review the complex and often inconsistent evidence provided by those who studied marketing to kids. Hastings, APA, Kaiser, FTC, IOM, Livingstone all did so confirming what Ward and his co-authors had pointed out 25 years earlier. In America, where ideology and law privilege market liberalism, the answer that congress came up with was 'no': there was insufficient evidence of harm to children's health caused by advertising alone. Yet in Britain the answer Ofcom offered was *a precautionary yes*: a ban on unhealthy food advertising to children under 16 was enacted as part of the Labour government's broader strategy to improve the health of the young.

Spokespersons from the industry in both countries have strenuously resisted an ad ban arguing that current advertising practices were changing and that the relationship between advertising exposure and obesity was unproven. Dominic Lyle (2004) chided the All Party Obesity Task Force in Britain, for example, stating that the 'only clear consensus to have emerged from this debate so far is that the role of marketing on children's diet and health warrants closer scrutiny and more detailed research'. This is because 'the causes of obesity are many and complex and that no-one yet really has a clear understanding of what the real causes are'. Most researchers would agree that the body of research on advertising's effects suffers from many weaknesses, both theoretical and methodological. Inconsistencies abound in the data, and researchers disagree on the processes and explanations of results. Scientific progress in any field emerges from disagreements, after all. But to say that the only consensus is the need for more research denies the now considerable weight of evidence that shows that advertising is one influence among many, which contributes to children's preferences and requests for food and that food preferences are a factor in children's weight gain. In what follows I offer an overview of the kinds of research that led most reviewers to conclude that despite its limitations there is sufficient evidence of advertising's modest contribution to children's weight status.

Early evidence that advertising influences children's consumer knowledge and choices

One criteria that many researchers believe strengthens a body of evidence is what is often referred to as triangulation. When similar relationships are found across studies with different methodologies and in various populations, the confidence in generalizing about them is greater. One strength, then, in the assessment of the contribution of marketing to children's weight status is that it includes three different methodologies: experiments, surveys and longitudinal studies. Experimental research has often demonstrated the strongest persuasion effects because the independent variable is exposure. One classical study was undertaken at a summer camp by Gorn and Goldberg (1982) who set out to isolate the impact of TV ads for a range of snack foods by embedding specific ads within a viewing context. For two weeks, children aged 5–8 watched a half-hour cartoon each day, with just under 5 minutes of advertising embedded. In this way exposure to the specific ads could be controlled. One group was exposed to commercials for orange juice and various fruits each day and another was exposed to commercials for Kool-Aid and various highly sugared snacks such as candy bars. Each day, after the TV exposure, the children were given a selection of fruits or candy bars from which to choose, as well as a choice of orange juice or Kool-Aid. Their snack and drink choices significantly differed after 10 days depending on their TV viewing exposure. Advertising could have both positive and negative impact on children's diet, but given the preponderance of unhealthy products on TV advertising the authors suspected that the risks outweighed the educational benefits of advertising.

Using a classic experimental design Jeffrey et al. (1982) also conducted a controlled before and after study examining the effects of low nutrition, pro-nutrition and toy ads by comparing 48 4–5 year olds with those of 48 9–10 year olds. Before the experiment these children were asked about how much they liked a list of different snack foods as well as a series of questions about nutrition and balanced diet. Younger children were both more credulous about ads and less knowledgeable about diet. In the low-nutrition exposure situation children saw an ad for Pepsi and Froot Loops. In the pro-nutrition they saw ads for carrots and milk and in the toy condition they saw ads for Nerf balls and Bonkers which were embedded in a 7-minute segment of the Jetsons. By observing these children they found that attention to the screen did not vary in the different exposure conditions but they did vary in terms of their consumption after viewing when offered a tray of snacks. Although both groups could identify the foods on the tray, the younger children were less able to recall them by name. Measurement of the choices and calories consumed from the array of more (grapes, carrots, apple, milk) and less healthy snacks (Fritos, Chips Ahoy, Honey Comb, Pepsi) did reveal some influence of advertising exposure. Boys who saw low-nutrition ads did increase their total caloric consumption as well as the amount of low-nutrition snacks when offered their choice from a tray after viewing. The researchers note that 'low-nutrition advertising does increase the recall, purchase, and consumption of products' (Jeffery et al. 1982: 89) – but only in males. They also found that age did not mediate the effects of advertising on snack choices among those boys in spite of their greater nutritional knowledge as well as their advertising literacy. The pro-nutrition ads however, did not improve the selection of snacks. In this study the advertising seemed to effect children negatively more than positively.

These conclusions were confirmed by field research. Using a survey method, Atkin (1975, 1978) found significant correlations between children's exposure to TV advertising and several dependent measures such as frequency of requests to parents and preferences for heavily advertised cereals. Atkin found that those young respondents aged 8–12 who watched the most children's TV also reported making more requests for advertised toys, cereals and fast foods. Heavier viewers also reported eating the most frequently advertised cereals more (r = +.41). However, the association between TV watching and eating less-advertised brands was still significant (r = +.27), which implies that a preference for cereal, whether advertised or not, was more common among those children who watched more television. Isler et al. (1987) used diaries from 250 mothers of 3–11-year olds to track the relationship between food advertising and children's purchase requests. This study reported that cereal and candy were both most advertised on children's TV and most requested by children who watched TV the most. Not all children therefore are equally at risk depending on their use of TV. Advertising effects should only be expected where exposure is greatest.

In a longitudinal study of generalized advertising effects on consumerism, Moschis and Moore (1982) note that the idea of causality requires three kinds of evidence: a correlation between ad exposure and a consequence, a temporal sequence that implies exposure causes the effect and the elimination of other mediating factors (gender roles, family communication, peer influences, materialism, consumer knowledge) that can explain the outcome besides the exposure to an advertisement. Moreover, rather than simply take the teens' reported weekly TV viewing as the measure of exposure, they developed scales that measured the interest and motivations of viewing ads. Their study of consumer learning therefore used a natural longitudinal design (over 14 months) examining the relationship between advertising and consumer knowledge and behaviour among 211 adolescents. Although correlations from the first wave revealed very little impact on materialism, consumer roles and consumer activity, when studied 14 months later there were interesting impacts on consumer activity and materialism – especially on those that initially scored lower on these measures. Both family and peer influences were also found to moderate the impact of advertising on materialism and consumer activity. The researchers conclude that advertising does seem to contribute to the development of materialistic values and consumer roles, decreasing 'the likelihood of performing socially desirable consumer behaviors, but only among those adolescents who are not likely to perform such activities in the first place' (1982: 285). However, they suggest that familial discussion can moderate the effects of advertising on consumerism by promoting greater awareness of economics.

More recently Lewis and Hill (1998) conducted an experiment in the UK with 103 children aged ten who saw a video with either five food ads (cereal, confectionary, snacks) or five ads (toiletries, household cleaners, pet products) which were embedded in a 15-minute Rugrats cartoon programme. Overweight and normal weight children were assessed for eating preferences, body image and self-perceptions before and after viewing the videotapes on different days. The study found that the self-perceptions of overweight children were influenced differently by viewing food advertisements: overweight children felt more healthy and expressed decreased appetite for sweets after the food ads, whereas normal weight children felt less healthy and more like eating sweets. This study implies that the effect of food commercials on children may depend upon their weight status as well as their understanding of advertising. Different children watch ads differently but unfortunately the most vulnerable to advertising are those most at risk for 'obesity'. Their own interest in unhealthy foods seems to be a risk factor in the mediated marketplace.

Taras et al. (2000) report a field study of 237 families drawn from San Diego preschools who completed a TV survey in winter and spring of 1991. Parents were asked to list each of the foods by brand that their preschool children had asked for in the preceding 6 months that might have been a result of television advertising. Parents reported that children made 2.5 requests for food items as seen on television, but the variety of brands included 176 different 'brand name' products. Parents also reported whether they had purchased those products. Foods were categorized into one of 17 different product type groups, which were compared with an independent sample of children's targeted Saturday morning and weekday afternoon television in the winter of 1993. A test score was calculated and correlations indicated that the more frequently advertised products were more requested and more purchased. The most heavily advertised foods were sugary cereal, restaurants, chocolate, low-sugar cereal, and fruit juice; these were also the ones most often requested. The most purchased products were sugary cereals, restaurants, fruit juice and candy. The correlation is strongest for the two most advertised products (sugary cereal and restaurants) but is less convincing for less frequently advertised products, particularly chocolate and fruit juice. The authors acknowledge that the parents viewing the commercial directly may have influenced the food purchase (i.e. pleasing the child) as well as other brand familiarity effects.

Crespo et al. (2001) used the nationally representative Third National Health and Nutrition Examination Survey for 1988 and 1994 coupled with an in-person medical examination to investigate the relationship between television watching, energy intake, physical activity and obesity status in US boys and girls, aged 8–16. The study of 4069 children sampled Mexican Americans and non-Hispanic blacks to ensure reliable estimates for these groups. They found that the prevalence of obesity is lowest among children watching one or fewer hours of television a day and highest among those watching four or more hours of television a day. Girls engaged in less physical activity and consumed fewer joules per day than boys. A higher percentage of non-Hispanic white boys reported participating in physical activity five or more times per week than any other race/ethnic and sex group. They reported that 'television watching was positively associated with obesity among girls, even after controlling for age, race/ethnicity, family income, weekly physical activity, and energy intake'. Having controlled for other factors, they conclude that food advertising most influences the girls' energy intake.

Advertising literacy: Savvy or duped?

Children's limited ability to understand advertising as a form of persuasive communication and to critically evaluate the claims made about products is the bottom line for regulating children's marketing. Buckingham has critiqued whether Ofcom's review of advertising effects for providing insufficient evidence that children constitute a 'uniquely vulnerable class of consumers'. If children are incapable of understanding advertising and processing market persuasion, then they do not meet the neoliberal criteria for being 'informed consumers' because they cannot be construed as granting informed consent to market transactions. For example we don't allow children to have credit cards because the contracts between lender and borrower cannot stand the test of mutual agreement in the courts. As John (1999) stated, the question of vulnerability came down to five complex issues: 'children's ability to distinguish commercials from television programs, children's understanding of advertising's persuasive intent, children's ability to recognize bias and deceptions in advertising, children's beliefs about the truthfulness of advertising, children's knowledge of advertising tactics and appeals, and children's use of cognitive defence against advertising'. So the state's responsibility to protect vulnerable consumers has propelled considerable research interest into the question of whether commercial content is clearly identifiable as such by the child audience, whether they can identify the source of the message and their intent to persuade and whether they are capable of discounting its claims.

Putting this question to the empirical test, most early researchers discovered that many children under eight years had trouble distinguishing advertising from programming (Ward and Wackman 1972; Atkin 1975). These of course are the heaviest viewers of children's time programming and the targets of many of the special kids marketing techniques. Robertson and Rossiter (1974) distinguished between children's capacity to read ads as product information as opposed to persuasive social influence. Using open ended responses, most of their under eight respondents could only describe ads as short and funny programmes, but rarely as trying to get people to buy something. Although many children don't take advertising as being 'truthful', few had a deeply sceptical attitude to advertising or recognized the techniques that were being used for persuasion. Fewer still had any sense of the commercial financing of television or understood who paid for commercials or programming. In terms of children's understanding of persuasive communication, age eight seemed to be a crucial developmental cut-off. Given the legal uncertainties surrounding marketing to young children, it is important to note that there is broad agreement that the majority of children under the age of eight do not exhibit sufficient advertising literacy to be considered competent consumers (Young 2003). As John (1999) concludes her review of the empirical evidence: 'there is little reason to believe that the vast majority of children younger than seven or eight years of age have a command of advertising's persuasive intent'.

But what about older children? Because they watch a lot of TV, by eight years of age most children learn to identify an advertisement as a distinct persuasive communication form that is intended to sell them something. Although their younger respondents demonstrated little understanding of what advertising was, it was also clear that most 10–12-year olds understood advertising's intent to persuade and were somewhat sceptical of advertising claims (Rossiter and Robertson 1974). Indeed, by the time

children reach their eighth birthday negative or mistrustful predisposi-
tions towards advertising are well established. However does the ability to
recognize an ad as such make them less susceptible to branded advertising?
As Robertson and Rossiter pointed out, although older children have the
ability to recognize persuasive intent in commercials, this 'should not be
taken as implying immunity to all commercials' (1974, p. 19). As Brucks,
Armstrong and Goldberg echoed, to be informed consumers children 'need
more than just a sceptical or critical attitude toward advertising. They also
need a more detailed knowledge about the nature of advertising and how it
works' (1988: 480–1).

Boush, Friestad and Rose (1994) studied the development of advertising
literacy among 426 adolescents in middle schools (grades 6–8) in the Pacific
Northwest, testing at the beginning and end of the school year. Their measures of scepticism about marketing included knowledge about advertising's
persuasion techniques, its intended effects, incredulity (belief in advertisers
truth claims) and mistrust of advertiser motives. They found that by age
11 children are somewhat mistrustful of advertising, compared with adults
and business students. But consumer susceptibility to persuasion was not
significantly related to mistrust and was negatively related to disbelief in
advertising. They did find that older children were more sceptical than
younger ones, and all children grow more sceptical during the school year,
yet 'there was a lot of room to grow after middle school', especially in their
understanding of advertising tactics and persuasive appeals used. They conclude that 'sceptical attitudes precede more sophisticated knowledge structures', and that the emergence of the 'schemer schemas about advertisers'
persuasive attempts start with general attitudes and then are filled in with
more specific beliefs' (1994: 172).

Using a 9-item SKEP scale, Obermiller and Spangenberg (2000) found
that scepticism was in part socialized in the family – particularly related to
fathers. Although children were less sceptical about advertising than their
parents, their scepticism about advertisements was related to general doubt
about other marketing communication forms, with ads considered the
least believable of all marketing sources. By age 12, many children seem
to have an understanding of the nature of commercial persuasion and the
economic transactions that enable advertisers to communicate with child
audiences. Many can competently decipher the selling points and recognize
some of the persuasion techniques. Yet even at age 12 their understanding
of the role that advertising plays in the broader media system is vague. In
this respect, researchers note that children's comprehension of the classical
tactics and appeals used by advertisers isn't consolidated until early adolescence (Moschis and Moore 1979; Obermiller and Spangenberg 2000).

A study by Dubow (1995) suggested that television advertising had a
considerable impact on the brand recall of 13–17-year olds despite high
levels of scepticism about advertising. These teens showed evidence of

advertising literacy and remained sceptical of advertising generally, yet the impact of advertising on their brand recall is greater than that of adults. The implications are twofold: firstly that scepticism and advertising literacy are irrelevant to brand persuasion processes and secondly that recall is crucial. Many industry and academic commentators argue that the current generation of kids growing up in a multimedia world are more media literate and that schools' media education is making them less naive. Yet as Drotner has found in a series of in-depth interviews with adolescents looking at ironic Guess jeans ads, many apparently sophisticated teens do not fully comprehend the complexly layered irony of commercials directed at them (Drotner 1992). Moreover, as Hobbs (2004) found out, teenagers who went through an ad literacy course did not necessarily become more effective, rational or wiser consumers. But many did think less of advertising generally.

In a meta analysis of the 23 studies involving 2934 children, Martin (1997) finds an *r* of 34–40 between age and children's understanding of advertising's intent to persuade. This correlation means that advertising literacy and scepticism both develop as children get older. But when all studies are combined, the evidence indicates that younger children are limited in their understanding of persuasive communication generally. They do not fully understand if an advertising source has different perspectives and interests from them; that the commercial message is designed to persuade them to do something; and that the messages are potentially biased by the seller's interest. Yet by the time they enter their teens most children know what advertising is and are guarded in their judgement of the veracity of advertisers' claims. Although this evidence is strong, Martin comments, there is still considerable variation in the studies, which means that we still have limited understanding of children's development of understanding of ad intent. Noting that advertising literacy is a function of changing social context and marketing practices as well as cognitive development (age), Martin goes on to suggest that some of the ambiguity can be explained by the way advertising intensity and practices changed between the 60s and 90s. Other socio-demographic factors (family structure, one-parent families) also influence children's consumer socialization.

Does branded affect subvert cognitive defences

McNeal (1999) notes that brands are increasingly important in children's lives. Even if children are sceptical of advertising, they do actively choose to watch commercials, not only because they are fun but also because ads provide them with one of the few sources of information about those products they are most interested in (snacks, treats, cereals, movies, toys and games). Brands determine how kids shop, how they communicate what they want to parents and how they exhibit pride of ownership to peers. The influence of advertising therefore starts with its effect on brand recognition, which with repetition implies brand recall and the formation of brand attitudes – and ultimately preferences. By the time they are five, however, many children exhibit a consistent preference for specific brands, which implies a brand construct as well as some product knowledge. Also he notes that brands that are first used in childhood are likely to be chosen in adulthood because brand effect lays the foundation of the long-term food preferences and taste.

As Young (2003) has argued, the relationship between advertising exposure and weight gain is marginal because 'The reality is that food advertising to children is designed to increase or maintain the sales of a particular brand, rather than to increase the consumption of a particular category of food'. Given that branded advertising is concentrated within the HFSS categories, the development of strong brand preferences could still be associated with a less healthy diet. As the previous chapter illustrated, the advertising techniques found in children's food advertising are less directed at informing the child about the product's nutritional qualities, risks or benefits than at drawing children's attention and bolstering positive brand attitudes.

To examine the relationship between general advertising scepticism and specific attitudes to branded advertising, Rieken and Yavas (1990) conducted a study that deployed Rossiter's ideas about advertising literacy by measuring truthfulness, scepticism and perception of advertising's bias. Subjects consisted of 152 children aged 8–12 who were asked for both their general attitudes to advertising as well as their orientation to advertising of specific sectors: toys, cereals and over the counter drugs. The results showed that 75 per cent of these children are media literate – they question advertising's truthfulness and recognize its positive bias to sell them something. Many don't like advertising much because it breaks into a programme and 66 per cent find many ads in poor taste. But when it comes to toy ads or even cereal ads, more than half have positive attitudes towards these products whereas medicine ads are viewed more negatively, implying that children have different ways of responding to ads based on their orientation and interest in these products. Overall, they are interested in learning more about food and toy ads because they like these products generally and are less sceptical about the advertising of these products. But when it came to specific brands, their negative attitudes to advertising were not generalized, for example 40 per cent had not formed a positive or negative attitude towards Alphabits whereas 73 per cent had a positive attitude towards Cheerios (a frequently advertised brand).

The formation and consequences of brand attitudes in children has been a focus of much discussion in the advertising industry (Bahn 1986; Derbaix and Bree 1997; Achenreiner and John 2003). Pecheux and Debraix (1999) found evidence that the affective component of a brand provides the link between the ad and the product. They developed a scale for general measurement of brand orientation and found that affect is much stronger than utility in predicting the product involvement and loyalty of children aged 8–12. They argued that hedonic rather than utilitarian dimensions of product meaning and attitudes characterize children's general relationship to goods being marketed. Across a range of food, clothing, toys and media products these researchers found that children either like the brand or not, regardless of their attitudes to advertising generally and their awareness of intent to persuade. There are a number of reasons why scepticism and puffery filtering may not help to reduce the persuasive impact of advertising on the formation of brand preferences and loyalty. Advertising has been shown to increase brand awareness through affective rather than cognitive channels by establishing liking for the ad (Hitchings and Moynihan 1998) so that scepticism and knowledge of intent to persuade are irrelevant. The first is that enjoyable and lively ads are more engaging and remembered better. The second is that advertising contributes to the formation of preferences based on the transfer of affect from ad to brand. If children like watching the ad, they orient more positively to the brand, regardless of whether they believe its claims or not.

Phelps and Hoy (1996) tested the psychological mechanisms of branded persuasion that potentially circumvent the cognitive resistance of children, noting that because of prior exposure to food advertising, children's brand familiarity needs to be accounted for in studies of the formation of brand preferences. The affective transfer of positive attitudes to the brand from watching a likeable ad can explain why older children who are sceptical are still impacted by advertising in the formation of their brand preferences and requests. Their study of this issue was based on 43 children aged 8–9 and 69 aged 11–12 in the Midwest of the US who were assessed in class for a set of snack (candy bars, cookies) and cereal products, some of which they were familiar with. A week later they were exposed again to the ads for those products and retested for their liking of the ads and brand preferences as well as their purchase intention (measured by the likelihood of asking a parent for the product). Results indicated that prior preferences for the brand accounted for 40 per cent of the variance in the brand attitudes whereas liking the ad contributed 9 per cent of the variance after controlling for the prior attitude for familiar brands, but 26 per cent of the variance for the unfamiliar brands. This means that the effect of advertising on familiar brands is cumulative in the consolidation of brand preferences, with new products benefiting most from likeable ads.

Although the two age groups were both sceptical and somewhat media literate, comparisons in their response to the ads were revealing. Although familiarity with the product predicted their attitudes to the brand equally, when controlled for, the younger group's liking of the ad accounted for 5 per cent of their brand attitude whereas it predicted 10 per cent of the variance in the older group. But when it came to unfamiliar products it explained only 13 per cent of the third graders' but 37 per cent of the sixth graders' level of brand preference. Clearly the older children, who are more sceptical, are more influenced by advertising they like, especially for products they have no prior exposure to. Yet when it comes to making requests for familiar brands a positive brand attitude explains 68 per cent of the variance in requests for sixth graders and 75 per cent for third graders. But when it comes to the prediction of requests for the brand, it was estimated that liking the particular ad predicted only 2 per cent of the intent to purchase a familiar brand and only 1 per cent of the variance of an unfamiliar brand. The authors remark therefore that 'Based on previous research … the third graders in the unfamiliar brands condition should have been the most "vulnerable" to advertising's influence on purchase intention given their generally immature cognitive defence skills coupled with their lack of product experience' (Phelps and Hoy 1996: 82). Even if a child likes an ad, forming the intent to ask a parent for the product is most likely for the brands which the child is familiar with. The younger children were less influenced by ads they liked than older ones, implying that either the younger children need more than two exposures to the ad in order to form a brand preference or that the particular ads used didn't have strong enough appeal.

Ewing et al. (1999) examined children's day after recall (prompted and unprompted) of branded food advertising as well as their ability to describe the commercial by using telephone interviews with 200 South Africans in a natural experiment which measured the effects of daily exposure to different food campaigns. Contrary to the researchers expectations, liking the ad accounted for 58 per cent of the variance in recall – an effect which proved much stronger than that of media weight and frequency. This study found significant differences on both liking and recall among all categories of foods, perhaps indicating that children's interest in and prior orientation towards the food facilitates retention of the brand. Those foods high in fat, oil or sugar (chocolates, sweets, desserts) are liked more and recalled better than ads for proteins, bread, rice and pasta. In other words, it would appear as if advertising for the fun or 'sin' foods is generally more effective from the point of view of branded recall than for the 'serious' or healthier foods.

Borzekowski and Robinson (2001) conducted a controlled experimental study where poorer Californian families were recruited from a head start programme. Forty-six 'preschoolers', aged 2–6, participated. Children were randomly assigned to watch a videotape of a popular children's cartoon in small groups. One tape had an educational segment with no commercials inserted, while others saw the same cartoons with several commercials of different branded food products embedded in the programme content. Shortly afterwards, they were asked if they wanted one of two food items which were similar in packaging, but one had been shown to the child before, during the experiment. Children in the experiment showed a significant preference (on most product categories) towards the item they had just seen advertised on the videotape. Background information given by parents indicated that the effects did not vary according to previous exposure to media, including regular viewing of TV ads, suggesting that the effect of exposure can be on brand preferences.

Bradford Yates (2001) applied the elaboration likelihood model to test whether the media literacy of a message recipient acts as a moderator of brand persuasion. The central route to persuasion implies cognitive elaboration and information processing are more important, whereas the peripheral route implies image processing and affective responses impact brand attitudes more. The ELM suggests that since attitude towards the ad can influence the brand attitude more than thoughts about the product, media scepticism could be a buffer against persuasion on the affective level. 148 fourth and fifth grade students were shown a Pringles potato chip ad and asked to fill out a questionnaire that recorded their thoughts about the commercial, their attitudes to the product, both positive and negative, and the arguments made about the product in the ad. General attitudes to advertising were also measured. Subjects then either received a media literacy training video or a control video, and watched versions of the commercial that presented strong and weak arguments. They were then tested for the persuasiveness of the arguments. The results revealed that media literacy training did not make the subjects scrutinize the arguments made in the ads more, but their attitude to the product, to the ad and to advertising generally was more negative. Although all subjects were sceptical of advertising, the ad literacy training did make them more negative about the benefits of advertising. The author concludes that the media literacy training may have taught children to have a more negative opinion of advertising rather than to be more cognitively sophisticated consumers.

In reviewing these findings therefore, Livingstone and Helsper (2004) concluded that advertising effects on children's brand preferences and requests are not confined to the youngest children, who are assumed to be most 'vulnerable' by their lack of advertising literacy. These studies support a few generalizations: first, children watch and learn from ads; second, children who watch more television are more likely to ask for advertised brands; and third, children form preferences for those brands which are most advertised regardless of their scepticism about advertising. Moreover some studies indicate that older children's preferences were more impacted in spite of their greater advertising literacy. But they also admit that 'we know surprisingly little of how media affect children differently at different ages'.

But are things changing?

Industry critics have objected that most of the evidence about scepticism is both out of date and American, arguing that advertising techniques and levels of scepticism of children today could be quite different than found in earlier studies. Yet recent research undertaken mostly by health researchers since those policy reviews has provided similar evidence that advertising influences children's branded food preferences and choices. Halford et al. (2004) suggest that motivated viewing can influence the effectiveness of ads by comparing normal and overweight children's responses to different ads. Studying a group of British school-aged children before exposure to both food and non-food ads, these researchers reported that while there was no significant difference in the number of non-food adverts recognized, the obese children did recognize significantly more of the food adverts. Recognition of the low-fat savoury snack is the only one that did not increase after viewing food ads. Moreover, recognition of the food ads did significantly correlate with the amount of food eaten after exposure, indicating that overweight children attend more to food ads and consume more than normal weight ones. Exposure to food advertising therefore promotes consumption in both groups, they conclude, but more so in the overweight ones because they attend to food advertising more avidly and remember it better. Chaplin and John's (2005) research further suggested that as children get older they increase the number of self-brand connections, peaking between 8 and 12 years of age, and begin to see brands as having personalities and symbolizing group membership. It is perhaps because of the way they process ads by assimilating the brand to self-concept that explains why teens, even though they are sceptical are still deeply impacted by advertising campaigns.

Valkenburg and Buijzen (2005) suggest that we have a poor understanding of the relationship between the cognitive capacity of children to recognize, process and retain brand constructs in the market and their formation of preferences and habits of eating. To further understand younger children's vulnerability in the market they undertook interviews with 196 children aged 2–8 to examine their cognitive capacity to recognize, process and retain brand constructs. Overall, younger children have much lower brand recall, and generally boys demonstrate higher recall than girls. The youngest children (<4 years) could recall one brand logo but recognize 8 of the 12 they were shown. Eight-year olds could recall five and recognize all the brands. The researchers found that the amount of children's TV viewing was a significant predictor of brand recognition, but not recall, and mother's brand recall was related to the child's. They also noted that the extent of brands recalled was associated with the Social Economic Status (SES) of the family. They concluded that it was important to distinguish between brand recognition – which is visual – and recall, which like requests to parents, requires linguistic and cognitive elaboration, in assessing the impact of TV. They suggested that the mechanisms for consumer evaluation of brands consolidated at age 7–8 because of cognitive development but was also impacted by family circumstances.

In a study of the effects of branding on food choice, Robinson et al. (2007) studied 63 children aged 3–5 from low-income families who were allowed to taste from 5 pairs of identical foods (hamburger, chicken nuggets, French fries, 1 per cent milk, and carrots) served in either a McDonald's or an unbranded package. Children were asked to identify which food in the pair came from McDonald's and to take a bite from each and to say which one tasted best. Each child was also assessed by the parent for the amount of TV they watched and whether they had asked for any food products during the week. Results indicated that over 306 paired samples the child preferred the taste of the food identified as 'McDonalds' more than the one in the plain wrapper. The effect was particularly strong for fries (77 per cent) but less strong for carrots (54 per cent) and hamburgers (48 per cent). The number of television sets in the home (but not the amount of time spent viewing them) and the frequency of eating at McDonald's were both positively associated with a higher proportion of McDonald's brand preferences. The authors conclude that brand effects are likely to be a result of 'past direct and/indirect marketing exposure as well as past experience with McDonald's products or packaging' (Robinson et al. 2007: 796).

A study by Chernin (2008) on children's responses to advertising confirms that savvy does not imply resistance to advertising's brand appeals. Chernin undertook an experiment on 133 children between ages 5 and 11, finding that exposure to embedded food commercials for Sprinkle Spangles and Tang increased children's assessment of the advertised products. The product assessments were done in a series of picture presentations that compared the product with similar ones asking the children that if they could eat it the next day, which would they choose. The results indicated that children not only responded positively to the Sprinkle Spangles and Tang ad (which they were more familiar with) but that, seemingly 'savvy' older children, who understand persuasive intent and possessed sceptical attitudes necessary to resist contemporary brand strategies, were equally persuaded towards the brand as the younger ones. The author suggests that perhaps critical skills are of little use in 'resisting' the persuasive influence of branded food marketing anyway, because branded persuasion is not much influenced by 'puffery filtering'. Moreover, gender differences in persuasiveness in these ungendered ads (boys exposed to ad were much more favourable) suggest that perhaps attention to the programme material, which featured a male character, increases attention to the ads.

Risk analysis of advertising exposure

An important distinction in the consideration of the evidence linking advertising and child obesity is the difference between a cause and a risk factor. Causes are necessary conditions which reliably contribute to a behavioural outcome, like weight gain, whereas risk factors are contributing variables which interact with other mitigating variables in a complex multifactor system. Adapting the epidemiological approach to communication research, health scientists have used multifactorial regression modelling to assess the risks associated with advertising exposure by controlling for some of the intervening variables that influence children's health status. Using regression modelling to examine the relationship between children's television advertising spends in the US, Australia and eight European countries, and the prevalence of overweight among children, Lobstein and Dibb (2005) reported a significant association between the proportion of overweight children and the weight of food advertising ($r = 0.81$, $P < 0.005$). A weaker, negative association was found between the proportion of overweight children and the number of advertisements encouraging healthier diets ($r = -0.56$, $P < 0.10$), suggesting that the content as well as the frequency of exposure explains the impact on diet.

Although such research shows that advertising can contribute to weight gain as Brian Young (2003a) has noted, 'The route from advertising to obesity is a long and tortuous one – from advertising being a dietary influence of sorts, and diet itself being only one element in the balance between energy in and energy out. So where does that leave advertising?' he asks. 'We have seen that advertising can influence food choice and preference but with several qualifications made about the role of other more important and powerful determinants of what children eat. And what children eat is just one of many other multi-factorial sources of influence on what makes children fat'. The problem is that in the context of moral panic, the complexity of children's food consumption has been obscured. As Young says, 'advertising seems to have been effectively scapegoated as the villain of the piece' (2003: 24). Most problematically researchers interested in effects often ignored the 'compensatory influences' and 'mitigating factors' that are also present in the family.

A study of 548 ethnically diverse students by Boynton-Jarrett et al. (2003) used a longitudinal survey design over two years, which modelled changes of media use as a determinate of dietary preferences. Generally they found that those children that watched four or more hours of TV each day ate less fruits and vegetables and were much more likely to be overweight or obese. Overall BMI increased, although strenuous physical activity decreased with TV viewing. Controlling for other factors, including activity and family meals, they estimated that for each hour of TV viewed by individuals the amount of fruit consumption decreased by .16 units. TV, rather than total media time seemed to account for the increase in BMI. The implication is that their exposure to unhealthy snack and confection brands accounts for the trade-off with healthier foods in their daily diet, but this was not measured.

In a follow-up analysis of the Boynton-Jarrett et al. study Wiecha et al. (2006) report on the changes taking place in the total energy intake due to the increasing consumption among viewers of heavily advertised foods (sweets, fast food and sugary beverages). The comparison of energy intake with that at baseline showed that for each hour of TV an additional 167 kcals extra were consumed. When it comes to the relationship between television viewing and diet, although an increase in viewing was noted in only 43 per cent of the children, their increase in energy intake was associated with greater consumption of advertised foods by five servings per day: With each one-hour increment in television viewing, the number of servings of soda, fried foods and sweet snacks increased. The research supports the idea that television's impact on the increase in total energy is related to the heavy viewers' choice of snack foods. As the authors conclude, 'In conclusion, although children and youth are encouraged to watch what they eat, many youth seem to eat what they watch, and in the process increase their risk for increasing their energy intake'.

Using a combination of econometric and epidemiological research techniques applied to the longitudinal data set from the NYSTC survey in the US, Chou et al. (2005, 2008) estimated that a ban on fast food advertisements would 'reduce the number of overweight children ages 3–11 in a fixed population by 10 per cent and would reduce the number of overweight adolescents ages 12–18 by 12 per cent'. These estimates of 10–12 per cent of variance explained are based on children's weight gain between 1991 and 1998 regressed against exposure to fast food advertising while holding constant other possible contributing factors like SES, community and family.

Noting the specific rise of fast food advertising on American TV, Taveras et al. (2006) asked 240 parents of 2–6-year olds about their children's TV viewing and fast food consumption. These authors used a parental questionnaire with a detailed accounting of the child's viewing to provide a more reliable estimate of exposure to fast food advertising specifically, as well as demographic factors such as neighbourhood, income and ethnicity. The parents attitudes towards fruit and vegetable shopping were also taken into consideration as well as the main determinate variable, which was the number of times each week that the child eats at fast food restaurants such as 'McDonald's Burger King, or Kentucky Fried Chicken'. It was noted that older children ate at fast food outlets more than younger ones, but that older parents took their children to fast food significantly less often. Wealthier and better-educated families were significantly less likely to take their children out for fast food, although no attitudinal differences were revealed. Comparison showed that both the hours that children viewed on weekends and the overall media consumption during the week distinguished those families that took their children out for fast food more. Controlling for income and availability, they report an OR for the relationship between TV viewing and eating at a fast food restaurant of 1.55.

In a diary study in 234 Dutch households with children aged 4–12, Buijzen et al. (2008) investigated the associations between children's exposure to food advertising and their consumption of (a) advertised food brands, (b) advertised energy-dense food product categories, and (c) food products overall. They argue that the distinction between advertising effects at a brand, a product category and a total consumption level is vital in the debate about the role of food advertising with regard to children's diets. But it is only because exposure to a biased advertising system leads to more generic consumption of heavily advertised energy-dense food products that concerns are raised. If advertising exposure leads merely to brand substitution within a category of similar energy density, then advertising-induced changes in children's preferences would not be a risk factor in obesity.

In this study, the link between TV exposure to food ads and the consumption of food products was examined using multiple hierarchical regression analysis, while controlling for various child (i.e., age, sex, television viewing time) and family variables (i.e., family income and consumption-related communication styles). Results showed that children's exposure to food advertising was significantly related to their consumption of advertised brands (rho = .21) and energy-dense product categories (rho = .19), yet the relation between advertising exposure and overall food consumption only held in lower income families (rho = .19). Children's advertising exposure added 4 per cent to the explained variance in consumption of advertised brands, after controlling for age, SES and parenting and 3 per cent to the variance in consumption of energy-dense product categories. In addition, consumption-related family communication was an important moderator of the link between advertising and the food consumption variables. Socio-oriented family communication (i.e., striving for harmony and conformity) was particularly successful in reducing the link between advertising exposure and energy-dense food consumption. In low-income families, children's exposure to food advertising was also negatively correlated with overall food consumption. The authors concluded that food advertising not only affected children's brand choice but also extended to their consumption of energy-dense food product categories generally.

In a unique longitudinal study of the long-term effects of heavy television viewing on dietary intake, Barr-Anderson et al. (2009) report findings from a five-year 'follow on' study of 564 middle school students and 1366 high school students in the Project Eat study. They were assessed for television viewing, activity and dietary practices. The study found that in the younger cohort, heavy television viewing was found in 21 per cent of the population. Five years later, heavier viewers exhibited more sugared soft drink consumption and less fruit eating, compared with the low TV viewers. These results were independent of other factors like gender but not ethnicity. In the older group, only 16 per cent were heavy viewers (> 5 hours media use daily) yet they were more likely to report increased total energy consumed, comprised by higher consumption of snack foods and lower fruit. Their increased energy possessed a higher percentage of total calories from transfats and sweetened soft drinks. They also consumed significantly more servings of fried foods and snacks and ate more often at fast food restaurants. When analysed for ethnicity, black and Hispanic youth were more at risk of these TV effects than white teens. Although the mechanisms by which TV increases dietary intake are still not clear, the authors note that the categories of food in which the effects of heavy viewing are evident are those that are most heavily advertised on TV.

Moving targets: Cognitive defences and changing marketing strategies

The empirical study of advertising influences on children's food preferences has revealed the multiple interacting factors involved in the media-saturated household. The results, however, have been more or less the same as found earlier: although researchers produce some inconsistent findings the weight of evidence suggests that TV advertising targeting children influences some children's requests to parents, brand preferences and product choices depending on age, social economic status, parental influences and cognitive orientation of the child. There is little evidence of a reduction of advertising's influence among media-literate adolescents. Teenagers, who are supposed to be more sceptical of advertising, also watch TV more and show relatively similar, if moderate, effects of advertising exposure on their preferences. Thus, contrary to neoliberal views of media literacy, policymakers cannot assume that a child who is knowledgeable about or critical of an advertisement will not be persuaded to like the advertised brand. In which case a precautionary policy that includes adolescents may not be 'incoherent' based on the evidence.

Although it is clear that younger children seem to lack the critical skills necessary to recognize advertising's persuasive intent of brand campaigns, advertising literacy may be irrelevant in today's mediated marketplace anyway. McAllister and Giglio (2005) noted how both advertising techniques and media delivery systems that target children have changed dramatically since these early studies of advertising scepticism: techniques like cross-marketing, product placement, integrated network branding, 30-minute commercials and online marketing campaigns make it much harder for even older children to identify what is an ad, and what isn't, in the synergistic media marketplace. A market research study found that while 90 per cent of children aged 8–12 could identify a commercial on TV as a form of advertising, less than half 11–12-year olds could identify character toy cartoons as such and only two-thirds could identify a brand logo on a T-shirt as a form of advertising (Achenreiner and John (2003).

In a recent prospective survey of 827 third-grade students, Chamberlain et al. (2006) revealed a significant correlation between TV viewing and both toy r = .15 and food requests r = .16. Followed up 20 months later, the testing of 386 of these 8–9-year old Californian elementary students indicated a strong predictive relationship between prior exposure to advertising and requests for the toys, foods and drinks that were frequently advertised in media. Even controlling for the number of requests made at baseline as well as sociodemographic factors, the requests for heavily advertised foods was significantly related to TV time whereas for advertised toys, it was related to total screen time. The authors concluded that screen media are now a risk factor in children's requests for advertised products with differences between food and toys explained by the fact that films and DVDs are themselves commercially embedded media.

The escalating importance of online food advertising to children has provoked concern about the extent of children's new media literacies among advocates (Which? 2006). Sandra Calvert (2008) has recently summarized the reasons why policy debates about food marketing to children have heated up recently: 'Today, marketing and advertising permeate children's daily lives. Many products marketed to children are not healthful and promote obesity. Younger children often do not understand the persuasive intent of advertisements, and even older children probably have difficulty understanding the intent of newer marketing techniques that blur the line between commercial and program content' (Calvert 2008: 206). When it comes to the Internet, it is far from clear that children can avoid the pop-ups and pornography, distinguish the commercial intent of sites such as Neopets, avoid cyber-lurkers, or understand how the information they input is being used by marketers (http://www.media-awareness.ca) (Montgomery 2007).

6
The Disruptive Screen: Understanding the Multiple Lifestyle Risks Associated with Heavy TV Viewing

In the previous chapter I argued that over the last 25 years social scientists have provided strong evidence of the limited health risks associated with exposure to branded advertising. The methods used have included both experimental and survey studies. The largest effects have been noted in experimental studies where exposure to advertising is carefully controlled. Weaker effects have been noted in cross-sectional and longitudinal field studies where exposure to advertising is measured by total TV viewing. The evidence of marketing risks has been based largely on evidence of a statistical relationship between two measurable variables in the US – TV viewing time and BMI. This relationship was examined across a number of studies. Reviews of this literature suggested that exposure to TV food advertising targeting children makes a small but consistent contribution to their weight gain by influencing their brand preferences and requests to parents. But as critics have stated, there are three limitations in this literature: the influence of TV advertising on diet is small, the effects can be mitigated by good parenting and TV advertising is not the only reason why heavy viewers gain weight. In short there are many other factors in children's lives that can moderate advertising's impact on children's weight gain including their parents' unwillingness to purchase what they ask for as well as their own regular participation in active leisure.

Each of these criticisms provides a valid qualification of the expectation that a ban on advertising would significantly lower weight gain. Figure 6.1 plots the relationship between TV viewing and obesity from the YRBS study (Youth Risk Behaviours Survey 2007) – a carefully representative national sample of over 13,000 teens gathered every two years in the US. In this data set TV viewing is significantly related to weight status, accounting for 3.5 per cent of the variance in BMI percentile. Putting aside measurement error (see Borzekowski and Robinson. 1999) we note that for every hour a teen watches there is an increase in BMI. But the increase is particularly strong for those who watch more than 3 hours of TV per day. Using this cut-off it is found that 46 per cent of obese teens watch more than three

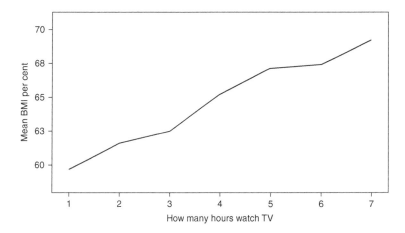

Figure 6.1   The relationship between TV watching and obesity

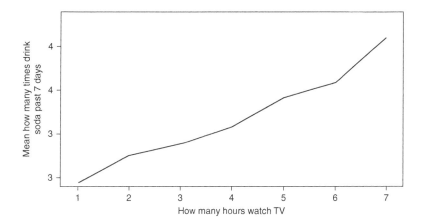

Figure 6.2   TV viewing and soft drink consumption

hours per day whereas only 32 per cent of normal weight teens watch this much. Those teens who watch 3 hours or more of TV are more likely to have BMI > 95 percentile. For the US teen population then, excessive TV viewing (> 3 hours per day) has an OR = 1.54. This implies that heavy TV watching puts some heavy viewers at risk.

Of the many concerns about food marketing it was the relationship between heavy TV viewing and soft drink consumption that was highlighted by the WHO. The linear relationship between hours of TV viewing and soft drinks consumed is illustrated in Figure 6.2. This relationship explains 4.6

percent of the variance in soft drink consumption which suggests a 'dose response' relationship predicted by exposure to soft drink advertising. This suggests that exposure to branded advertising on TV can influence teens' preferences for branded soft drink products.

Yet frequent soft drink consumption is only marginally related to BMI (OR = 1.1) and the relationship with obesity differs for males and females and holds only for those who drink more than 4 soft drinks per day as shown in Figure 6.3. Moderate soft drink consumption (as opposed to avoidance) even appears to be a protective factor. Moreover the influence of soda advertising on weight status is limited since weight gain depends on daily diet, of which frequent branded soft drink consumption is just one minor contributing element.

The implication of these findings is that heavy TV viewing teens are more likely to be obese for reasons that have little to do with advertising's direct impact on their diet including their fruit and vegetable consumption or their active leisure. The data confirms this suspicion: heavy TV viewing is correlated with failing to exercise moderately (r = –.05) and failing to exercise moderately is correlated with higher BMI (–.039). This implies that some heavy TV viewers are gaining weight because they are more sedentary rather than because of what they eat. Which is why critics argue that a measure of total TV viewing confounds the estimation of health risks associated with exposure to food advertising with those associated with TV viewers' sedentary lifestyles.

Indeed, the more closely one examines these interacting risk factors, the more complex the relationship between TV viewing and weight gain appears.

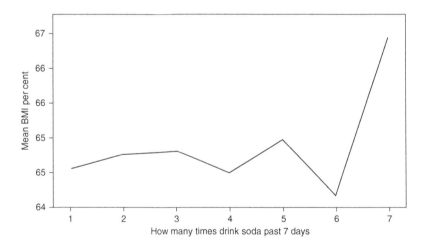

Figure 6.3　Obesity and soft drink consumption

Figure 6.4 indicates that for daily drinkers of soda, excessive TV viewing increases the risk of obesity slightly from 14 to 18.2 per cent (OR = 1.14) whereas for occasional soda drinkers, 5 hours of viewing per day increases the risk of obesity from 10.1 to 21.9 per cent (OR = 1.48). Moreover, among the heavy viewers, those that drink soda occasionally have a greater tendency to be obese than daily drinkers. Clearly soft drink advertising provides an unlikely explanation of why these heavy TV viewers weigh more.

What becomes quickly evident when studying the implications of food marketing for teen obesity is just how important social demographic factors are. The YRBS data analysed in Figure 6.5 suggests that Afro and Hispanic American teens are at greater risk of obesity than white teens. Whereas 18.5 per cent of Afro and Hispanic teens are obese only 10.8 per cent of white teens are (OR = 1.886). Afro and Hispanic teens also watch TV more. Whereas 54.5 per cent of them watch more than 3 hours daily, only 27.4 per cent of white teens watch this much. Does this mean that ethnic teens are more at risk from marketing then? Not necessarily. Despite their extensive exposure to TV, the impact of TV viewing on Afro and Hispanic teens' weight status is a modest OR =1.06 whereas among white teens the risks associated with heavy TV viewing are considerable (OR = 1.70).

	No TV	5+ hrs TV	OR
Drink soft drinks daily	14 per cent	18.2 per cent	1.14
Infrequent soft drink consumption	10.1 per cent	21.9 per cent	1.48

Figure 6.4   Assessing the risk of obesity at different levels of soft drink consumption

	Watch TV < 3 hours daily	Watch TV > 3 hours daily	OR
Afro and Hispanic	17.4	19.6	1.06
White	9.2	14.7	1.70

	Afro and Hispanic	White
< 3 hours TV	30.1	28
> 3 hours TV	40.6	48.2

Figure 6.5   Interactions between ethnicity, excessive TV viewing and obesity

The estimates of the impact of TV viewing on all teens therefore might understate the actual risks associated with the excessive viewing of a particular group. White teens seem to be more at risk of heavy TV viewing than Afro and Hispanics. Indeed the analysis of daily drinking of soft drinks among Afro and Hispanic populations has a modest relationship to TV viewing, whereas white teens who watch more TV are also much more likely to drink soft drinks frequently. This suggests that, although there are multiple risk factors in all teens' lives, those associated with exposure to advertising are relatively less significant (OR = 1.59) for Afro and Hispanic teens than for white teens (OR = 2.4). In view of demographic differences, generalized estimates of the impact of advertising exposure can both over and understate the risks to particular groups. Alternatively put, this data suggests that white teens are relatively more at risk from advertising's influence than Afro and Hispanic teens – perhaps because these demographic groups are at risk for other reasons such as poverty or culturally specific diet and activity preferences. Unless one sees weight status as a socially situated lifestyle risk, the explanatory value of TV time is bound to be very limited.

Estimating marketing risks

As I have argued, the use of total time in TV viewing as an independent measure in risk analysis can both understate the levels of specific children's exposure to advertising and confound those risks with others associated with the sedentary lifestyles and snacking. In a regression analysis of the US Panel Survey of Income Dynamics, Zimmerman and Bell (2010) attempted to estimate the specific contribution of TV advertising to child obesity by comparing diary data from children under 8 with those aged 8–13. The data set contained over 2000 children sampled in 1997 and again in 2002. It was found that older children watched more commercial TV (1.47 hours per day) than younger children (.88 hours) thus exposing them to advertising more. Their study shows that in the US, younger children who watched more non-commercial TV were also least at risk of obesity. Yet among them, those who watched more commercial TV were at greater risk. This data set also showed that older children were generally more at risk to obesity for multiple reasons: They were less active physically, watched TV more than younger children and ate in front of the TV frequently.

Zimmerman and Bell (2010) suggest that using total TV time in regressions may underestimate the degree of risk because it confounds advertising effects with those associated with sedentary leisure. The regression models they used to estimate the relationship between commercial TV viewing and BMI controlled for three factors: the children's initial BMI, activity levels and eating in front of the TV. For the younger children, after controlling for activity levels, exposure to commercial TV in 1997 accounted for about 3.3 per cent of the variance of BMI, whereas exposure to non-commercial TV was not related to children's weight status. For older children, exposure to commercial TV in 2002 accounted for 2.5 per cent of the variance in BMI whereas time spent watching non-commercial media was unrelated to BMI. Based on this analysis they concluded that 'Television viewing may be a sedentary activity but it is not for that reason that it is associated with obesity in children.' When controlled for exposure to commercial TV, non-commercial TV and physical activity levels, it was only the time spent watching commercial television which bore any significant relationship to children's weight status. The authors concluded that 'the relationship between television viewing and obesity among children is limited to commercial television viewing and probably operates through the effect of advertising obesogenic foods on television' (2010: 338). How else can we explain the difference in weight status found when comparing these two viewing patterns? Their findings also suggest that the protective factors of active leisure and advertising literacy may not be that important in older children.

But how much risk? In the YSRB study only 14.4 per cent of US teens are classified obese (BMI > 95 percentile). So if risks are associated with excessive viewing then at most 6.1 per cent of teen obesity (14.6 × .46) can be attributed to advertising exposure. But this means that 8 per cent of all obese teens are at risk for reasons other than marketing pressures on their diet. By breaking out the data it is found that 10.9 per cent of teens who watch no TV are overweight compared with 20 per cent of those who watch more than 5 hours daily. The risks associated with the heaviest viewing have an OR = 2.01. Those that watch five hours daily are twice as likely to be overweight as non-TV viewers. That increase can be attributed to TV viewing. Yet 10.9 per cent of those who are never exposed to TV advertising are still obese.

Consistent evidence of a modest relationship between advertising exposure and obesity was sufficient for Ofcom to propose a ban on TV advertising targeting children. Yet we should not expect a sudden drop in the incidence of child obesity in the UK. Firstly, because the estimates of obesity risks are based on the US experience where exposure to children's advertising and levels of media literacy are different. Secondly, because the degree of British children's exposure to commercials targeting them was already limited because of their greater viewing of non-commercial TV and the shift of food marketers into prime time or alternative media. This implies that given the greater exposure to advertising in the US research may overestimate the degree to which children are at risk in the British marketplace. And thirdly because there are other factors associated with TV viewing such as sedentary lifestyles and snacking that confound the estimates of TV's contribution to weight gain. In this respect it is worth remembering that the ban was based on a precautionary logic of child protection for reasons of developmental inadequacy rather than proof of harm done. Young children simply do not have the competence to make informed choices about lifestyle risks communicated in the market whatever the level of risk.

Forming branded preferences in the media-saturated household

Although modest risks from TV advertising may be sufficient reason for imposing a ban, there are other good reasons why we should not assume that the food marketers' targeting of children is always effective. As Young (2003a) has rightly explained, the theory of direct exposure effects 'implicitly assumed that the more frequently children see a TV commercial for a branded food then they will proportionately consume more of that food. Consequently the foods advertised on TV and seen by the child should have a direct effect on the foods consumed by the child. This is simply untrue and does not do justice to the complexity of food preference and choice and how advertising works within that framework'. Young points out that brand competition within the three most advertised core food categories – cereals, fast food and confections – is intense, implying that the nutritional implications of brand switching, should they break through the children's 'puffery detectors', could be health neutral (i.e. from Shredded Wheat to Quaker Oatmeal or from Frosted Flakes to Cocoa Puffs). Young goes on to note that 'even if ads prompt kids to make frequent requests, this doesn't mean that they get the unhealthy foods they ask for either. In short there are many other factors that need to be considered if we are to understand why there is only a marginal impact of food advertising on weight'.

In the modern family there is considerable divergence in the conditions in which children are exposed to and interpret advertising messages. Even if children have greater say in family choices these days, parents still make most of the provisioning choices for them – particularly young ones. A simplistic exposure-effects model of market risks fails to account for the ways SES, advertising scepticism, media use regulation, food tastes and parental guidance in the food and leisure choices of children influences their lifestyles. As Livingstone and Helsper (2004) noted in their report to Ofcom, the research into advertising effects has identified many environmental factors which 'mediate between advertising and children's food choice including gender, cost, birth order, cultural meanings of food, obesity levels, family eating habits, parental regulation of media, parental mediation of advertising, peer mediation of advertising, pro-health messages and pester power' (2004: 19). Their model, shown below in Figure 6.6, characterizes this complex system of interacting factors and levels of environmental influences which can moderate the 'direct influence' of advertising on children's food consumption.

Families differ in the amount and types of programming viewed, in the foods they like and in their ownership and use of media, all of which influences the degree to which children are exposed to food ads targeting them. They also differ in their interest in and scepticism towards advertising. Moreover because children acquire their taste for specific foods, and often brands, in the family, we cannot assume they attend to or like the most heavily advertised products.

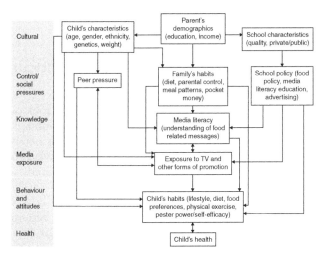

Figure 6.6 Model of factors that influence children's food choice, habits and health
Source: Livingstone and Helsper 2004.

Figure 6.7 Factors mitigating TV advertising's influences on brand choice

Some families prefer cereal for breakfast and some prefer toast, meaning the way they emotionally engage with branded messages varies significantly across the population. And ultimately most parents still buy and prepare most of their foods implying that children are not at liberty to eat what they like all of the time. Children's consumer power is discretionary in the sense that familial circumstances impose constraints and coach their choices until they leave home (and often long after) (Marshall et al. 2007, 2008).

Based on the literature reviews, Figure 6.7 identifies my own assessment of the key mitigating factors that must be considered in understanding why up to 5 per cent of variance explained provides a reasonable estimate of advertising's contribution to population weight status.

Discretionary power: Family dynamics and the mitigation of advertising

The following is an account of the research project which took place in the spring of 2004 in a primary school in Burnaby, British Columbia. This school was typical of an ethnically mixed, lower- to middle-class neighbourhood in Greater Vancouver. Over a five-week period, using surveys, diaries and interviews, a research team from the Media Analysis Laboratory at Simon Fraser University gathered both qualitative and quantitative data on the 475 students aged 5–12 at the school. We measured each child's TV viewing, attitudes and knowledge of advertising, eating and activity patterns and consumer behaviours as well as their height and weight. The data were gathered in the classrooms with teachers involved actively in the process. For expediency and clarity of exposition, the details of the questionnaires and analysis are excluded and interested readers are encouraged to read the methodological notes in the appendix.

Remembering that 90 per cent of Canadian children under 12 are *not* obese, my intent was to assess the moderating circumstances within the Canadian family that mitigate the impact of food advertising on children's preferences and choices. Similar to Valkenburg and Buijzen's study of the multiple interacting factors involved in brand preference formation, I used diaries and questionnaires, but with a few differences. Firstly by interviewing children rather than surveying parents, the Canadian study could assess their levels of media literacy, their attitudes to nutrition, and their likes and dislikes in brands. Secondly, by assessing their food preferences and tastes I was better able to determine whether a preference for energy-dense foods is independent of advertising. Thirdly, by using detailed diaries of children's media consumption, food and snacking behaviours (including media-related eating habits), sedentary lifestyles and activity levels efforts were made to control for the confounding factors associated with heavy TV viewing. Finally by operationalizing the power relationships and the dynamics of negotiation I could explore the ways that children exercise power over family consumption or become empowered to make purchases on their own.

In this school only 6 per cent of the children were obese as defined by the BMI > 95th percentile for age and gender criteria. Another 8 per cent could be classified as 'at risk' meaning that under 15 per cent of this sample could be deemed overweight. Not only is it 14 per cent lower than the Canadian average but much lower than those rates typically reported in both the US and the UK. Yet other evidence also suggests why British Columbian children are slightly less at risk of obesity. In BC, children watch the least TV in Canada and they are more active physically – for both climate and cultural reasons. Moreover the population base is almost 40 per cent of Asian origin. Perhaps this is why BC males have recently achieved the distinction of being the longest lived in the world – and BC women third. In short this population must be considered to be one of the least 'at risk' of obesity in the developed world. Although children in British Columbia are exposed to television advertising on both US and Canadian networks, I found a very modest if significant correlation between overweight and the amount of TV use in this sample explaining about 1.8 per cent of the variance. I am reluctant to generalize about the effects of branding from this small sample from one school in Vancouver. Yet if one is looking for the ways families encourage healthy lifestyles of their children this Vancouver sample offers promise.

The analysis that follows excludes the children from grades 1 to 3. These children are typically aged 5–7. When I comment on the situation of these 183 younger children I will mostly make reference to the interview and focus group data. The main reason for excluding them was their stage in cognitive development. Children of this age have difficulty understanding the broader context of market persuasion – they can recognize logos and characters but they don't understand that advertising is intended to sell. Although they often express negative attitudes towards advertising, their discussion of food and advertising rarely gives evidence of informed choice. The literature has shown that they have brand knowledge, it is less clear that they possess nutritional knowledge and stable preferences, that they can recall advertising information and have much influence on their parents. Moreover, although questionnaires can be designed to accommodate their limited ability to write, when it comes to activity, media and diet diaries, I was not convinced that these quantitative measures were reliable. Other researchers use parental reports when studying 5 and 6 year olds, but without uniform measures it would be too problematic to combine younger children's responses with older ones. Another limitation of the regression analysis was that because data was gathered over five separate weeks, many of the students did not complete all of the data sets. What this means is that although there were up to 204 students who had completed enough to be reported in some of the findings (amount of TV viewing, preferred snacking, brand knowledge etc.), only 150 had completed all instruments necessary for the risk analysis.

Media consumption routines

Examining their media use on a typical weekday, these children prefer to watch TV and play video games after school and after dinner. 45 per cent of the total TV time is accounted for by after-school viewing – especially among younger children who prefer to watch children's programming and non-commercial stations. Breakfast time viewing is reported at least sometimes by 54 per cent of the sample, accounting for 15 per cent of the viewing time. The total time spent using media is about 95 minutes per day, with over 68 minutes accounted for by TV viewing – most of it commercial. Although both PBS and Canadian educational stations are available, the older children largely watch commercial stations, especially in prime time. Boys spend about 15 minutes more with media than girls. Much of this is accounted for by video game playing, which on average takes 20 minutes longer than girls, who preferred using the Internet. TV time tallied for morning, after-school and evening accounts for 60 per cent of the variance of time spent in all media use. Again gender differences in media-use preferences are evident. Boys generally also like to play video games more than girls. Children tend to watch more TV on weekends than during the week, bringing their average weekly TV use to about 11.5 hours. Given their low average weekday viewing time, estimates of exposure to advertising found in FTC data seem overstated for these young BC viewers simply because they watched less TV. Yet because they tend to watch TV mostly after school and on Saturday morning – when they are targeted by food advertisers – they are likely to be exposed to some ads targeting them.

TV after dinner is enjoyed by all genders and age groups – perhaps because it competes less with homework and active play – accounting for about 40 per cent of the viewing time. Obviously on weekends this pattern of viewing changes. TV watching is not only a regular but also a much enjoyed after-school activity. After doing their homework, watching TV is not only the most frequent but also their preferred activity. Whereas 10 per cent of the sample stated that they don't really like watching TV 26 per cent said that they liked watching TV 'a lot'. Those that enjoy it more, also report watching it more ($r = .23$). Yet there was little difference in the enjoyment of TV between boys and girls or age groups. Boys however report playing and enjoying video games more than girls do.

Children develop genre and programme tastes fairly young. They don't simply watch whatever is on, but choose particular programmes that they are interested in. 95 per cent were able to state three favourite programmes by name. In the interviews they would often talk about them at length. The younger boys preferred the child-oriented 'cartoon' programmes and educational shows. Less than 20 per cent of the favourite programmes in the 8–12 age group are child oriented. Mostly boys like cartoon programmes; when they are younger it is Yugi Oh and Spiderman and among the older it is South Park and King of the Hill. The Simpsons was the most popular general audience programme with all children. The vast majority of older children watch general audience (American Idol) or adult-oriented commercial TV shows (Survivors, Fear Factor). In a sports-crazed province however, it was surprising how few children mention sports among their favourite TV genres. For those who hoped that broadcasting sports would inspire greater involvement in sports participation this might be a warning. Older children (10–12 years) watch fewer children's programmes than younger children (8–9 year olds), and few of them ever watch the news.

Advertising literacy

Children not only exhibit preferences for TV programmes and genres but also for ads. Many children show evidence of an avid interest not only in products and brands but in the ads. The ones they like most present goods and experiences of interest to them. They feel motivated to watch ads that have things that are 'for them', that are 'interesting' or 'funny'. In the interviews, children can describe ads at great length – even quoting funny bits or singing the jingle. It is hardly surprising then that 76 per cent of children mentioned at least one favourite ad and 32 per cent could identify three. When asked which ads the children 'like the best' there was a wide range of responses although playthings and foods topped the list. However, clothing (GAP, la Senza) and beauty products (Revlon, Herbal Essence) receive some mention mainly among older girls for whom these products are beginning to have relevance. Yet food has the broadest appeal, comprising 42 per cent of all branded ads mentioned. Playthings and media product ads accounted for 21 per cent of all branded ads mentioned positively. Clearly children aged 8–12 are not merely exposed to food commercials but engage actively with ads because they are meaningful to them in some ways. They also discriminate among ads, paying attention to some and ignoring others. They even report disliking some ads. But having a 'dislike' for some ads does not mean they are media savvy.

Based on open-ended discussion of the commercial media system and advertising's place in it, we found little evidence of advertising literacy among the younger children (e.g. see Figure 6.8). This is not to say that they are dupes, but rather most of them simply don't understand the economics of commercial persuasion. By age eight most can distinguish ads from programming, but 45 per cent seem lacking in basic advertising literacy (defined by intent to sell, awareness of product persuasion). When it comes to knowledge of the economic arrangements of commercial media systems, only about 15 per cent of the students know how advertisers 'buy' audiences, can say what a product placement or cross-marketing arrangement is, or know that celebrities are paid to be in advertisements. Advertising literacy is associated with age and with those who watch TV more. The 10–12-year olds mention 'selling intent' more, but curiously scepticism about claims was found in only 5 per cent of all children and was not related to age. The implication is that scepticism of advertising may be related to family coaching rather than cognitive capacity.

Branded affect

The correlation between TV viewing and advertising literacy implies that children learn about advertising by watching it. Even if they are sceptical of the claims, they may be learning about the brands. When asked about

	Percentage of all children exhibiting literacy level
Scepticism	6%
Understand selling intent	44%
Ads as product stories	42%
Limited understanding of commercial TV	10%

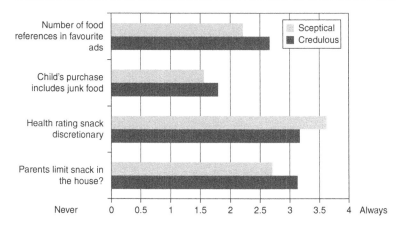

Figure 6.8   Media literacy levels of British Columbian primary school students and its relationship to food choice

favourite ads, many children mentioned branded foods by name. The more they watched the more likely they were to refer to food ads as favourites ($r = .23$). Given that many report that watching commercials is a pleasurable experience, it is hardly surprising that children form affective relationships with some brands they are exposed to. The transfer of affect from ad to brand implies a common mechanism that spans both adult and child responses. Moreover in Figure 6.9 we see that many children report feeling hungry when they see food and drink ads, that when they see ads they sometimes want to buy the product and that they sometimes ask their parents for branded products that they see on TV. 58 per cent of the students say that watching a food ad makes them feel hungry or thirsty while 12 per cent say that never happens. While 8.7 per cent report never having thought about buying something that they saw on TV, 64.5 per cent say that it happens sometimes or often.

Clearly children feel themselves to be impacted by advertising in many ways. Moreover, those who watch more TV report having these experiences

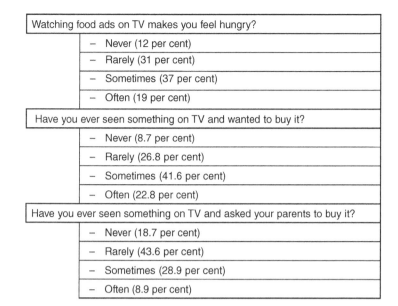

Figure 6.9 Children's perceptions of their relationship to advertising

more. These correlations suggest that the psychological dynamics through which advertising exposure gets translated into pester power is a dynamic system of related possibilities. Whereas 18.6 per cent of the children say they never ask parents for advertised stuff, about twice as many (37 per cent) report doing it often or all the time. Those children that make more requests watch TV more, are more likely to report wanting things they see on TV, are older and male. Male heavy viewers, who have higher rates of obesity, also seem to translate exposure to ads into requests more.

The extent of children's active engagement with branded advertising is evidenced in what children learn in front of the screen. Many can identify brand names with the slogans of the most often repeated campaigns. Of these, McDonald's is the most familiar: 91 per cent of the children could correctly match the name with the slogan. Tim Horton's also scored high on slogan recall (54 per cent) as did Nike (48 per cent), although Pringles Chips, Dairy Queen (fast food) and Volkswagen were accurately identified by less than 20 per cent of the students. Only 4 per cent of the children couldn't correctly identify any of the slogans of the most heavily advertised products. Obviously, repeat exposure is an important component of children's formation of brand knowledge and preferences. When a total score of food brand knowledge was calculated, it was found to be significantly correlated with total TV viewing ($r = .235$) and with older children ($r = .383$). It was unexpected, however, that among those who correctly identified every slogan, there were some who said they never watched TV. To some degree this may indicate the degree to which advertising has become embedded in the conversation of youth peer groups. Although advertising literacy was associated with higher levels of TV viewing there was no evidence that it reduced their interest in advertising. In fact the more media literate the more brand knowledge, as measured by their ability to recall slogans.

Discretionary consumption and branded affect

While watching commercial TV, children not only acquire brand knowledge but also consolidate their brand preferences as they form an affective relationship with the ads. Although their knowledge of goods is not exclusively derived from TV (peers, siblings, shopkeepers and catalogues all play a role), the ads do provide a constant flow of information that most of them pay attention to. One of the obvious consequences of the constant exposure to food advertising then is that children will learn about and make requests – but mostly for brands in food groups they like. Branding is about communicating on the level of affect, which means that cognitive defences and poofery filtering are incidental.

Yet children's tastes and interests vary not only in entertainment and play but in the food they like to eat. By age eight many have established favourite brands which they report eating regularly. When asked about their favourite type of cereals, snacks and beverages (core category products) the majority responded by mentioning brand names. But when it came to favourite types of bread, milk and ice cream (less advertised products) they responded with generic favourites (i.e. rye, 2 per cent, chocolate). Few children referred to their favourite bread (13 per cent) or milk (5 per cent) by brand name. This means that branding is not only about forming a new preference but also naming the affective relationship to a product. The consolidation of brand preferences in front of the TV is what enables children to respond to ads and communicate with parents about what they want.

Consumer empowerment in the family

The corollary of responsibilization of marketers is the empowerment of child consumers – the degree to which parents enable them to exercise control over some of the goods they consume by granting discretionary power. To understand the dynamics of family power, I asked children to indicate the kinds of foods and eating occasions in which they had most say. Their responses indicated that cereal, treats and foods eaten out of the home are the ones they get to choose most often and most freely. Children indicated that their parents shop for, and ultimately decide on, most of the daily diet. Both lunches and dinners were largely chosen by parents (albeit taking children's preferences and requests into account). Nor can we assume that the requests children make are only for HFSS products: fruits, carrots, rice and noodles were also common things children asked for. When they asked for healthy foods such as fruit and favourite vegetables, their parents were happy to buy them. When it came to 'desserts' as well as breakfast cereals, snack foods, and treats – precisely the types of foods that are disproportionately advertised on children's TV – many children had success in getting what they wanted as well. Parental complicity in lifestyle risks is dependent then on how they respond to children's expressions of taste.

This power dynamic can be witnessed in relation to one of the most targeted food sectors – breakfast cereal. The research explored this issue by asking children to list a typical breakfast, leaving it open ended as to whether they used product or brand name categories to describe what they ate. In this sample 48 per cent of the children reported that they normally ate cereal for breakfast. Yet three quarters of them, including those who ate cereal occasionally, could name a preferred brand of cereal. Children clearly develop branded preferences for cereals while watching ads on TV: 75 per cent of the heavy viewers named a favourite brand, whereas 57 per cent of the normal viewers did so. Moreover, the brand preferences they exhibited were precisely those cereals that we find most heavily advertised on TV – Froot Loops and Frosted Flakes followed by Cheerios and Rice Krispies. Although some children mention moderately healthy cereals (All Bran, Just Right, Special K) they lean towards the less healthy brands with an excess of sugar and limited protein content.

In this study, the formation of a branded preference for cereal implies a health risk. Whereas 85 per cent of breakfasts are either healthy or moderately so (eggs, sushi, pancakes), 46 per cent of the cereals fall into these two categories, 44.5 per cent into the minimally healthy and 9.2 per cent into the junk food energy-dense category. But it also must be remembered that children rarely buy cereals for themselves; rather they must convince their parents to buy the brands that they want. Perhaps this is why there is no consistent relationship between the amount of TV that children watch and the health rating of their breakfasts. In fact, there was a slight but not significant tendency for children who watch TV the most to eat healthy breakfast cereals – perhaps due to the mitigation of parents. Clearly the majority of children do not get to have most of their preferences fulfilled. But those that do are put at risk by their exposure to branded advertising of cereals.

Discretionary snacking

Many children also reported having a regular say in snacks purchased for the home. 26 per cent of this sample said that that they made most of the snack food purchase decisions in their household. An additional 23 per cent said that they negotiated with parents influencing some snack food choices. 51 per cent said it was the parents who decided and bought the majority of snack foods consumed in the home. While just under half the households granted children influence, a complex relationship was found between the amount of TV viewed and the discretionary power of kids. Families where negotiation over snacking choices takes place are also the heaviest viewers. Discretionary power is also related to the more frequent making of requests to parents: 48 per cent of children who can decide for themselves also resort to pester power whereas only 29 per cent in families where parents provision the snacks actually report asking for things that have been seen on TV (see Figure 6.10). It is these branded product requests that many brand advertisers set out to influence and which parents resent most because of the conflict it potentially causes.

With the importance of children's brand preferences in mind, the research set out to investigate children's consumption of snack foods by asking them generally about what they purchased with their own money. The argument that discretionary consumption provides a good test bed for estimating the influence of branded advertising on children's preferences is based on the idea that although there are many factors (taste, peers, nutritional knowledge, parental negotiation and advice) influencing children's food choices, snacks are the product domain in which branded advertising should have the greatest influence. The snacks a child buys with their own money, I would argue, is the best indication of their discretionary power.

When asked about what they buy with their own money, children discussed a range of things from toys, clothes and sports equipment to video games. But prominent among them was snack food including mostly drinks, chips, ice cream, candy and snacks. Indeed 67.3 per cent of the children use their pocket money to purchase snacks (33 per cent choose toys or games). When analysed for nutritional quality, these snacks tend to be of the less healthy variety. Although some children buy fruit or water, the vast majority is energy dense and salty – chips, chocolate and drinks being common. 12 per cent of all snacks received a health rating of high or moderate healthiness, 31 per cent in the low health category and 57 per cent were in the junk food category.

The data also indicated that those children who watch more TV after school are more likely to purchase food, especially junk food with their pocket money ($r = .303$); both the health rating and the frequency of junk food choices are related to the number of food references that are found in their favourite ads ($r = .14$). 75 per cent of the heavy viewers purchase food with their own pocket money whereas 66 per cent of the normal viewers do. Moreover 66.7 per cent of the heavy viewers purchase junk food whereas 55.4 per cent of the normal viewers do. Those children who watch TV almost every day also make more frequent discretionary snack purchases than moderate and occasional viewers.

Favourite ads contained	Percentage of children
No food references	37
One food references	33
Two food references	22
Three food references	8

Discretionary purchases by Canadian children	Percentage of snacks with health rating
High health	1%
Medium health	11%
Low health	31%
Junk food	57%

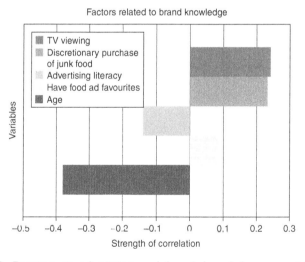

Figure 6.10 Exposure to advertising and brand knowledge as contributors to unhealthy discretionary food choices

Coda

The research described above set out to clarify the importance of the familial factors mitigating the risks of the TV diet. Firstly, the vast majority of children live busy lives and have their TV viewing restricted: only one in five are 'exposed' to advertising at a level putting them at risk. Yet children's tastes and interests vary, and even those who watch a lot of commercial TV do not always prefer sweets and snacks. Although many of these heavy viewers understand the advertisers' intent to sell, advertising literacy provides little defence against brand affect. Children who watch TV most like and remember ads and gain brand knowledge. But perhaps most importantly, even if children form preferences for unhealthy snacks and soft drinks in front of the TV, their requests to parents may go unheeded. Less than one in four of these Canadian children reported having a great say in their family's snack foods. These children's daily diet revealed parents' firm imprint on lunch and dinner. Their positive orientation to fruits, oatmeal and less advertised products like yoghurt implies that many children are more or less immune to ads. Once these mitigating circumstances are accounted for, it is quite understandable that exposure to branded advertising is only a modest risk factor in obesity. But at the same time, there was evidence that the indirect effects of advertising on children's knowledge and brand preferences are considerable. The impact of advertising on their unhealthy consumer choice is only evident however, when the decisions are made by the children themselves – in their discretionary consumption of snack foods. Not all kids are allowed to buy what they want with their pocket money and not all want snacks even if they can. But those who watch TV more make junk food purchases significantly more. The empowerment of child consumers therefore leaves some of them at greater risk to branded HFSS advertising.

Part III
Beyond Blame: Unpacking Media-Saturated Domesticity

In Part I of this book I documented the way epidemiological advocacy galvanized growing press coverage of the lifestyle risks associated with weight gain in child populations. Food and public health groups not only intensified their research efforts but circulated their results widely to raise awareness of the fast food diet and sedentary lifestyles that were putting children's health at risk. As population health studies showed, some individuals were more 'at risk' than others. Their diets were inferior; their daily lives more sedentary and dependent on TV. Although class, gender and ethnicity were clearly associated with the distribution of obesity, in the press, it was children that were identified as most at risk. The risk factors causing obesity have been widely publicized in the media. So US judges have concluded that adults have sufficient awareness of what it takes to stay healthy. But in the grip of media panic, the politicized battle over blame for children's obesity became a zero sum game. Health officials and parents argued that food advertising was a risk factor in children's obesity and therefore vulnerable child consumers needed to be protected from irresponsible TV advertising. The policy debate hinged on the empirical question of children's status as 'vulnerable' consumers.

In Part II I discussed the ways that public policymakers in Britain and America re-examined the research to assess whether it was necessary to protect children against food advertising targeting them. The review of research backed the health advocates' claim that there was an unhealthy TV diet that contributed to their weight status. The more children watch TV, the more they 'prefer', ask for and choose branded products heavily advertised there. The food industry naturally opposed any regulation of advertising on the grounds that the same evidence showed that brand advertising has only marginal impact on children's health and ignored the other lifestyle risk factors involved in weight gain. Given the complexity of the interactions between exposure to ads, sedentary lifestyles and snacking associated with heavy TV viewing, industry spokespersons suggested that if some children were overweight, it was parents who ultimately were to blame for buying the foods and failing to turn off the TV set. They were stating the obvious. Children are not 'autonomous' consumers. Given that parents buy the foods, define the viewing rules and teach children about healthy lifestyles, of course they are implicated in what goes on in the media-saturated household. Until they are teens, children's risky choices are largely made by or in conjunction with parents.

In this sense both sides had a case. The literature provided strong evidence of advertising's weak impact on children's food consumption. Yet as Young argued, the influence of advertising is 'operative against a backdrop of an already established set of food preferences and choices that is primarily determined by influences from the cultures of the family and peers' (Young 2003b). As my research has shown too, the very modest relationship between TV viewing and obesity is understandable given the many protective factors which shape young Canadians' daily eating, activity levels and media-use patterns. Although children enjoy, remember and talk about ads with friends, the impact of this exposure on brand preferences is modest, changes with age and depends on a variety of familial lifestyle issues which mitigate the impact of advertising on their diet. The majority of children, guided by their parents, develop healthy food preferences and reasonable controls on their snacking; if they are influenced by advertising, parents do refuse their persistent requests for unhealthy foods. By limiting their children's viewing, by encouraging their children to be sceptical of advertising and by educating them about nutrition parents were counteracting advertising. So it seems fair to say that by focusing on the 10–14 per cent of children that are put at risk of obesity in front of the screen, the press coverage lost sight of the 86 per cent that weren't because their parents were successfully mitigating their obesogenic lifestyle choices. Given that most kids are not obese, we must conclude that the vast majority of parents deserve considerable credit for mitigating the risks and preparing their children for life in the consumer culture. But some don't. And here lies the problem, for given the power to choose for themselves, children's discretionary snack purchases turn out to be more branded and less healthy.

Managing media-saturated domesticity

As Brian Young (2003b) has stated, 'There is no disagreement amongst any of the authorities I have read that obesity is a multifactorial issue'. I agree. Researchers' attempts to statistically isolate the degree to which TV advertising independently contributes to children's weight gain is a question framed by the blame game, rather than the risk analysis. Any estimate attributing weight gain in children only to advertising will be confounded by other risk factors associated with heavy TV viewing, including snacking while viewing and sedentary lifestyles. Part III of the book sets out to situate the mitigation of child obesity within the analysis of media-saturated domesticity. The negotiations and power dynamics of the family system defines the context of both protection and socialization of young consumers. Families are systems of gradual empowerment, and until they are teens, children's lifestyle choices tend to be decided by or in conjunction with parents. Preparing children for making their own decisions about their lifestyles – including the risks that they encountered in daily consumption – matters in the risk society. In short, consumer socialization is the crux of the matter. By giving children freedom to choose, the parent was also exposing them to lifestyle risks.

In Chapter 7 therefore I overview what is known about the complex ways that heavy TV viewing, lack of exercise and a diet high in energy-dense foods jointly put children at risk. Three general research approaches have been deployed in the study of the system of relationships between media and obesity. The most common are epidemiological studies that use large national samples to study the risk factors associated with obese populations. The benefit of this approach is that in using large samples they provide fairly reliable estimates of the risks. However, this approach is limited because risk estimates are not directional and large surveys often use very general self-report variables to measure items such as overall TV viewing. Other researchers offer smaller-scale studies, which provide in-depth information that enables more complex exploration of attitudes and perceptions (self-esteem, body image, brand affect) and more valid measurements of complex risk factors (such as 24 hour diet recall, actual TV diaries, activity levels and exertion). The limitations of these studies hinge on the potential population biases that exist in small samples and the inability to explore complex interaction effects due to the small numbers of subjects. The third approach is experimental, clinical or prospective field studies that compare cohorts or individuals over time. These studies are costly and often suffer from drop-out in the sample. The cumulative evidence however suggests that media are the key to obesogenic lifestyles because their use is associated with both sides of the energy balance equation – eating patterns and sedentary lifestyles.

The fast food frame in the media not only overstated the health risks associated with the marketing of foods but distracted the policymakers from the fact that these were socially distributed. Yet the moral panic did at least alert many parents to the multiple lifestyle risk factors their children face daily. Media literacy, nutritional knowledge and active leisure were becoming more important aspects of consumer socialization in contemporary families, in large part in response to the media-provoked angst arising from the globesity panic.

Noting the disparity between expert and public risk perceptions, Chapter 8 explores Canadian parents' strategies for managing the risks associated with children's obesogenic lifestyles. Reporting on qualitative research I note that many parents were deeply concerned about and mindful that the excessive snacking, a lack of exercise, too much media use and freedom to buy what they want needed to be monitored and discussed. A survey of 200 Canadian parents explored the diverse ways they attempt to encourage children to consume TV moderately, to cultivate healthy food preferences and help children learn to spend their own money wisely. Through regulating media, talking about nutrition, instilling advertising scepticism, encouraging active leisure and providing consumer education, these parents seem keen to raise healthy children. But families are widely divergent in their values and their styles of parenting. And it is in this respect that parental perceptions of environmental risks matter most because parents who protect and negotiate most mitigate the risks and foster healthier consumer decision making in children. My research is intended therefore to contribute to the notion of the 'health-promoting' family as an antidote to the epidemiological analysis of the 'obesogenic' one as suggested by Christensen (2004).

Obesogenic lifestyles and media-saturated domesticity

Consumer socialization in the modern family develops as an unfolding familial 'negotiation' in which children are consulted, coached and coerced to be competent consumers in a sequence of age-graduated experiences of the material world. In Chapter 9, I review the literature on consumer socialization noting that risk management starts with eating but quickly spreads to leisure time. Play and media become crucial zones of consumer socialization where parents teach children (or fail to) to make healthy lifestyle choices. Goods – from clothes and toys to music lessons and candy – are given to children as rewards, as signs of parental love, as attempts to teach moral values, to allow choice and give scope to personality and self-expression, to improve their health and well-being and often to simply give them freedom to choose. But they are also vehicles of risk communication. As children get older they are encouraged to learn to make responsible choices for themselves. They are given allowances and taken to stores to learn the skills and attitudes necessary in a consumer culture. These outings become occasions for risk communication too. In this respect, I agree with Valkenburg and Cantor (2002) that our concern with the development of children's cognitive defences has to some degree deflected researchers from the important ways that parents continue to educate and prepare children to be self-regulating and self-expressive consumers. The chapter continues by reporting on the findings from the Vancouver study that suggest that parental efforts to protect and educate children about risks associated with snacking and media consumption does contribute to children's ability to maintain a balanced lifestyle by making more risk-informed consumer choices.

It is often said that those who fail to learn from history are destined to repeat it. As I have argued, the obesity panic exposed the limits of the neo-liberal ideology to appropriately reconcile the anomalous situation of child consumers in a mediated marketplace. The assumption of young children's competence has revealed itself to be the empirically invalidating chink in the armour of commercial free speech advocacy. I agree with Buckingham that Ofcom's definition of media literacy is deeply flawed because it fails to teach children about the lifestyle risks associated with media consumption. Having reviewed the literature on consumer socialization, I think it is time to challenge this narrow view of media literacy invoked by the policy debate about advertising. My own objections are threefold: first neoliberalism reduces media literacy to the cognitive ability to distinguish ads from programming and to understand the ads 'intent to persuade'; second, it assumes the economistic conception of the child as an autonomous consumer failing to recognize the family and state as agents of socialization; and third, it has a narrow conception of the requisite competences necessary for market transactions required which include the 'risk-cost-benefits' calculus in the risk society. The chapter closes therefore with the discussion of primary school interventions which use a media education to challenge students to become aware of and reduce their own lifestyle risks. We can empower children as consumers by teaching them about lifestyle risks but the lessons are urgent, for by the time they are teens, risk taking has become a part of their culture.

7
Obesogenic Lifestyles in the Media-Saturated Household

I have argued that the medicalization of consumer choice is implicit in the obesity debates. As a media analyst, it is impossible to ignore the role that medical rather than communications researchers played in study of TV as a lifestyle risk. Nutrition and kinesiology are the two health sciences that have contributed most to the medical establishments' diagnosis of the underlying lifestyle risk factors contributing to weight gain – vying with each other to set the 'risk agenda' by explaining to what degree fast food or sluggish kids were most responsible for weight gain. However, in heavy TV viewing both nutritionists and kinesiologists found a risk factor which they agreed on. Dietz and Gortmaker's (1985) epidemiological research on over 6000 12–17-year olds was one of the first to find that the likelihood of 'overweight' in adolescent populations increased by 2 per cent for each hour of television viewed. This hallmark study concluded that television viewing is a 'major health concern at which counselling should be directed' because it promoted both increased food consumption and reduced activity. The relationship between amount of TV viewed and obesity persisted when controlled for prior obesity, region, season, population density, race, socioeconomic class and a variety of other family variables implying that it was a risk factor independent of all other population variables.

A subsequent study conducted during the early 1990s estimated that up to 60 per cent of the overweight in children aged 10–15 may be due to excessive television viewing. Analysing the data from a national prospective survey between 1988 and 1994, Gortmaker et al. (1996) found that the 26 per cent of children who watched four or more hours of television a day had significantly more body fat than those who watched less television. The odds of being overweight were 4.6 times greater for youth watching more than 5 hours of television per day compared with those watching 0 to 2 hours. These risks persisted even controlling for mothers' overweight, SES and ethnicity. These authors recommended a reduction in viewing time as the means of preventing chronic health problems in the future.

As Robinson and Killen (1995) reported, the mechanisms by which TV viewing influences weight gain can vary, however, depending on the ethnicity and gender of the teen. In their study of 1912 ninth graders, African Americans and Hispanics had the highest BMI and whites the lowest. Generally speaking, boys who watched more TV were more physically active and ate more high-fat foods than girls – except among African Americans. African Americans experienced multiple risk factors in their lifestyles: they watched significantly more TV, were less physically active and ate more fatty foods than the other ethnic sub-samples. Whites reported the least TV viewing and the lowest rates of obesity. Although they found little evidence that activity was displaced by watching TV, heavy TV viewing was significantly associated with dietary fat intake among both boys and girls. Overall, their study suggested that TV viewing is most associated with increased dietary fat intake rather than displacement effects in teen populations. However, as the authors note, 'cultural factors' may influence the susceptibilities of children and adolescents to the effects of television viewing.

These early studies of the health risk factors produced one consistent finding: controlling for gender, SES and ethnicity; the more time children spent watching television, the greater their BMI. Three competing explanations for the relationship between media dependant lifestyle and obesity have been offered. Those interested in leisure activity, children's sport participation and fitness became concerned about the displacement of time and effort spent in active leisure by TV viewing and other media. Meanwhile nutritionists and food researchers documented how the exposure to fast food marketing while watching TV promotes energy-dense food preferences and requests for unhealthy snacks and drinks. And family lifestyle researchers noted that sedentary lifestyles and food were linked through the unhealthy media consumption practices themselves that involved eating and snacking patterns.

TV and fast food culture

In the US, where the relationship between media use and obesity has been most studied, children's food consumption has been associated with heavy media use in ways that cannot be accounted for by direct exposure to advertising and media content. A number of behavioural eating trends, including larger portions, more frequent eating at restaurants, ready-made dinners, skipping breakfasts and energy-dense snacking have been found in the obesogenic family. Of these, eating dinner while viewing television may be the most important. Gillman et al. have shown that TV dining is related to the types of food consumed in the household and the caloric intake of children. In a cross-sectional study of 16,202 children aged 9–14, Gillman et al. (2000) found that almost 20 per cent of children never ate dinner with their families, whereas 43 per cent did so every day. Households where family meals were frequent were more likely to eat five servings of fruits and vegetables, eat less fried foods at restaurants and also drink less soft drinks. Children in those households ate .8 more servings of fruit and vegetables than those where family meals were infrequent. Their explanations of the healthful benefits from family eating concern the possibility that ready-made dinners, which are lower in nutrients, are more common in families that don't eat together as often. Also it is possible that family discussion of nutrition takes place around the dinner table. In this respect, a major limitation of the study was that it was conducted on health professionals who were mostly white and conscious of the importance of nutrition.

Coon et al. (2001) examined the meals of 92 children in Washington using dietary recalls for three days to construct nutrient intake profiles for children aged 7–12. Their research compared families consuming two or more TV meals (41 per cent of households) with those who keep the TV off, finding that families who watch TV during meals consume 6 per cent more energy from meats, 5 per cent more from pizza and snacks and soft drinks and 5 per cent less from fruit, vegetables and juices. Caffeine consumption was also higher in these households. They suggest that there are 'fundamentally different dietary patterns for children whose families have incorporated television as a habitual part of the food cultures'. Controlling for ethnicity and SES, they show that TV dining is negatively associated with mothers' education, and is more frequent in one-parent families and those that frequently eat 'ready meal suppers'. They also found a relationship between television and foods not ordinarily advertised, namely fruit, vegetables and red meats. These effects were independent of ethnicity and SES of family. The authors argue that 'it is possible that selective promotion of certain types of foods may crowd ignored foods out of a typical diet over the long run', especially where parents are concerned that their children eat something they like.

Karen Cullen et al. (2002a, 2002b, 2003) reported results from a survey of 287 school children aged 8—12, finding that 42 per cent of dinners eaten at home were consumed while watching television. TV dining was reported in 50 per cent of the overweight children, but only 35 per cent of the normal weight households. It occurred in 62 per cent of African American and 42 per cent of Hispanic households compared with 21 per cent of Asian households. Cullen suggests that children who eat while watching might be less aware of what and how much they are eating, whereas families who eat together tend to discuss and educate their children about nutrition and health at the dinner table.

Researchers have also suggested that TV exposes children to more than fast food advertising, however. It is a window into a normative social world in which food and body image are crucial elements in young peoples' identity (Wilson and Blackhurst 1999). Looking at the psychosocial explanations of the relationship between problem eating and TV, Burggraf et al. (2001)

found that TV was also a factor in adolescent girls' development of eating disorders. Their survey of 374 girls aged 10–14 found that problem eating and dieting were associated with BMI, watching situation comedy, total time spent watching TV and having siblings who diet. Bar-On (2000) similarly explores the psychological relationships between girls' body image and frequent TV watching arguing that eating disorders arise in a context of the interaction between media, body image, self-esteem and dieting. Field et al. (2001) report that the combined influences of media and peers on weight concerns increase during adolescence.

Based on an ethnically diverse sample of 124 third- and fifth-grade students Matheson et al. (2004) set out to assess the kinds of foods and eating occasions that linked TV watching and problem eating. Higher BMI was associated with consuming more energy while watching TV. The researchers note however that foods which are more advertised, such as soft drinks, cereal, fast food and sweet snacks, are not necessarily they ones eaten while watching TV. Using 24-hour food recall diaries, they found habits relating TV and eating were different on weekdays and weekends. 74 per cent of third graders and 76 per cent of fifth graders reported eating while watching on weekdays and 63 per cent (58 per cent of fifth graders) on weekends. On weekdays 17–18 per cent of total energy was consumed while watching, and on weekends it rose to 26 per cent. Other leisure activities, from video games to reading and doing homework only accounted for 3 per cent of energy intake. 60 per cent of the children eat TV snacks, 45 per cent have dinner while watching and 23 per cent at breakfasts in front of the TV. The energy density of meals eaten while watching do not differ from those served with the TV off. This study suggests that it is the type of food eaten while watching television, not the serving size or frequency, which is associated with weight status.

Noting that most studies focus on the direct effect of eating promotional foods while watching, Francis and Birch (2006) suggest that eating while viewing TV can also distract children and disrupt their ability to regulate the amount of food consumption. They tested this idea out in a small-scale quasi-experimental study of 24 children aged 3–5. Some of the children were exposed to TV while eating and the others formed a control group, which did not watch television. The experiment took place over six weeks and the children were fed both a lunch (pizza, carrots milk and apple sauce) and a snack (crackers and banana chips) in their normal day-care surroundings. The calories consumed were measured carefully in both TV watching and non-TV watching conditions and parents provided background information about home viewing and snacking patterns. Results indicated that children were actively engaged in TV viewing. They oriented to the screen 96 per cent of the time and in doing so, lowered the amount consumed in both the snacking and lunch conditions relative to the no-TV condition. Children ate more lunch and snack foods when the TV was off. Yet when the amount consumed by children who regularly snack in front of the TV at home was compared with those who don't, the result reversed. Children who snacked at home consumed more lunch and snack food while watching TV at day care. This suggests that children must learn to combine food consumption with viewing.

A Canadian survey of diet (Garriguet 2004) suggests that the risks associated with fast food promotion may have been overstated. This national survey found that 70 per cent of children aged 4–8 regularly eat the recommended servings of fruit and vegetables. By comparison, only half of adults do. Moreover although concern about sugary cereals is often cited, on average, children consume about 18 per cent of daily calories at breakfast. Lunch and dinner account for over 55 per cent of children's caloric intake and, generally speaking, lie within Canada's nutritional guidelines. It is only when it comes to snacks, that is food and drink consumed between meals, which account for just over 25 per cent of children's caloric content, that there seems to be a problem. For Canadian children snacks account for more calories than breakfast and about the same as lunch. Snacks however are not necessarily high in sugar, fat and calories. Vegetables and fruit make up 13 per cent of calories from snacks and diet soft drinks are commonly consumed. The proportion of calories derived from snacks peaks among 14–18-year-olds at 30 per cent for males and 28 per cent for females, and then falls with advancing age to around 16 per cent among seniors aged 71 or older (Taylor et al. 2005).

Eating out is thought to be associated with overweight. Yet only one in four Canadians reported that they consumed something at a fast food outlet on the previous day. Among 14–18-year-olds, the figure is one-third; at 39 per cent, the percentage is highest among men aged 19–30. Moreover children are relatively less likely than adults to consume food at fast food outlets and the highest-income households are more likely to eat more fast food. It clearly is not young children who are most at risk of fast food marketing. Nor should all out-of-home eating be classified as 'obesogenic'. Only 40 per cent of patrons of fast food establishments choose a pizza, sandwich, hamburger or hot dog. And only 25 per cent had a regular (as opposed to diet) soft drink. Fast food consumption peaked in the 19–30-year old category at 39 per cent of males and 34 per cent of females. Young adults are therefore more at risk from fast food marketing than children.

To assess children's food-related behaviours and their relationships with eating while watching television, Marquis et al. (2005) collected data from 534 10-year-old French-Canadian children. A self-administered questionnaire was used. Almost 18 per cent of girls and over 25 per cent of boys reported eating in front of the TV every day. Although, overall, the boys' eating pattern was less healthy than the girls', all of the children's food choices deteriorated with increased frequency of eating in front of the TV. Compared with girls, boys gave more importance to coloured and attractive foods, and selected foods similar to those eaten by others. Over 50 per cent of children received negative weight-related comments from family members. For boys, significant correlations were found between the frequency of eating in front of the TV, the importance given to a food's appearance and their requests to parents for advertised foods. These results suggest that gender should be considered in attempts to understand children's food motivations and behaviours.

Sluggish kids in the media-saturated family

Weight gain can indicate the consumption of too much of the wrong foods. It can also indicate too little exercise. TV seemed to influence both. This simple biological fact implies that TV's impact on diet alone is not sufficient for explaining weight gain in children. Media's role in children's sedentary lives is another potential risk factor contributing to the rising incidence of overweight children because they are inactive while watching and because the time they spend watching is at the expense of active outdoor play. TV has long been implicated in the formation of sedentary lifestyles. Children's waning participation in informal sports and active leisure, which troubled the Kennedy administration, grew into a cultural truism during the 1980s. Sedentary lifestyles are thought to form as the low-energy enjoyment of TV (or video games) dominates children's leisure time 'displacing' regular participation in vigorous outdoor activities, games and sports. Yet the displacement hypothesis assumes children are naturally active. It is equally plausible that TV (and video gaming) competes with other sedentary activities like chess, homework, window shopping or listening to music. Moreover heavy exposure to sports or health promotion (i.e. *The Biggest Loser*; PSAs for healthy living) could conceivably lead to active lifestyles – for example through fitness awareness or identification with celebrity sports stars. It is also plausible that overweight children develop a preference for sedentary leisure activities for psychological reasons having to do with their weight status (feeling lethargic or having low self-esteem). In brief, the relationship between TV and sedentary living is as complex as its relationship to diet.

Many environmental factors have made families more sedentary as urbanization, automation and cars defined domestic consumption around ease, speed and convenience. Active leisure provided only five per cent of daily energy expenditure and driving a car, office work and watching TV made the largest contribution to energy expenditure (Dong et al. 2004). In this redefined family environment, children's lives were changing too: kinesiologists found the total energy burnt by physical activity was decreasing with children's growing preference for indoor activities and their declining engagement in regular intense exercise (Marshall et al. 2004). Children no longer ride bikes or walk to school, their street play is disappearing and the drift towards less physical activity is compounded by the fact that physical education, once an important part of every child's school day, has been cut back at many schools. Less than half of US schoolchildren have access to daily physical education classes (Squires 1998).Without playgrounds and gyms, and with the cutting of fitness programmes at school, the state was a risk factor in the obesogenic environment. Population studies found that lack of physical activity was a socially distributed health risk too. The poor and ethnically defined segments of the population were especially impacted by restricted access to sports and physical education facilities.

In the US, children aged 8–18 spend more time (44.5 hours per week) in front of computer, television and game screens than at any other activity in their lives except sleeping (Kaiser Family Foundation 2010). An early study of the bodily effects of watching TV found that during television viewing metabolic rates were significantly lower than during resting periods for a group of obese and normal weight children, aged 8–12 (Klesges et al. 1993). Early studies found that children who watched most TV played outdoors less, got driven to school more and participated in organized sports teams less (Tucker 1986; Dietz 1991; Hernandez et al. 1999; Bar-On 2000). The correlations between heavy media use and inactivity suggested that the time spent using media not only reduced daily energy expenditure but also displaced active leisure and sports (Taras et al. 1989). Subrahmanyam et al. (2000) studied the impact of home computer use on children's activities and development, reporting that children who use a lot of electronic media and have them in their bedrooms have lower activity levels. Cummings and Vanderwater (2007) showed that this had to do with complex trade-offs between adolescents' preferred leisure-time pursuits.

Berkey et al. (2000) studied approximately 10,800 boys and girls who are children between the ages of 9 and 14 using a longitudinal design that could better account for increases in BMI attributed to various factors including media use, activity levels and food consumption practices. The results of a regression analysis indicated that BMI gain in girls was predicted by higher caloric intake and lower activity levels, but most significantly by screen time. For boys BMI gain was predicted by screen time and marginally by physical activity. Overall just under 5 per cent of the variance of BMI change was accounted for by screen time (total use of media including video games but not Internet). Although the sample is large the population base is skewed: 97 per cent of the families were health professionals who are white and educated about many health issues.

Most studies have suggested that the displacement of active play, a bedroom culture and the spread of digital media into the home are all implicated in the rise of child obesity. Yet the predicted relationship was modest and the factors in the home shaping media consumption little understood (Dennison et al. 2002). Their study of preschoolers (aged 1–4) for example, found that a child's risk of being overweight increased by 6 per cent for every hour of television watched per day. If that child had a TV in his or her bedroom, the odds of being overweight jumped an additional 31 per cent for every hour watched. Preschool children with TVs in their bedroom watched an additional 4.8 hours of TV or videos every week. These authors conclude that 'Television viewing and television in bedroom associated with overweight risk among low-income preschool children' (Dennison et al. 2002).

Tremblay and Willms found that TV watching and video game use play a role in the formation of sedentary lifestyles and obesity in Canadian children too (Tremblay and Willms, 2003). Their survey found that heavy media use of both types is associated with reduced participation in both organized and unorganized sport and are also associated with higher BMIs. Adolescents who watch more than three hours of television a day are 50 per cent more likely to be obese than those who watch fewer than two hours. Sedentary lifestyles seem to become regularized as leisure-time preferences form around media at the expense of participation in vigorous outdoor activities, active games and sports. These researchers conclude that 'more than 60 per cent of overweight incidents can be linked to excess TV viewing' through the dual mechanisms of metabolically reduced activity and the displacement of active leisure.

A US survey of teen respondents revealed that it is vigorous physical activity (rather than light) that is reported less among heavy TV viewers. Although, for girls, highly active leisure generally declines with puberty, this trend is more prevalent among the heaviest TV viewers (Eisenmann et al. 2002). Although low-exertion activities like playing video games, watching TV and listening to music are regarded as sedentary, it is difficult to explain why media reduces liking and time spent engaged in active outdoor leisure and sports. One suggestion is that displacement depends on a screen culture linked to the spread of digital media into the bedroom. Vandewater et al. (2004) assessed the role of traditional media as well as computers separately. They found that trade-offs between media consumption and active living are confounded by the exchanging of TV time for computer gaming among boys. A stronger relationship was found between playing electronic video games and childhood obesity in school-aged Swiss children by researchers from The Children's Hospital of Philadelphia and the University Hospital Zurich (Stettler et al. 2004). The decrease in physical activity associated with increasing time spent using computers persists into adult life, argued Gordon-Larson et al. (2004).

Marshall et al. (2004) performed a meta-analysis of 52 studies investigating the sedentary lifestyles of children. They found that correlations between media use and body fatness (measured either by BMI or skin-fold thickness) are in the order of .084, explaining less than 3 per cent of the variance. For video games the correlation is .128. The researchers comment that this relationship is rather modest compared to the claims often made, and warn that such findings may have little clinical relevance. They also evaluated the trade-off between TV, video games and active leisure and report slightly larger negative correlations for physical activity levels of .13 for TV and .14 for video games. Their study shows that these negative correlations are strongest for vigorous exercise, for girls and for older children (–.152). They suggest therefore that it is possible that TV viewing only displaces vigorous activity. In this respect it must be recognized that this meta-analysis combines research from studies undertaken in very different environments and cultures. The relationships between media use and obesity in Japan and Mexico may be different than in the US due to variation in other lifestyle factors like diet, age, gender and resources available. Without measuring what children ate, whether they got driven to school, participated regularly in sports or rode their bikes, it was difficult to state exactly what the mechanisms were. Although many believed that screen dependence enhanced sedentary lifestyles through trade-offs with activity, it was important to acknowledge the many other factors that mitigate the strength of the relationship between children's activity levels and media use. Diet and family guidance as well as community resources (parks, schools, malls) could all influence the impact of TV on energy balance.

The importance of these other demographic and lifestyle factors was demonstrated in a longitudinal study of the transition in Australian girls' lifestyles between 12 and 15. Hardy et al. (2007) found that sedentary behaviour increased from 45 per cent to 63 per cent of their discretionary leisure time. Screen media consumption, which was their favourite pastime, accounted for 33 per cent of their sedentary time, while homework and reading accounted for 25 per cent. On weekends, hobbies and computer use increased their sedentary leisure time by 3.3 hours. Viewed through the lens of sedentary activities, the authors note that for girls the transition between early and mid-adolescence marks a major lifestyle change that requires more research. Attention to the sharp decline in active leisure among teen girls is important because a lack of exercise can impact children adversely. Early childhood is a time of tremendous growth for children and the amount of physical activity positively affects the strength and amount of bone mass developed. A study of preschoolers found that girls who watched more television measured lower in the amount of hipbone density implying health consequences that can compound with adult obesity (Janz et al. 2001).

Leatherdale and Wong (2009) point out the complexity of studying BMI in relationship to active and sedentary behaviour, which are not necessarily mutually exclusive. Defining sedentary as spending more than 2 hours in low energic activities (like watching TV or playing video games) and highly active as performing more than 90 minutes of moderate intensity activity per day, they argue 'youth could be considered both highly active and highly sedentary' depending on how they allocated their time. Their study of 25,060 Canadian students found a complex relationship between media viewing and activity levels. 16.3 per cent were low, 68.7 per cent moderately and 15 per cent highly active, whereas 10.3 per cent were low sedentary with 32.4 per cent being highly sedentary based on a mean media use score of 2.7 hours. Although low sedentary boys and girls tended to be equally active, five per cent more girls were both sedentary and inactive.

In this sample, 13.3 per cent were overweight, but low active/high sedentary boys were 1.5 times more likely to be overweight. Similarly, low active/high sedentary girls were 2.24 times more likely to be overweight than high active/low sedentary girls and 1.91 times more at risk than high active/high sedentary girls. In the case of girls, the role that media play in developing sedentary lifestyles seems especially important: high active/high sedentary are more likely to be overweight than highly active/low sedentary girls. For girls, thinking of oneself as overweight was also associated with low active/high sedentary lifestyles. Among boys and girls, there were mitigating factors, which reduced the risks: parents that encouraged active living and team sports were negatively associated with being a low activity/high sedentary teen.

The disruptive screen: TV, diet and sedentary lifestyles

All media, but especially TV, are implicated in the routines of domestic consumption. From the 1980s the health implications of media use by children has been given intense scrutiny. And as William Dietz (1986) suggested early in the study of TV as a risk factor, 'although the behavioral correlates that link these risk factors to childhood obesity remain unclear, inactivity and increased dietary intake of fat appear at this time to be the most logical foci for preventive interventions. Television viewing, which promotes both increased food consumption and reduced activity, represents a major concern at which counselling should be directed'. Using epidemiological methods, a few researchers have tried to understand the complex dynamics linking media use, diet and activity levels of children.

Crespo et al. (2001) used the nationally representative Third National Health and Nutrition Examination Survey for 1988 and 1994 coupled with an in-person medical examination to examine the relationship between television watching, energy intake, physical activity and obesity status in US boys and girls, aged 8–16. The sample of 4069 children included Mexican and non-Hispanic African Americans to ensure reliable estimates for these groups. They found that the prevalence of obesity is lowest among children watching 1 or fewer hours of television a day and highest among those watching 4 or more hours of television a day. Girls engaged in less physical activity and consumed fewer joules per day than boys. A higher percentage of white boys reported participating in physical activity 5 or more times per week than any other race/ethnic and sex group. Television watching was positively associated with obesity among girls, even after controlling for age, race/ethnicity, family income, weekly physical activity and energy intake.

Veugelers and Fitzgerald (2005) studied 4298 fifth grade students in Nova Scotia, reporting that approximately 10 per cent of the 10–12-year old population were obese. Like other researchers, they found that TV watching of more than 1 hour per day was strongly related to overweight. Their regression analysis shows that TV is a risk factor best explained by the displacement of physical activity by sedentary leisure in these Canadian children. Excessive time spent sitting in front of screens was a major problem in families that didn't compensate for sedentary behaviour by encouraging children to play actively. But they also note that TV is a risk factor which interacts with diet too. Children who ate supper in front of TV five times a week were at greater risk (OR = 1.44) whereas those that ate supper with the family three or more times a week were at reduced risk (OR = .68). The researchers note although 'eating behaviours in the home associated with TV dinners ... are risk factors, but the frequency of eating fast food was not'.

These authors also point out that environmental and family factors were both related to obesity: 'in keeping with other studies, we observed a gradient whereby children of socio-economically disadvantaged families were more likely to be overweight or obese' (2005: 612). Moreover divorce put children slightly more at risk whereas a parent's university education put them less at risk. Schools were implicated in these 'environmental' risks too: those that had physical education classes two or more times a week experienced OR = .61 reduced risk whereas those that bought lunch at school were at greater risk (OR = 1.39). Moreover soft drinks and vending machines in schools were not important risk factors and surprisingly eating at a fast food restaurant more than three times a week actually lowered the risk of obesity (OR = .86).

With the complexity of health risks associated with TV in mind, Buijzen et al. (2008) used a questionnaire and food consumption diary to test the three competing explanations of the link between heavy TV viewing to obesity – advertising effects, displacement of active leisure and unhealthy media-related eating habits. In this study 234 parents of children aged 4–12 years were surveyed and interviewed to provide indicators of

(1) the amount of time spent watching TV (mean = 12 hours/week) adjusted for estimated advertising exposure to food ads (but not actually their exposure to advertising),
(2) the total daily food intake (mean =15.25 products) as well as the amount of energy-dense food products (mean = 2.56) heavily advertised on TV (but not what and how often food was consumed while watching) and
(3) a measure of active outdoor play time (mean = 6.52 hours) per week (but not intensity and nature of activities) as well as weight status, parents' weight status and family income.

Their results indicated that food advertising exposure on its own was not related to total food intake but did explain 6 per cent of the variance in the consumption of those energy-dense products advertised on television. This relationship between advertising and energy-dense food consumption held only for those older subjects, which they suggest can be explained by the fact that older children have more influence on family consumption choices. When it comes to displacement the study found that 5 per cent of the variance in outdoor playtime can be accounted for by the amount of television viewing. Those who watched more TV played outside less, although, as they note, this could be explained by the development of a preference for sedentary leisure generally, as well as direct substitution of media for play. With regard to eating while viewing they found that total food intake actually decreased as a function of increased television viewing although the amount of energy-dense food consumed remained equal. Unfortunately this study did not really operationalize eating while viewing in a way that could meaningfully estimate the amount and types of food eaten in front of the TV.

Despite these shortcomings of design and measurement, the researchers were able to use regression analysis to estimate the implications of these variables for children's weight status controlling for child's age, parental weight and family income. Although parental weight status, family income and outdoor playing time significantly correlated with weight status, these relations were diminished when television viewing time was entered into the equation. They report that television is the most important predictor of weight status (5 per cent of variance explained) and that for younger children (< 8) that 11 per cent of the variance of weight status is explained by television viewing. 'A possible explanation for these differential findings is that television viewing is more disruptive of younger children's activities, because they are physically more active overall.' Since older children are more sedentary the impact of television on their weight is more likely to happen through dietary preference than displacement of activity, they suggest.

Laurson et al. (2008) report a longitudinal study of 268 10-year old children, comparing BMI gain over a 18-month period testing whether physical activity, screen time and dietary habits including soft drink consumption account for BMI gain. This study included differences in these behaviour variables tracked over time as well as the BMI variable. Their result indicates the relative stability of BMI over the period but shows that weight gain is slightly greater in overweight children. Tracking of behavioural variables however revealed moderate levels of stability, perhaps due to changes or otherwise due to the unreliability of self-report measures. Their regression models found that only baseline BMI predicted weight gain; differences in screen time, activity levels or dietary practices were not associated with significant increases in BMI for either boys or girls analysed separately. Although insignificant, for girls a decrease in physical activity was most closely associated with increased BMI ($r = .11$) followed by eating with the family ($r = .08$).

Commenting on the failure to confirm associations between behavioural factors and weight gain, the authors point out the limitations of BMI in longitudinal studies of children in this age group whose body morphology is changing due to maturation. They conclude with the thought that 'although the magnitude of the associations found here is small, it is most likely that several etiological factors acting independently or together at any point in time may trigger paediatric obesity in each individual case. Thus, one may argue that obesity can be attributed to small changes in several environmental factors acting and interacting with each other' (2008: 799).

The research undertaken since the 1980s has clearly implicated TV as a lifestyle risk factor in development of children's weight gain. In their study of New Zealand, Hancox and Poulton (2006) found that BMI and the incidence of overweight in children aged 3–15 was significantly related to the amount of TV viewed, especially in girls. They conclude that although the effects size appears small, it is greater than that often reported in studies of either nutritional intake or regular exercise. The health scientists therefore had confirmed what many parents knew and practised. Encouraging active leisure and healthy diets were vital for their children's health and well-being. But both were related to TV use. As moral panic increased the press coverage of the risk factors, parents became anxious about their excessive media use; their TV snacking and their lack of outdoor play became lifestyle risks that need to be watched. And here is where risk analysis gets really frustrating. Although health sciences could demonstrate that the risks associated with media saturated lifestyles did exist, they couldn't tell parents what to do other than ban advertising, provide fruit as snacks and take kids to the gym (Campbell et al. 2001).

8

Panicked Parenting: Managing Children's Lifestyle Choices in the Risk Society

Before they can influence their parents or make rational brand choices, children must not only distinguish their likes and dislikes for goods but learn to communicate them (Ekstrom et al. 1987). Guided by social norms, most parents will become deeply involved in helping their children acquire language competence by talking, singing and reading to the child, modelling the production of sounds, rewarding the child's efforts, playing games that associate sounds and actions and ultimately sending them to school to be formally instructed as competent members of their language community. The process of managing children's consumption starts in the high chair too, where the negotiations about taste and health begin. Even before they learn to say 'no, I don't like that spinach', children have become engaged in a complex negotiation over their own preferences.

Paralleling the learning of language, the ultimate goal of consumer empowerment is a self-regulating subject who can express his or her own ideas, feelings, preferences and values. Like all language games, this one consists of strategic negotiation. The feeding relationship quickly becomes an intimate experiment in mutually agreeable taste as parents offer a variety of flavours and textures testing out what the child likes within the edicts of nutritional requirements. In this way feeding lays the pattern of an intimate strategic dialogue where the parent looks to the child's face to decode the child's emotional experiences of consumption. Children are learning to influence their parents about their preferences while the parents are finding ways of managing their children by pleasing them. If the child smiles and eats, the parent feels successful. If the child frowns and spits out the food, the experiment continues or conflict ensues. Not surprising therefore, that children become strategic about getting what they want at a very early age too by using language to refuse foods they don't like and gain access to ones they do. These discussions of food preference become more animated as parents seek to balance pleasing children with their excessive demands for candy or refusal to eat healthy vegetables.

Cultivating taste and managing nutrition

Good nutrition and healthy eating have been prime issues in parenting throughout the century but have become a more important aspect of child-drearing in the post-war years as TV became integral to domestic lifestyles. Berey and Pollay (1968) found that child-centred mothers were especially reluctant to yield to children's brand demands because of their concerns over nutrition as well as their image as good mothers. In their overview of the literature related to the nutritional factors which put children at risk, Birch and Fisher (1998) and Ventura and Birch (2007) review US family dietary practices influencing children's development of self-regulation of energy intake. Their concern was that beyond the genetic disposition, family environment shapes patterns of food preferences, food consumption and physical activity that predispose children to weight gain. Their work focused on fat as a proportion of total caloric intake not only because nutritional surveys show that children acquire greater than 30 per cent of their energy from fats but also because their high-in-fat diets also have lower than recommended fruit and vegetable intakes. Their purpose was to discover to what extent the relationship between child and parent obesity in obesogenic families can be explained by the ways that parents cultivate preferences for energy-dense foods in their children.

Their review notes that parents shape their children's eating in a variety of ways: through the patterns of taste established from birth; through the foods they make available; through modelling, controlling and moderating food knowledge and advertising; and by the management of the contextual factors of eating (snacking, TV dinners etc.). Food and dietary restrictions are founded on notions of 'good' and 'bad' foods, which can be ill informed and emerge as a parental response to the perception of the child's weight status or developing food preferences (too many sweets). But dietary strategies that encourage or control children's eating of certain foods can boomerang on the parents: mothers reported restricting their own foods more when their children's BMIs were greater. Birch and Fisher's studies of children's preferences have shown that using foods as rewards and punishments might make those foods more desirable to children, implying that 'restricting children's access to foods may actually promote over-consumption of those foods' (1998: 544). Particularly they found that maternal restrictions on girls' snack foods were related to girls' (but not boys') consumption of those snacks in an unrestricted eating setting.

Birch and Fisher also point out that parental restrictions on eating may ultimately undermine children's development of self-regulating mechanisms for energy imbalance and satiety. Monitoring the caloric density of foods consumed in a first course, they tested the ability of children to regulate the caloric content of a second. Their hypothesis was confirmed that children responding to the energy density of the first course would consume less in the second course, revealing that children do have a natural ability to moderate food intake in relationship to the energy density of the food. Yet when children were given competing instructions about desirable eating practices – one tuning them to internal cues and the other to rules for cleaning one's plate – it was found that the self-regulation mechanisms no longer worked. As they conclude, these findings suggest a powerful role for the child-feeding practices of the family in shaping not only how much they consume but their responsiveness to increasingly energy-dense diets.

Hill's (2002) review of the issues surrounding parental guidance of food choice also suggests that neither strict control nor laissez faire parenting seems to work. The determinants of what children choose to eat are complex, and the balance changes as children get older, yet adults clearly occupy a central position in this process. Parental behaviour shapes food acceptance, and early exposure to fruit and vegetables or to foods high in energy, sugar and fat is related to children's liking for, and consumption of, these foods. Some parents are imposing child-feeding practices that control what and how much children eat. He argues that over-control can be counterproductive because it teaches children to dislike the very foods we want them to consume and potentially undermines self-regulation abilities. 'Children should be neither the only focus of nutritional interventions nor expected to solve the nutritional problems with which adults around them are continuing to fail' (2002: 259). He also notes that by the time they are 12, children have established quite strong ideas about what is enjoyable and suitable for them to eat. Up to one-quarter of young adolescent girls report dieting to lose weight, their motivation driven by weight and shape dissatisfaction. For some, dieting and vegetarianism are intertwined and legitimized as healthy eating. For others, striving for nutritional autonomy, the choice of less-healthy foods, is not just for their taste but an act of parental defiance and peer solidarity. Evidence from families with older children show that family food rules imposed at an early age may indeed predict healthier eating habits at adolescence. Yet as Coveney et al. (2002) have suggested, this may result less from the efficacy of family food rules *per se* than from failure of communicating them appropriately to children in a family setting. The importance of risk communication in the family cannot be ignored.

Benton (2004) provides more recent evidence of the salience of studying parental influence on food preferences in young children. Because tastes such as sweet and salty are biologically established, children have a predisposition towards learning to like foods with high-energy density. Yet preferences result from trial and testing. Food aversions can be learnt in one trial, and towards the second year of life, there is a tendency to avoid novel foods. In the process of developing food preferences, parental style is a critical factor, in which emotional atmosphere, modelling and positive encouragement plays a role. Traditionally, attempts to impart basic nutritional information accompany the introduction of less energy dense and more nutritionally balanced diets. Research has shown that repeated exposure to initially disliked foods can break down resistance, although forcing a child to eat a food can decrease their liking for that food. Obviously, the dinner table is an important site of taste formation: the attitudes to food, the stabilization of preferences and the modelling of eating behaviours all happen there. But as children grow older they are given greater autonomy and greater responsibility in relationship to food. They eat at friends more often, go out for meals and eat with peers at school. The increase in out-of-home food consumption means that parents must educate their children to make healthy food choices in a context where they are not present.

Carruth et al. (1991) surveyed 887 10–12th grade students on the media's, peer's and family's influences on food choices and snacking, noting that not only are many teens helping with family food shopping but also preparing meals for themselves and others. 64 per cent report helping to decide what foods to buy in their families and 55 per cent go shopping for groceries with parents. Foods consumed in families then are largely a result of the training of parents. Yet by adolescence, snacking preferences are far less subject to negotiation: 72 per cent of teens report that they rarely talk about food advertisements and 71 per cent that they rarely asked parents advice about snacks. Talking about food advertising with friends is mentioned by less than 25 per cent of respondents, and 60 per cent don't discuss fast food choices with their peers. Snacking seems to be an autonomous zone of personal preferences.

Stratton (1994, 1997) interviewed members of British families individually in private and then with the whole family together, concluding that families talk regularly about both the practical issues and the preferences presented by food choice. Children have a role to play in determining family diet, he argues, but it is far from the popular version of parents feeling pestered to give their children inappropriate foods. Parents did not see their children's influence as contentious and were more concerned about maintaining enough variety in the face of their children's likes and dislikes in order to stop them from becoming bored. Many parents also reported that their own diets were strongly influenced by what they provided for their children. Within the practical issues raised, nutrition and health issues were low priority. Parents are mentioned in about a third of children's discussions of food. Other family and peer influences are also mentioned frequently. Interestingly, the economic factors (price, marketing issues such as advertising, pack information and supermarket ecology) are mentioned rarely and constitute only 15 per cent of the replies. Stratton rebuts the 'myths' of children and food advertising such as the idea that families see advertising as distorting the pattern of their children's eating. They were well aware that children's food advertising concentrates on snacks, drinks and cereals but did not see these categories as distortions of their children's diets (Stratton 1997: 14). Mind you, this study was completed long before the British press galvanized around food politics.

Obesogenic families are characterized not only by their energy-dense diets but by a number of food-related behaviours including eating while watching TV, a lack of family meals, missing breakfast and of course a preference for energy-dense foods. Reviewing the literature on food socialization, Kyung Rhee (2008) summarizes the many ways that parents can impact their children's food consumption both positively and negatively. Family food traditions are shaped not only by negotiated provisioning choices but also through parental modelling of food attitudes and behaviours, the atmosphere surrounding food, their restrictions, explanations and responses to unhealthy eating and their general parenting style including their sensitivity and their expectations of maturity in their children's behaviours. Rhee also notes that that despite the protective benefits of family meals, lifestyle factors that impact children's weight status such as TV snacking and nutritional knowledge are socioculturally distributed. Higher rates of obesity in Black and Hispanic families may have a lot to do with food-related behaviours therefore independent of advertising exposure.

Managing media, leisure time and sedentary lifestyles

But food is only the first battleground in their parents' long struggle to teach their children to be safe and healthy. It may start with the stove is hot and keep your fingers out of the electric sockets but it gets progressively more complex in the media-saturated world. Children's understanding of lifestyle risks associated with consumerism takes place through a broadening negotiation of wants, costs and risks associated with goods generally, including entertainment activities, toys and clothes. Risk management takes place as a complex game played out between parents and children in the increasingly in which certain things are sanctioned and others prohibited. For example toys are given to children at birth as the privileged tools of early learning. Not only are they the first 'commodities' that children come to own but the templates for learning about social roles, cognitive and physical skills and identities. But they also are laying the foundation of indoor leisure preferences and sedentary lifestyles.

Using an experimental method, Prasad et al. (1978) set out to study the ability of parents to mitigate the influence of TV ads on children's preferences for toys. In this study, 64 8–10 year old boys were exposed to television commercials for two different equally attractive toy products embedded in a TV programme. After viewing the ad, mothers talked with the child about the toy giving assertive negative information, reasoned negative information or no negative information (control). Children then played a game and were allowed to choose a toy 'prize'. The results showed that parental counter information made no difference to product choice but did extend decision time in the control condition. Results also indicate that the more attractive ad produced more requests regardless of negative parental comment, whereas when it came to the weaker ad, reasoned feedback influenced choice. Obviously parents can intervene in the product decision process. Yet an assertive negative negotiating style can convince the child that the advertised toy is more attractive.

Since children's response to TV food advertising is to make requests to their parents about advertised products (Reid and Frazer 1980; Winman 1983) one way to intervene in the flow of influence from marketing is to regulate children's access to TV (Reid 1979). Although teaching children advertising literacy has marginal impact on their discretionary consumption, parents can moderate the impact of marketing by controlling children's free time by creating rules for viewing or mandating other activities – either sedentary or active. It is worth remembering that toys are highly valued not only because play is regarded as constructive but also because toys are enjoyed by children. Before they go to school, keeping children busy is a central problem for many parents. In this respect, toy play which preoccupies the infant is usually followed by other media forms including books, TV, video games and music in managing the child's free time. With playrooms full of toys, video games and TV many children develop a preference for the low-energy intensity activities of indoor leisure. Tucker (1986) reported on the relationship between TV, obesity and physical fitness among 379 high school males. In this study, physical fitness was measured by a series of tests using push-ups, pull-ups, sidestep, long jump, sit-ups, and jog-walk. Results showed that although light viewers were not significantly less obese than moderate or heavy viewers they did score significantly better than heavy viewers on a composite fitness index. Demographic variables had little influence on the associations found between viewing and fitness.

It is not just advertising therefore, but TV watching generally that requires parental attention, argued family life educators Christopher et al. (1989). They undertook a series of in-depth family interviews to explore the relationship between attitudes to television, discussion of television and the qualities of family life. Positive attitudes to children's television were associated with more TV viewing and more TVs in the home. Television may also be used as a reward for completion of chores or homework or a privilege that may be taken away if these activities are not completed. Negative attitudes to television were associated with stricter regulations on all fronts. If parents perceived the TV as interfering with children's well-being they talked about it more with their children. Strict regulation of television was therefore associated with an open family atmosphere where children were encouraged to express their feelings. Moreover the more negative the parents' attitudes to TV, the greater the family cohesion, expressiveness and participation in active recreation. Regulation of TV therefore was a means that parents used to keep children active.

Durant et al. (1994) observed the activity levels of 191 3–4-year old children while TV viewing as well as while playing outside. They report that physical activity was lower during television watching and that children sustained longer and more active bouts of exercise outside. But in this young sample, body mass was associated with physical activity but not with the amount of TV viewing. Hofferth and Sandberg (2001) have noted that children's free playtime dropped by an estimated 25 per cent between 1981 and 1997 replaced by the time children spent in structured activity. But as Canadian research by Tremblay and Willms (2003) has shown, although 3+ hours of TV viewing puts children increasingly at risk of obesity, regularly playing unorganized sports (but not sports teams) and high SES are protective factors which interact with media use. Single parenting on the other hand is a compounding variable which increases both the time spent watching TV and obesity.

Regulating TV

It is well understood by most parents that children are learning lots from television from brand names to ways of coping with growing up. But the strategies and reasoning deployed in managing this learning process varies considerably and is constantly changing. Family regulation of TV takes a number of forms including content limitations, time-based regulation, enforced educational quality and co-viewing. As Atkin et al. (1991) noted, younger children are generally more tightly regulated in their media use for a variety of reasons including the profusion of new technologies and TV in the bedrooms. Although parents claim to strictly monitor and co-view with younger children, evidence from the older ones reveals that they either ignore, subvert or work around the rules. Other studies of leisure have confirmed the salience of family media monitoring and regulation as media proliferated and bedrooms became media sanctuaries (Livingstone and Bovill 1999).

Weintraub et al. (1999) undertook a study of the motives for mediating the tube, arguing that direct and indirect control is enforced by four means: rule making, modelling, normative legitimation and active discussion. In a survey of 255 parents they examined whether the frequency of mediation (frequent vs. rare) and the valence of the interaction (positive vs. negative) distinguished family media regulation patterns. In this study parental attitudes to TV mattered. The amount of prime time TV consumed, the frequency of co-viewing, concerns about content were all significantly related to types of mediation practised. Moreover 9 per cent of the variance in the 'trust in advertising' variable is explained by the cynical TV mediation style of parents. The authors conclude that it is important to study both positive and negative mediation of TV in the family as the later is associated with protective motivations and the learning of critical viewing.

Studies since have found diverse styles of television mediation among American families. Despite a growing awareness of media risks, the majority of US parents adopt a laissez faire attitude to media – even for young children. Mostly parents simply talk to their children about their TV use. Perhaps this why viewing statistics are higher in the US than Britain and Canada. The Media Q study (Gentile and Walsh 2002) reported that 57 per cent of parents feel their kids are being adversely affected by TV. Yet their restrictions were modest. Although most American parents claimed to monitor their children's media use, and many established rules, there was a clear lack of parental involvement in the television programme selection process and infrequent use of co-viewing as a mediation technique. The rules applied were also arbitrary and followed by inconsistent enforcement. Perhaps that explains why the high levels of exposure to advertising in the US results in greater preferences for energy-dense foods. American parents may be failing to reduce children's exposure in the best way possible: turning off the tube.

Parenting styles and consumer socialization

Protecting children from lifestyle risks while preparing them for making informed purchases are the contradictory ideals that dynamizes consumer socialization. Clearly children's food preferences, media use and attitudes towards healthy living depend largely on what is modelled, provided and discussed in the home. But a wide variety of parenting styles are reported in the childrearing literatures depending on gender, ethnicity and region. Moreover the problems facing the media-saturated family are multiple, including the management of children's discretionary consumption, their leisure time, their nutrition and exposure to market persuasion.

Based on studies of factors influencing teens' consumer decisions (Moschis and Churchill 1978; Moschis and Moore 1979; Moschis et al. 1984) George Moschis (1985) goes on to explore the little-understood processes of family communication on young people's consumer socialization and behaviour offering a social-psychological model which distinguished the interpersonal power relationships (parent-child) from the educational means (through talking and modelling attitudes to products, brands, money, stores etc.). These two dimensions provide a family dynamics typology which predicts four possible parent–child family types: laissez-faire, protective, pluralistic and consensual based on their degree of social and conceptual orientations. Whereas laissez faire families exert little power over children (no restrictions) and engage in little communication about consumption advising them of choices and preferences, consensual families are both controlling and discussing consumption extensively. Protective families on the other hand stress control but not conversation, whereas pluralistic families stress communication but not restrictions. Aspects of control and negotiation are diverse and variable but include mostly price quality, managing money, comparative shopping, savings and using sales, parental involvement in decisions, materialism and values, brand preferences, product categories, consumer skills and financial strategies, store preferences and information, modelling restraint or savings, encouraging learning from experience, motivations and critiques of market/advertising/stores.

Moschis (1985) suggests that three dimensions of parental style influence the child's acquisition of consumer skills, brand preferences and consumer values: direct, indirect and mediating. Additionally, the forms of control can be intentional (restrictions or instructions), passive (observations or rewards) and mediational based on the family's control of other sources of influence such as peers and advertising. Moreover, the review suggests that variation across social demographic factors (such as social class and ethnicity) as well as across product categories (food vs. clothes for example) is to be expected. Moreover given variation in the way families intervene in influence processes (stores, peers, media exposure) and the diversity of communicational styles in family (modelling, restricting, discussing and letting children learn for themselves) means that the effects of family practice on consumer socialization is likely to be complex.

Noting the importance of parents in the mounting public debate about television's impact on the consumer socialization process, Carlson et al. (1990, 1993) complemented Moore and Moschis' study of adolescents' perspective on consumer socialization with a survey of 491 mothers of children aged 5–11, studying their approach to consumer socialization. Although most researchers acknowledge the subtle interpersonal dynamics within consumer socialization, these researchers notice that parental concern about food advertising resulted in greater control over many aspects of their children's consumer socialization. Adopting findings from studies of political socialization, they distinguished two important dimensions of parents' roles (see Figure 8.1). Firstly, the socio-orientation was associated with the degree to which parents promote deference to authority and overt restrictions on children's behaviour; and secondly, the concept-oriented dimension was associated with parents' concerns about educating the child, building a child's self-regulation and their emphasis on communication in order to foster a child's consumer competence.

	Low socio	High socio
Low concept	Laissez faire	Protectives
High concept	Pluralists	Consensuals

Figure 8.1 Comparing parenting styles

Scales were developed to identify parenting styles along these two criteria and their sample was fairly balanced in terms of four different patterns:

1. Laissez-faire parents neither monitor nor educate their children.
2. Protective parents monitor and control children but downplay negotiation. They are strict and brook no dissent.
3. Pluralist parents stress self-control and learning through negotiation and don't believe in policing children's consumption.
4. Consensual parents encourage children to explore consumerism on their own, yet they carefully monitor and control them as well, expecting compliance with restrictions.

The researchers then examined a series of hypotheses concerning the relation between these family communication orientations and a variety of consumer socialization variables including the setting of goals, media use and regulation, ad literacy, co-shopping, child influence and parents' response to children's consumer requests. The results showed that a child's influence on family consumption was greatest in pluralistic families even though the amount of TV viewing is lowest, because these families privilege teaching about consumerism. Rather than encouraging children to learn about consumption, protective parents acted more like gatekeepers mandating children's consumption than like teachers encouraging children to consume wisely. Consensuals on the other hand negotiated with their children, permitting most discretionary choices but denying children's requests. These families control media use most and focus on teaching their children ad literacy.

Building on the literature on familial styles of consumer socialization, Mangleburg (1990) suggested that three factors were impacting the development of children's agency within family decision making. First, the type of product advertised matters because children are 'interested' and 'informed' parties in some product areas and less so in others. For example, they can have substantial impact on breakfast cereals, toys, treats and clothes but only limited influence on other leisure activities (cable subscriptions, holidays) and products that are used by the whole family such as bread, furniture, TVs and cars. The extent of their influence and their methods of negotiation therefore vary by the product categories and whether they are informed enough to contribute to the decisions. Research has also shown that children have differential involvements at different points in the family decision making. They seem to have more influence in recognizing that a product is needed than in where and which brand will be chosen. Since price, product qualities and access also matter in family decision making and purchase, children's cognitive and linguistic abilities as well as the extent of their consumer knowledge of price, benefits and risks associated with the product can be a factor in their influence, involvement and the degree of parental yielding to their influence attempts. Thirdly, the parenting styles and ways of managing the child's development also influences the way they grant children money and power to buy or influence family diet and pastimes. Parents can yield to influence attempts made directly (or resist or negotiate), but also when they take into account children's known preferences (for example at Christmas) in making their purchases in order to reward, please or pacify a child (Beatty and Salil 1994).

Defining financial literacy as 'having the knowledge to be financially responsible', Clarke et al. (2005) note that the socialization of money skills, so essential to consumer socialization, is little understood. Noting that many American adults are living beyond their means and that surveys of young people indicate little understanding of money, they surveyed young adults for the following dimensions of the socialization of financial management: teaching the setting of financial goals, financial values, exploring career opportunities, budgeting, saving money, thrifty use of what you have, credit, purchase of domestic necessities, insurance, home ownership and maintenance, taxes and investments. Their data suggests that parents are the primary source of economic literacy, both teaching and modelling financial skills. Although parents model and teach general financial values, most of these young adults lack the basic skills necessary for wise financial management. Very little of support for learning consumer competence comes from outside the family.

Based on a survey of Estonian parents, Keller and Kalmus (2009) found that 'advertising was viewed as an archetypal institution of the consumer society which ... incarnates the symbolic themes of consumerism' (2008: 370). Given their concerns about advertising, Estonian parents tend to be relatively protectionist and normative about the consumer society. Yet hoping to go beyond the tired debate about advertising to children, these researchers go on to define consumerism more broadly as including all aspects of children's participation in the market including shopping, brand knowledge, value orientations and self-identification with lifestyles and brands. Older adults, steeped in the communist past, are less consumerist than younger ones but strikingly the perceived vulnerability of children to TV advertising is the one constant of generational value systems.

Parenting styles in Canada: Managing children's lifestyle risks

Given the anxieties raised about children's weight gain, the Media Analysis Laboratory at Simon Fraser University set out to discover how Canadian parents managed children's exposure to lifestyle risks in the media-saturated household. A pilot study began with our research team interviewing 18 British Columbian families. Each family had at least one child between the ages of 4 and 12. In-depth interviews with parents reviewed the family routines, parental aspirations, their values, their methods of discipline and their concerns about raising children in a risk society. The interviews included a walk through the home with a description of the negotiations governing both leisure time and snacking routines. Mothers were also interviewed in the kitchen with regard to general attitudes to eating, nutrition and diet. Children were interviewed in their bedrooms and also wherever they use media most often. All parents were informed about the problem of child obesity. Many cited news reports that made reference to research warning of health issues associated with weight gain. Some expressed concern about their own child's weight. Generally speaking these parents felt the challenge of both protecting their children while preparing them to make decisions on their own that would make them happy and healthy. Teaching their children to eat well, play freely, to become educated and stay active are very much at the forefront of their priorities for their kids while they are young. Protecting children from dangers they don't understand yet is a guiding principal most parents follow – although what that means in practice is different. Granting them freedom to explore the world, to buy things for themselves however, becomes an equally important learning objective as they get older. But it is neither easy or sudden. Restricting media, negotiating with children in shops, and where necessary, enforcing healthy regimes of eating and activity are the means deployed when children are young. Allowances and freedom to choose for themselves become more important for older children and adolescents. They are given more choice and input into family decisions. Children's empowerment is evident in their reports of discretionary purchases, open access to media, casual snacking and outdoor play.

The complexity of teaching children to want what is good for them was the central theme of these interviews. These parents eagerly discussed the challenges of preparing children as self-regulating citizens while granting them the freedom to explore their world. For younger children the parents are especially anxious about the nutritional quality of foods. But they acknowledge they use food to reward children for good behaviour and broaden their palates too. Most draw a line in the sand around cost, health and moral considerations in eating – but where this line gets drawn differs considerably. Family meals, snacking while watching, going out for fast food and rewards while shopping all get mentioned but not by everyone, and not in the same way.

Free time is another arena in which children are inducted into the moral and lifestyle orientations of the family. But again some families expect to watch TV, play games and talk together while others retreat to their own rooms or to a designated play space. Most parents are keen to help their children become wise consumers, taking them along when shopping and coaching them in the routines of selection and purchase from a young age. But they note too the influences of advertising on children's knowledge and requests.

Money is another tool that parents consciously use in the processes of consumer socialization. Teaching saving and spending by giving a piggy bank is a classic example of the way prudent money use is taught by traditional families. Many children are given allowances or pocket money and encouraged by their parents to save up for special gifts or spend it as they want. Children are also taught to buy things with their own money. They are encouraged to search through the aisles, compare prices and to be able to count the right amount of money and wait for change (Williams 2006). Television is often a sore point in family life, associated with conflict and discipline. Many parents acknowledged the guilty pleasure they felt when they used TV to pre-occupy their children while they took a break from parenting. Many claimed to coach their children to watch quality kids programming and made rules around its use.

Because of the cross-cutting expectations of entraining freedom and responsibility, raising children was regarded as a challenge. Although most parents mix instruction, guidance and rewards for children's learning with specifying rules, wielding love withdrawal, issuing warnings, providing sanctions and meting out punishments, they find no easy formula and no deus ex machina. Helping children learn about pleasure, happiness and self-restraint in the marketplace is never easy. Some complained that they lacked information about how to handle difficult circumstances. But most clung to a set of 'values' that they felt were important in their parenting. Parents unanimously value children's play and are eager to have their children learn to enjoy reading. But they also have concerns about too much and the wrong kinds of play, particularly when their children exhibit a reluctance to be active. Many parents were also concerned about their neighbourhoods, refusing to let their children just go out and play in the park or streets. They felt safer if the child was indoors and preferred to drive children to sports, recreation centres or clubs than let them free form outside. Many were aware of the irony associated with their fears of the street: they remembered their own more free-ranging childhoods, but also were anxious about granting their children the freedom to bike, go to the park or visit with friends on their own.

Given their awareness of the growing risks of obesity, these parents' anxieties about media seems to have forced some rethinking of parenting styles and philosophy. Yet rather than the conceptual model suggested by Moschis, three parenting styles seemed to best characterize their overall approach to the risk management strategies applied in these households. I have called these the mandated, permissive and negotiative approaches to lifestyle risk communication. What is missing in my typology is the 'laissez-faire' category hypothesized by Moschis. This makes sense given that all parents we talked to were clearly striving to both educate and protect their children from multiple lifestyle risks – even if they did so in different ways. But none were hands off. Although a consistent style across all lifestyle risks was rarely found, the grid shown in Figure 8.2 was used to assess the parenting style for the four risk behaviours separately.

Generally speaking, permissive parents believe most in giving children the freedom to explore pleasures and make choices with minimal constraints. But this is not because they don't care. Permissiveness is a strategy for enabling children's learning just like rules and constant negotiation are.

	Media use	Snacking	Activity and sports	Discretionary consumption
Permissive	few restrictions	choose for self	free play is encouraged	spend own money
Negotiative	media education	nutritional guidance	guidance and advice mainly	consult on important purchases
Mandated	time and content rules	choose among what is offered	enrolled in programmes	purchases specified within range

Figure 8.2   The matrix of lifestyle risks management

Mandated parents on the other hand imposed rules on risky behaviours and expected compliance. Of course they knew these rules had to be explained. Negotiative parents seemed caught between these two strategies preferring to not only explain the rules but also their concerns in order to educate them to be 'aware'. Although instructing children is prioritized and rules applied in all families, when it comes to learning about taste, discretionary consumption and how to spend their free time, parents communicated about risks differently emphasizing rules, education or self-discovery. But they did not do it consistently.

Managing lifestyle risks

The insights from these interviews informed the development of a questionnaire[1] which asked 200 British Columbian parents about their strategies for managing the lifestyle risks associated with media-saturated domesticity. Of the respondents, 88 per cent were women, more than half of whom were in their 30s. 76 per cent were born in Canada, 19 per cent were immigrants, most of whom were born in China. Their household incomes spanned from 20 per cent under the Canadian mean to 27 per cent (who reported more than $100,000 per year). 66 per cent of the children included were 8-years old or younger and 33 per cent were 9–14-year olds. The children's gender distribution was 52 per cent boys and 48 per cent girls.

Family values provide the guiding principles of childrearing (see Figure 8.3). In this sample, developing a moral compass is at the top of the list scoring (4.78), followed by developing a child's self-esteem, being active and healthy (4.58) and spending time with family. Less important were the maintenance of cultural heritage (3.19), preparing children for life's difficulties, playing sports and having freedom to explore their world. Clearly protection

Preparing the future (20.5 per cent)

> learning to save money
> learning to use money wisely
> learning to understand work
> protecting my child from social ills
> establishing house rules
> eating meals together
> doing well at school

Family oriented (14.5 per cent)

> developing a moral compass to guide him/her through life
> developing his/her self-esteem and confidence
> spending time talking and doing things together as a family
> having leisure time to enjoy being a child

Active freedom (10 per cent)

> having the freedom to explore the world on his/her own
> participating in sports
> being active an healthy

Exposure to the worldly (7 per cent)

> making friends with other children
> media enables my child to learn valuable lessons
> developing a sense of autonomy
> preparing my child for adulthood by exposing him/her to life's difficulties

Familial dialogue (7 per cent)

> my child regularly participated in decision making for family leisure choices
> explaining the ideas behind my actions
> maintaining the cultural heritage of our family
> acting as a role model for my child

Total variance explained is 59 per cent

Figure 8.3 Cluster analysis of the family values scale items

triumphed over freedom in their parenting. Parents of children older than 6 differed on only two issues: they stressed education and acting as a role model less. Parents considered explaining one's actions and exposing children to life's difficulties more acceptable for boys than girls. A factor analysis of these items indicated that preparation for the future was a central concern explaining 20.5 per cent of the variance in this sample. It is interesting to note that establishing house rules and eating together are viewed as modalities of learning. Instilling morals, bolstering self-esteem and spending time together are crucial to their family orientation, explaining 14.5 per cent of the variance. These families also varied in relationship to the support of children's active freedom, their exposure to the broader world and their emphasis on talking with children.

Managing media access

Media are a fixture of family life although parents had very different interpretations of the degree and nature of the 'dangers' that TV, video games and Internet presented. 40 per cent of parents actually have a positive view of TV, maintaining that it allows their children to learn some valuable life lessons, whereas 25 per cent strongly disagree with this statement. Most parents have some concerns about children's TV viewing and many have multiple concerns. The relative strength of these concerns is illustrated in Figure 8.4.

As Figure 8.4 indicates, although parents have strong concerns about TV watching, the issues raised by the obesity pandemic – the ads – were the lesser of these parents' media anxieties. These British Columbian parents seem most alarmed by violence and adult content in the TV programmes. Only 60 per cent expressed concerns about their child's exposure to commercials. Concern about frightening images was expressed most by parents of younger children. Other than that there were no gender, age or SES differences. The overall level of concern about TV was not related to children's media use although those parents who are specifically concerned

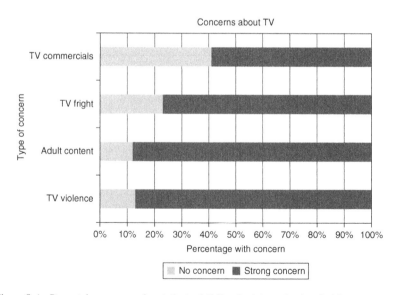

Figure 8.4   Parental concerns about their child's television viewing habits

about commercials and violence report that their children watch TV and use video games less.

In this sample, parents report that their child's TV viewing averages less than 1.8 hours per day. Only 19 per cent report that their children use media more than 3 hours per day and 21 per cent report their children use media less than 1 hour per day. Only 4 per cent report children use video games or the Internet more than three hours daily. 36 per cent had a TV in their bedroom and 10 per cent had a computer. Only 5 per cent had both. Children's use of media is somewhat socially distributed. Poorest households spent the most time using media. Age and gender were unrelated to amount of viewing time. Girls and older children generally were slightly more likely to have a computer, while boys were more likely to have a TV in their bedrooms. Those children who had a TV or computer in their bedrooms spend significantly more time using them – and those that had both, even more so. In those households where children use media most conflict over media is greater. Yet the parents generally seemed comfortable with the idea that TV taught something useful, especially those parents who allowed them to have a computer in the bedroom. Ethnicity was another factor, with Internet use higher in households of foreign-born parents. The amount of time children spent playing video games was higher for boys, and the amount of time on the Internet was greater for older children generally.

Managing leisure in a media-saturated household

How children spend their free time is an important arena of child empowerment. Toys and media are ways that parents teach children to manage time. Most parents believe that children should be given some scope to make choices about how they spend their free time for themselves. Almost 70 per cent of the children are granted a say in the choice of activity often or always. Yet less than 20 per cent of children in this sample would be considered 'at risk' due to heavy viewing. Relative to US norms, their children's media use does not seem excessive and their activity levels seem adequate. Perhaps the reason is the rather hands-on approach to media. In this sample 68 per cent of the parents report imposing time limits on their child's viewing often or always and only 29 per cent are allowed to view whenever they want. Older children however are less regulated than younger ones. The Internet use is regarded as least problematic and conflict is mostly about children's video gaming, not TV. 65 per cent of parents say TV viewing never or rarely interferes with their children's exercise while 78 per cent say it rarely interferes with children maintaining friendships. In short children's sedentary lifestyles do not seem to be a great concern in this British Columbia sample, perhaps because TV, video games and the Internet are mostly regarded as distraction and entertainment. Ultimately problematic content motivates restrictions more than advertising exposure and sedentary lifestyles. Those parents with concerns about media displacement did impose time based, rather than content-based rules more – but they were few in number.

Parents perceive and respond to the challenge of managing media differently. The qualitative research indicated that three parenting styles – mandated, negotiative and permissive – dominated the way risks were communicated in the family. The survey corroborated this distinction. The survey found that most parents understand that it is important to establish rules and provide guidelines for media use as part of family values. And most parents claim to have established rules governing media use (see Figure 8.4.). Mandateds control media by not only talking about rules but by enforcing limits. Negotiators talk constantly about TV watching with their children while trying to be a role model. They tend to favour co-viewing and dialogue as strategies of control. Permissives believe that children will learn best by being given the freedom to choose for themselves because they know the rules. Parents that are most concerned about TV are also most likely to adopt the mandated strategy for children's media use. And when parents place direct restrictions on what and when children can watch, children in fact spend less time with TV. Yet ironically, talking to children about media use and discussing the programmes also reduces the amount of time that children spent watching TV. Media literacy more than media use seems to be a class issue however. Income is not related to restrictions but it is strongly correlated with concern about commercials and the importance of teaching scepticism. Only the permissive approach is associated with significantly higher levels of TV watching. Parenting style proves to be a more significant determinant of TV viewing than either income, ethnicity, gender of the child or age.

Family rules are the prime means of guidance of media use (see Figure 8.5). Children with TV in the bedroom, those who get to choose for themselves, those with TV on during dinner, those without time and content limits, all watch significantly more TV. With regard to the enforcement of restrictions, families favour withdrawal of privileges and rewarding compliance, but scolding and being send to the room are common strategies. 88 per cent of parents claim an explanation accompanies any attempt to control the child. Few actually punished children for violations of TV rules and conflict over TV and video game use is reported in only 12 per cent of the families. Since parents are most concerned about content, their dialogue with children can have a positive effect.

TV and discretionary snacking

The 'globesity pandemic' made many Canadian parents anxious about their children's TV viewing and its relationship to diet. In this sample, the data reveals a high level of concern with children's nutrition. 90 per cent of parents claim to be very careful of what they feed their children. Many report

Parental strategies	
Talk about choices	14% always
TV on at dinner	34% never on
Use of rating	8% always
Time limits on media	37% always
Co-viewing	11% always
Talk about content	18% always
Set specific hours	19% always
Content limits on TV	41% always

Figure 8.5 Parental strategies for controlling children's media use

reading the nutritional information on the package and trying to only buy healthy foods for their children. This seems to work: 70 per cent report that they have no trouble in getting their children to eat healthy foods. Yet these decisions are not made without input from the child: 85 per cent consult with children about the foods the family will eat. Children, especially the younger ones, get taken with parents on shopping trips where negotiations over nutrition are frequent. 50 per cent of the parents report that they are accompanied by children often or always whereas only 7 per cent say children rarely go shopping with them. 67 per cent report that negotiations take place mostly while on these trips and only 28 per cent say they rarely give children a snack while on these outings.

Provisioning snack foods is different than the daily meals. Snacks are used as rewards in 62 per cent of families. When it comes to snacks, parents' preferred strategy, especially for younger children, is to buy healthy snacks and let the child choose among them. Compared to daily foods, however, snack foods are less healthy. Only 42 per cent say they mostly buy snacks that are healthy and 75 per cent admit that they buy snacks because their child will eat them. There are some limits however on snacking while shopping (23 per cent) and in the home. 25 per cent don't allow TV snacking and 32 per cent limit the child's choice of TV snacks often or always. The power to chose for themselves increased with age and experience. Younger children choose their own TV programmes less and when they request snacks they have seen in advertisements they get them less often than older ones. Younger children also get to choose their TV snacks less than older children. Some of the risk factors associated with unhealthy eating were being managed: TV is on during dinner in only 19 per cent of households. Snacking while watching, however, is less controlled and 66 per cent of children get to choose what they snack on.

Where TV is watched more, children also snack while watching, choose their snacks more, watch TV while eating, have parents less concerned about healthy snacking and less concerned about the effects of commercials or teaching them to be sceptical. This pattern is characteristic of permissive parenting. Of the demographic variables associated with media risks, gender and ethnicity are less important than the age of the child. Older children have parents who are willing to buy TV snacks they ask for, spend less time shopping with parents and are allowed to choose their own snacks more. With their own money they buy discretionary snacks, spend on active leisure and save less than younger children. The lower-income families are more hands on with money management, teach advertising literacy less and have children who spend their own money on toys. About half of the parents report that they rarely or never buy the advertised snacks that children request.

Generally children get the snacks they ask for in families where more TV is watched. Parents who allow their children to view lots of TV, not surprisingly, report feeling pressured by peer opinion more, but are less concerned about buying healthy foods and snacks. They also are more likely to allow children to pick their own snacks while shopping. Those parents who find it hard to get their children to eat healthy foods are generally less concerned with health anyway and more concerned with peer pressure. Parental food awareness is a significant factor in a child's discretionary choices. Parents concerned about nutrition have children who buy fewer snacks with their pocket money. These parents also tend to be more concerned about the effects of commercials, generally buy healthy foods and encourage scepticism about advertising, but are less willing to give in to pester power, to allow the child to pick out own snacks while grocery shopping, to let the child to snack while watching TV, choose their own TV snacks or to buy snacks as a reward for the child. In short, those parents most concerned about TV adopt a 'precautionary' approach to food too, encouraging children to be mindful of their snacking. The children whose parents are most concerned about buying healthy snacks tend to watch less TV but buy snacks more often with their own money.

Discretionary spending and consumer empowerment

The parenting style research suggests that consumer empowerment is one of the most controversial aspects of childrearing. And Canadian parents are divided on how to manage children's discretionary choices. Learning how to use money wisely, both saving for special goods and spending on things they really want, lies at the core of consumer socialization. Most parents use an allowance as the medium for teaching children about the marketplace, giving them money and the scope to use it as they mature. 53 per cent of the children receive an allowance, which averages 5 dollars per week. Younger children receive 4 dollars per week on average, and the older ones 9. But a family's approach to children's empowerment clearly differs. Most parents give money with strings attached. Their freedom to choose is mostly counterbalanced by the responsibility of doing chores and homework. Children's allowances increase with family income and with age, but not gender. The freedom to spend also depends on the parenting style. Permissive parents give their children more allowance and freedom to use it than mandated parents.

Parents report that children's spending was a trade-off between food and toys. According to the parents, 24 per cent of children save their pocket money, 58 per cent spend it on toys or media, 34 per cent of children buy food and 14 per cent spend on active leisure (multiple responses are possible on this question). Of course these choices depend on what the parents already provide in the home so the figures may indicate the tendency of parents to provision sports and snacks. It could also genuinely indicate children's preferences. Older children are less likely to save, buy discretionary snacks more and are more likely to spend their money on active leisure than younger ones. Boys and more affluent children buy toys most often. Younger children save more than older ones. Children who save are from wealthier families where they receive more and have parents who talk to them about what they should buy less. Gender and ethnicity are not related to the ways children spend their discretionary pocket money other than the tendency for Canadian born children to spend more on active leisure than immigrant children.

Parenting style and lifestyle risk exposure

Epidemiological research suggested that media management is the key element in a precautionary strategy for reducing lifestyle risks in the obesogenic family because it intersects with diet, activity and discretionary consumption. Although most parents are granting children more freedom and autonomy, they are doing so in a world impregnated with risks, including those associated with media. Other than the value of preparing children by exposing children to life's dangers, no abstract family values are related to the child's TV viewing. As we have seen, family strategies for lifestyle management supplement the communication of values, and these guidelines, negotiations and restrictions are often directed at shaping children's media use, eating, active leisure and discretionary consumption.

Generally speaking, in households where children watch TV most a constellation of parental choices put them at risk. Those who rank high on the media permissiveness scale believe in preparing children by giving them scope to learn for themselves. They are willing to expose children to risks, not because they don't care, but because they think experience provides the best opportunities for learning. They are least concerned about commercials and are least likely to teach advertising literacy. TV is on at dinner more, family meals stressed less and being active valued least. They are worried about TV time displacing friendship time, yet not generally concerned about healthy eating. They are also more willing to buy advertised snacks that are requested while shopping. At home they allow TV snacks more and let their children choose the ones they want. They don't try and provision the house with healthy snacks and rarely read nutritional labels. Yet they are also most likely to have children who spend their own money on toys and active leisure goods – rather than snacks.

Parents who negotiate with children about media most believe strongly in freedom to choose too, but they are most committed to talking with their children. They explain their ideas to children and eat meals together more. They are concerned about commercials more and stress learning to use money wisely and advertising literacy as points of conversation. They co-view with the child more often, impose restrictions on both time and content and favour the strategy of buying children healthy snacks from which they can choose. They are concerned about commercials on TV, most likely to examine nutritional labels but are generally less concerned about displacement of leisure or friendship in front of the screen. The result is that their children are less likely to buy discretionary snacks.

Media mandated parents are also concerned about commercials, value family meals and permit TV to be on during dinner less. They are strongly concerned about buying healthy foods and with active sports and health. Freedom and autonomy of children are not big issues but they like to explain the value of money and importance of a moral compass. Their notion of discretionary consumption is one guided by advice about how to spend their own money and rules about what they can buy. They teach advertising literacy and talk with children about snacks often. They try and buy healthy foods generally, and don't let their child choose snacks when shopping, or while watching TV. They don't allow TV snacking and prefer to buy children's healthy snacks before allowing the child to choose. The more mandated the parenting, the less TV that is viewed by the children.

Permissive parents believe that children need autonomy and freedom to be children in order to grow up healthy. They worry less about the effects of media, advertising, snacking and lack of exercise and encourage their children to 'decide for themselves'. So they allow them to buy, eat and watch TV as they like. Not that there is a lack of rules and negotiations in these households but rather that they choose to communicate about lifestyle choices differently. Given these differences, it is interesting that permissive parents are less concerned about media use and report the least conflict over TV; thus they are more willing to give their children scope to learn for themselves in the face of a risky world. Mandated parenting on the other hand was not only associated with considerable anxiety about play and media use but with conflict over media use.

Market literacy and consumer socialization

The empowerment of children to choose snacks and pastimes depends on how parents perceive and manage children's growing ability to manage their own lifestyles. Clearly the competences that children need in the risk society go beyond a narrow view of advertising literacy invoked by the 'tired' policy debate about child-targeted marketing. My own objections to this way of theorizing protective factors in the family are multiple. First it conflates media and advertising literacy, reducing the former to the cognitive ability to distinguish ads from programming and to understand the ad's 'intent to persuade' when obviously managing media use is a key to familial strategies of risk mitigation. Second it subsumes an economistic conception of the child as an autonomous consumer failing to recognize that parents remain the primary agency of consumer socialization. And third, the range of competences required for lifestyle management implies a more robust understanding of the 'risk-cost-benefits' calculus necessary for 'informed consent'.

Based on this survey it appears that parents are aware of the risks associated with media-saturated domesticity and fostering an awareness of media as a complex lifestyle risk. Market literacy, the composite capacities presumed by the notion of consumer competence is defined by three elements (Kline 2010: 247). The first is *media literacy*, which not only includes scepticism about advertising but an ability to understand media institutions and manage their use of screen media. The second is *economic literacy*, that is the financial knowledge of competitive markets and the money skills necessary to compare and evaluate competing goods along a standard yardstick of monetary value. The third concerns the question of *consumer literacy*, which includes the capacity to make informed lifestyle choices based on a comparison of the relative benefits and risks associated with using specific products. What is heartening from the survey of parents is that the majority of parents are broadly aware of the challenges facing childrearing in the risk society. To make thoughtful choices in the consumer marketplace, parents are trying to teach kids about the three 'M's – media, markets and money.

9

Consumer Empowerment in the Media-Saturated Family

All societies face the challenge of socializing children and childrearing practices are the primary means by which familial norms and values are transmitted across generations. As psychoanalyst Eric Fromm (1947) argued, 'In order that any society may function well, its members must acquire the kind of character which makes them want to act in the way they have to act as members of the society or of a special class within it' (1947: 66). Fromm applied Freudian psychoanalysis to the 'market orientation' of post-war America arguing that human personality formed in two ways: 'by acquiring and assimilating things' and 'by relating to people (and himself) in a process of socialisation' (Fromm, 1947: 66). Not only were the individual's relationship to things becoming more important to family life but a child's character was increasingly formed through material rewards, through the negotiation of tastes and preferences, through shopping and through the management of money. Recognizing that American children were growing up in an environment where materialism was valorized, he identified consumer empowerment as the paradoxical problem underlying changes in post-war socialization practices through which parents strive *to make children freely want the things that parents want them to want.*

David Riesman (Riesman et al. 1950) was among the early sociologists to reflect on the broader implications of the changing dynamics of child empowerment. Riesman highlighted the profound changes taking place in childrearing practices in post-war America as mediated popular culture eroded the Protestant valorization of hard work and self-discipline while promoting an 'other-directed' character structure of mass consumerism. Parents were becoming more concerned with teaching the skills and knowledge required in the mass mediated marketplace – the ability to enjoy life, to play, to experience freedom, and to save, shop for and find a good buy among the vast array of goods – rather than with enforcing modesty, hard work and thrift. The new regimes of American childrearing, he warned, were creating an 'other-directed' culture that was eroding the moral basis of self-regulation of the American family. No longer fearing idleness as the 'devils work', American parents became preoccupied with empowering children, hoping that goods, freedom and leisure would cultivate happy, autonomous and self-expressive individuals: the dynamics of power within the family were changing (McDonald 1980).

Children are introduced to the materialism of the American family very early. They are showered with gifts from birth and material rewards are given (or denied) to control behaviour as they grow older, implicitly communicating family values and lifestyle. The goods of children, including toys, food, clothes and furniture are part of a complex process of teaching the lessons of materialism, including ideology of ownership rights, status and pathways to happiness. Caught between the risks to children's health and the desire to help the child become an autonomous, self-defining subject, many parents find that healthy tastes must be negotiated beginning with the child's first refusal of strained carrots. As the child grows older, consumer socialization also takes place around TV viewing through rules governing use, lessons about media literacy and responses to requests for toys or foods seen there. These negotiations are often staged in stores as well since young children often accompany shopping parents. Realizing this constant dialogue over consumer socialization, marketing researchers have studied the influence of children by looking at parent–child interactions while shopping (Atkin 1978; Galst and White 1976). Generally speaking, younger children, who most often accompany parents on shopping trips, make more attempts than older ones to influence parents to buy a product. They are often refused. But the older they get the more effective children are in their influence attempts. They may ask for fewer things but get what they want more often. Gradually, through a series of negotiations around the table, in front of the TV and shopping with parents, they learn to communicate their preferences to parents. But this negotiation is two-sided: both children and parents become more strategic in their negotiations over healthy lifestyles.

During the 1990s, younger children seemed to be gaining more consumer power – both influential and discretionary (Reid and Frazer 1980; Belch et al. 1985; Ekstrom et al. 1987). Empowerment implies parental recognition of children's own subjective, motivations and desire within the lifestyle choices they negotiate. As James McNeal (1999) reports, their first purchases are generally made by age 6 in the presence of a coaching parent. By age 7, many children exhibit a profound knowledge of brands and price points. By age 8 many are 'active shoppers' in their own right, searching through toy catalogues, using pocket money for discretionary purchases, window shopping, chatting with sales personnel, carefully investigating their favourite products and learning to influence their parents to buy what they want. During the next few years their empowerment increases as they successfully negotiate a wider range of family purchases (cars and holidays) while having (and sometimes earning) more of their own money. Many 8-year olds receive allowances to spend freely on discretionary items. Some save for something special while others buy playthings, snacks, clothing and entertainment depending on their interests, SES, gender and parenting style. Although empowerment was a new dynamic in family life, it also raised flags for health researchers. Recognizing the health issues associated with children's eating of sweets, dental researchers began studying the interactions between parents and children in relation to discretionary snacking. Since food is among the first consumer products that children attempt to influence their parents to buy, and noting that older children are good bargainers and get more of what they want, Roberts et al. (2003) surveyed children aged 7–8 and their parents in Manchester about their snack consumption, allowances and influence in decisions about what sweets they eat (both influence on family provisioning and discretionary choices). Their research found broad agreement in families that children have considerable influence over what treats they consume. Although older mothers limited children's access to sweets more than younger ones, their children were likely to attribute these limits to lack of money rather than health. Mothers, especially younger ones, seemed reluctant to communicate about the nutritional issues surrounding 'treats'.

This may indicate that circumstances and family values have changed over the last generational cycle leading to ineffective strategies for managing consumer empowerment in pre-teen children. Noting evidence that generation Y spends more time in commercial environments and plays a greater role in familial consumption decisions, Dotson and Hyatt (2005) set out to explore the relation between the five most important influences shaping children's consumer decision making: TV ads, parents, peers, shopping and branding. Their survey of 663 children and youth aged 8–14 confirmed that the amount of TV watching is directly related to both children's liking and acceptance of advertising as well as their peer orientation to goods, but is negatively associated with their parents' involvement in their consumer decisions. No relationship was found between the amount of TV viewed and children's brand involvement, however. The survey also showed that age, gender and the amount of available pocket money are important factors in children's consumer socialization. For example, older children are more likely to be influenced by peers rather than parents. Boys are more likely to not only watch TV more but to accept and enjoy advertising more than girls. Girls are more likely to be peer oriented in their shopping decisions, but are equally brand oriented as boys. Children with less spending money enjoy shopping less, do it less often and are less influenced by peers and more by parents (upon whom they are probably dependent). Those with more money to spend, however, are more brand conscious.

Laura Flurry (2007) surveyed over 1400 mothers of children in grades four to five exploring the idea that changes in the sociology of family life were further empowering millennial children as consumers. Her study examined parental perceptions of children's influence at various stages of consumer decision making. She argues that children's influence on family life was not only evident in product categories such as toys and restaurants but extends to larger purchases like holidays and cars. The survey indicated that sociological factors, from divorce to ethnicity, significantly shape the extent of children's decision-making power in purchases. For example, children in smaller households also had more say over child-oriented goods (toys) and divorced parents indulged their children's requests more for both child and family goods. Overall it seemed like gender and age matter less in familial negotiations and that wealthier parents incorporated their children's opinions in consumer decision making more often. Yet parenting style matters too. In families where the parents exert less control over childrearing the children's initiation and search efforts for goods is greater.

Nutritional literacy

Family shopping trips are major occasions of consumer socialization (Brody et al. 1981). Observing 142 family groups while grocery shopping at 11 diverse neighbourhood supermarkets, O'Dougherty et al. (2006) found that pester power is not dead. Overall, negotiation of food choice took place in 55 per cent of all selection episodes, and 63 per cent of all discussions about food resulted in the child getting a sweet or snack. Only 13 per cent of the selections were parent initiated but in all cases what parents chose were accepted because they were 'treats'. In just over 50 per cent of the family food choice negotiations, the child initiated a request for a product of which 55 per cent of all requests – refused or yielded to – were for sweets or snacks. Moreover, 28.6 per cent of all food negotiations involved branded or heavily advertised foods, and on 21 per cent of occasions the child mentioned a brand by name. The researchers noted that when asked, 47.8 per cent of all requests were yielded to by parents, and yielding was equally likely for sweets or other foods. Most parents, when refusing the child's request, provided a soft reason, although ignoring the child or a stern refusal were witnessed as well. Occasions were observed where parents refused children's requests for fruit and vegetables and other healthier foods as well. Indeed children were actively engaged in the act of shopping, learning to read and name the fruits and vegetables and parents liked to encourage the children by asking them about foods. This study provides a clear view of the two-way power dynamic that structures domestic lifestyles as parents strive to teach children to be autonomous but self-regulating consumers. Many parents have learnt to countermand marketing risks by regulating TV use, by making their children aware of advertising and by negotiating with children while shopping about the nutritional value of foods.

As children approach their teens their consumer power increases as do their opportunities, scope and resources to take lifestyle risks. Although their nutritional knowledge is essential in evaluating the risks associated with diet

(Weiss and Kien 1987; Pirouznia 2001), surveys of teens have shown that despite the obesity pandemic in the news, courses at school and pro-health PSAs, most US adolescents lack sufficient understanding of body metabolism and diet (Keirle and Thomas 2000; Hart et al. 2002). UK studies have found that 10-year olds cannot evaluate snacks and drinks in terms of their caloric content (Halford et al. 2004, James et al. 2004). Marketing research on British teens suggests that many have an ill-formed conception of healthy eating, as well, and little awareness of nutritional guidelines. When pressed for explanations of snack food choices, Dixon found confusion in all age groups as to what constituted 'junk food'. Teens in this study snacked on chips and soft drinks because taste and brand preferences matter more than nutritional quality or price point. Given strong brand preferences and considerable discretionary power around snacking and leisure, perhaps heavy TV viewers' propensity to make unhealthier lifestyle choices is a result of their limited understanding of nutrition.

It is in the context of their empowerment as adolescent consumers that parental strategies for negotiating sedentary lifestyles and TV snacking habits get more complex (Marquis et al. 2005). Yet studies of adolescent nutrition knowledge and attitudes by Gracey et al. (1996) also found that teens' understanding of fats and energy intake were particularly deficient from a scientific point of view. As they remark, 'serious misconceptions indicated difficulties in translating nutrient advice into food choices'. Moreover, their survey of 391 11th-grade students revealed that this lack of understanding of nutrition was greatest in those teens at the lower SES schools and among those who watched the most TV. Although TV viewing was not associated with BMI or fat intake, the amount of fats consumed was related to their control over the foods purchased, heavy TV viewing, alcohol consumption and being male. Although these teens reported a fair degree of control over their food consumption, the barriers to better eating were perceived as parents' control over food at home rather than their own ignorance of health. Additionally, they note that the health beliefs, values and motives of these teens were gendered, with girls more interested in weight control and dieting than in fitness.

As we saw in Chapter 8, by educating children about nutrition and by cultivating a healthy taste in both food and activity many Canadian parents also seek to counter the seemingly corrosive influence of TV on their children's health. Although most parents encourage and support children's discretionary consumption, we have seen that their means of doing so differ. As children gain freedom, parental strategies for managing lifestyle risks associated with TV change. In addition to media literacy, many parents are communicating about the lifestyle risks associated with energy imbalance – particularly those associated with food preferences. Their parenting styles consist of a combination of restrictions, modelling and explanation that they hope will equip the child with the means of making healthy choices on their own. During adolescence, consumer socialization involves constant negotiation lodged in a power dynamic intended to produce autonomous self-regulating individuals. But teaching about a balanced lifestyle is no easy matter. And the result is rarely predictable.

Mitigating the disruptive screen: The Vancouver School Study

Research into 'obesogenic' families identified the risk factors associated with TV, whereas the Vancouver School Study noted that the strategies used by many British Columbian parents seemed to be effectively reducing their exposure to media risks by regulating its use. These children had fairly low rates of obesity (6 per cent), moderately good diets and enjoyed active leisure. In the following discussion I set out to explore the ways that cultivating a taste for healthy living, communicating about lifestyle risks to children and managing their discretionary consumption can support children's development of balanced lifestyles in the media-saturated family. To this end we asked children aged 8–12 about how their parents influenced their snacking and leisure choices. Children generally reported they had a modest say in family meals but were given greater influence in the selection of cereals, snacks and treats. Although many had their media use regulated, they were also freer to choose toys and sports. And when it came to their pocket money, most reported having considerable discretionary power.

Scales were developed to identify three aspects of this family power dynamic. The first was the degree to which children felt their parents controlled the decisions about foods and snacks. The second was the degree to which children felt they could influence their own consumption of snacks. Third was the degree to which they felt their parents responded positively to the requests they made. These scales were used to classify the power dynamic from the child's point of view. Permissive parents were seen as encouraging their children's freedom of choice. In mandated families, children felt their food choices were largely governed by the rules and restrictions imposed on them. In negotiated families, children felt their parents talked to them and made trade-offs according to a variety of criteria including nutritional considerations. Overall the dominant parenting style was negotiated (52 per cent of families), while 17 per cent of the children reported permissive parents and 30 per cent said their parents largely provision and choose all food and snacks.

Obviously, consumer empowerment is a power dynamic in which children are granted influence within familial decision making and control over their own lifestyles. In Figure 9.1 we can see it is a gradual process in which parents widen the scope of children's consumption opportunities while coaching them about making healthy snacking choices and discretionary purchases. The strategies preferred by most of their parents included restricting the foods available for snacks (70 percent), talking to children about nutrition (66 per cent) and encouraging them to develop a taste for healthier foods like fruit and vegetables. It involves considerable negotiation with a singular goal: to help children make healthy food choices for themselves. No parenting style is pure, however: in all types of family, children reported having some influence and power to choose for themselves, which increases as they acquire more money and demonstrate more and more responsibility and understanding. For this reason, an indicator of nutritional self-regulation was constructed by combining items that indicated children's use of labels and their reporting of nutrition-based food choices as well as indexes of their preferences for fruit and vegetables and for energy-dense snacks.

We asked students about the basis of their own choices to determine to what extent nutrition and health considerations entered into their own decision processes. Although 80 per cent reported making decisions on taste and 17 per cent because of brand, 30 per cent also made choices on nutritional value, 15 per cent considered parental advice and 13 per cent chose snacks based on whatever was available at home. We, therefore, cannot assume that all children are unaware of the importance of mindful eating. Indeed, over half the children consider nutrition important and 30 per cent reported examining the label to ensure their chosen snack food was healthy. In light of these findings, we cannot assume that all of children's discretionary choices are completely without consideration of nutritional knowledge, or guided by branded preferences alone.

Cultivating a taste for healthy foods

Children's preferences for different branded foods is central to the problem of consumer socialization in the promotional marketplace (Robinson et al. 2007). Their choices are based on the liking for the branded product. Children who are allowed to choose for themselves reported taste as the reason for choosing snacks more and said they get what they want in the supermarket more often than those that are restrained. They also watched TV more, were more likely to snack while watching, and when they have opportunity to buy treats for themselves, they tended to choose less healthy ones. Those parents who mandated and negotiated children's selections, however, enjoyed multiple and seemingly interacting benefits: their children watched TV less, had greater nutritional awareness and made healthier snacking choices when snacks were bought with their own money. They also developed a taste for fruit and vegetables, whereas children who chose for themselves preferred energy-dense treats.

I have already mentioned that the daily diet of these Canadian children was moderately healthy. Despite their bombardment with cereal advertising, for example, just over half reported eating cereal regularly. From a health standpoint, their breakfasts were nutritionally okay: less than a quarter of the children breakfasted on highly sugared cereals, but the rest ate wholesome cereals, bacon and eggs, rice and kimchi, pancakes or porridge, which are considered a 'balanced' morning meal. Their lunches, largely chosen by their parents, too, also proved reasonable: a sandwich was typical with a few mentioning fast food or convenience foods (noodle, KD). Juice, water, yoghurt and especially fruit are mentioned often, with chips, candy and treats being less common. The reason was similar to TV usage, most of the foods they ate were supervised by parents: only 9 per cent of children reported that their parents bought them what they wanted to eat while 58 per cent said they never did. Overall, it seems, these Vancouver families enforce nutritional regimes and discuss healthy eating well into adolescence, which reduces the risks associated with TV marketing.

By modelling, talking about and mandating good nutrition, many British Columbian parents also seem to be gradually cultivating a taste for healthy foods (see Figure 9.1). When we asked children about their preferences for snacks we found that ice cream was on top (1.5) with fruit close behind (1.76) – both ahead of chips and chocolate. Cereal (2.33), vegetables (2.35) and bread

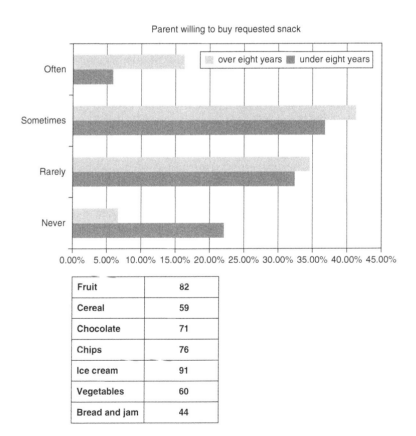

Fruit	82
Cereal	59
Chocolate	71
Chips	76
Ice cream	91
Vegetables	60
Bread and jam	44

Figure 9.1 Parenting and taste for healthy snacks as protective factors in snacking

and jam (2.90) were rated less favourably, perhaps indicating an overall preference for sweetness rather than savouriness. In light of the arguments about junk food advertising overriding a taste for fruits and vegetables, we note in this sample the relatively high popularity of fruits and vegetables: 43 per cent of children expressed a very positive attitude to fruit and vegetables, whereas only 46 per cent had a clear preference for the energy-dense side of the snacking spectrum – chocolate, chips and ice cream. The only gender difference in snack preferences was for fruit, which girls preferred significantly more than boys.

Media, eating rituals and snacking

The rituals that link eating and media seem to be well established – whether it is popcorn for a film or a beer and chips while watching the Super Bowl. Although family meals are largely chosen by parents, children's eating rituals are more flexible. Ten per cent eat breakfast in front of the TV every day, and 44 per cent do so often or sometimes. When it comes to eating dinner in front of the tube, although 55 per cent say they rarely or never do it, 45 per cent report they do it sometimes or often. TV snacking was most reported as an after-school activity – linked with the moment of relaxed freedom from school, with friends or siblings in front of the TV. Nearly two-thirds (64 per cent) of children snack while watching TV sometimes or often, and 9.3 per cent said they do so most days. Only 14 per cent said they never did so. Although the list varied greatly, it is worth noting that in an open-ended question about their preferred TV snacks, fruit, juice, bread and jam, cereal and popcorn figured equally with chips, candy and pizza pops.

Clearly children's consumer empowerment is associated with snacking. Even in the most traditional of families, snacking is the eating behaviour in which parents seek to teach self-regulation. With this in mind, we examined the week-long snacking diaries for the kinds of foods children ate in relationship to the activities undertaken. We found that eating while watching TV is the most common occasion for snacking. A snack or drink after sports is the second most-reported snacking occasion. Not all media, however, are equally associated with food. For example, heavy video gamers or Internet surfers rarely report snacking during their media use. In this sense, the formation of discretionary risk is linked with heavy TV viewing. 13 per cent reported that most days they chose their own TV snacks, while another 57 per cent reported that they sometimes or often chose the household snacks, remembering that their discretionary food choices were influenced by branded TV advertising, and perhaps, the limits of their parents' concerted attempts to cultivate a taste for 'healthy'.

Cultivating nutritional knowledge

Perhaps more than media literacy, teaching children about nutrition seems to be a way of mitigating the risks associated with TV advertising. Many parents see mealtime as an opportunity to teach children about nutrition as well as solicit dietary preferences. So too shopping excursions provide opportunities for consumer socialization. They are also occasions where children are allowed a say in the family diet. Only 8 per cent of children said they were never allowed to pick snacks while shopping. A scale was constructed that distinguished nutrition-conscious children from those who used brand and taste as their criteria for choosing a food. The food-aware index grouped children who reported that they were mindful of nutrition and read labels when making discretionary snack choices. Whereas 24 per cent were nutritionally savvy, 34 per cent reported that they never or rarely bothered about nutrition in making their food selections. Nutrition-conscious children, although in the minority, were more likely to report preferences for healthy foods (fruit and vegetables) and like treat foods (chocolate, ice cream and chips) less. Yet they were no different in their liking of cereal and bread and jam. However, nutrition-conscious children also spent more time with screen media, including TV and the Internet. Their interest in healthy food may be a buffer against the TV diet. Although they watch more TV, they are less likely to report feeling hungry when they see a food ad, wanting to buy the advertised product or asking their parents for it. Moreover, they snack significantly less while using media, and when they do, the snack is healthier.

Parenting style also matters when it comes to nutritionally informed choices, as 56 per cent of children from mandated households were high in nutritional awareness, whereas only 15 per cent of permissive children were. Mandated children are less likely to report snacking while watching TV or hanging out with friends, whereas the permissive and negotiated children are more likely to snack and eat during media use. Children of permissive families also report snacking at other times during the day more. Their lack of health consciousness is implicated in the foods children generally eat while watching TV. In families where parents controlled snack food availability, children were more nutrition conscious and liked fruit and vegetables more. This result implies that parental insistence on good nutrition may increase those children's liking of these foods. Perhaps the strategy of letting children choose snacks from healthy alternatives helps to mitigate the risks associated with TV snacking. Neither age nor gender was significantly related to the practice of nutrition-based choices or the liking of fruit and vegetables, although trends followed the expected direction. Girls were slightly more food conscious and liked fruit and vegetables more.

Although the data provided no evidence that frequent TV watching was related to the health rating of snacks eaten while viewing, it was noticed that media use was positively associated with snacking while watching (.235). This makes sense (see Figure 9.2). Those children who are heavy users have more bouts of media use in which to eat. But we also noted that frequent TV snackers chose the snack foods in their homes more (r = .375),

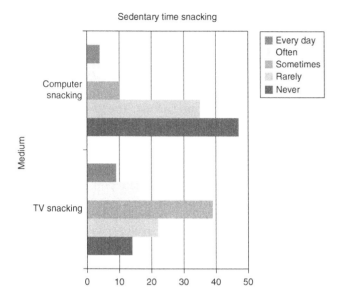

Figure 9.2   Eating behaviours which are differentially related to media use

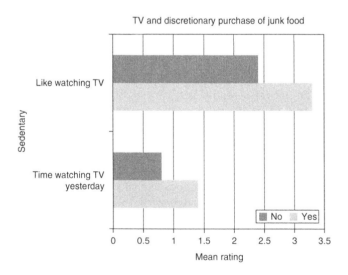

Figure 9.3   Liking and watching TV as risk factors in discretionary choice

and the nutritional quality of their snacks tended to be worse ($r = .237$). Of the snacks children chose for themselves only 17 per cent were either healthy or moderately healthy (see Figure 9.3). An examination of TV snack foods indicated why, for some children, TV snacking could be a source of excessive calories: while 57 per cent of children's snacking foods were very or moderately healthy, 29 per cent fell into the low-health category and 18 per cent were rated as junk foods. This implies that heavy media usage may contribute indirectly to the poor nutrition of children in those households where children are given licence to choose snacks for themselves and watch TV more. A child's access to television therefore becomes a key factor in their exposure to multiple lifestyle risks. For this reason parenting style matters.

Discretionary leisure and media

It is not just healthy provisioning and risk literacy that contributes to students' low rates of obesity in British Columbia. The survey suggests that many Vancouver children have developed a healthy preference for active leisure. 45 per cent report liking sports and exercise a lot; 48 per cent like such activities to an extent and only 7 per cent do not like them very much. But both their leisure preferences and their levels of activity are gendered. This 'taste' for active leisure is a step in the direction of active lifestyles, too (Bar-Or 2000). Those who liked sports and outdoor play spent more time in active pursuits whereas those that liked media and sedentary activities spent more time indoors with screen media, books and toys. Based on week-long activity diaries, 40 per cent are engaged in active leisure for more than 90 minutes daily. Their daily activity levels and enjoyment of outdoor play seems to be a protective factor. Only one in four children gets less than 30 minutes of active play each day. Leisure preferences however are gendered: 44 per cent of boys and 35 per cent of girls are highly active whereas 16 per cent of boys and 35 per cent of girls are spending less than 30 minutes a day in active pursuits. This means girls fail to receive as much moderate exercise on a daily basis.

Total sedentary time was also calculated by including time spent reading, playing with toys and playing video games. The after-school routines of media use seem to be implicated in children's development of sedentary preferences. Those that watch TV a lot develop a subjective preference for other 'indoor' low-energy activities like playing games, listening to music, video and other indoor games and just hanging around with friends. For these children, TV is the precipitating factor. Those that use other media watch TV more as well. Their total media use was inversely related to their liking of active leisure (r = .240). Gender preferences were predictable among the most sedentary children. Sedentary boys like playing sports, too, whereas girls enjoy shopping, talking with friends and doing homework. Although boys watch more TV than girls, 56 per cent of the heavy viewing boys are also active, whereas 58 per cent of the heavy viewing girls are inactive.

The importance of habitual TV viewing in the development of sedentary lifestyles was also indicated through an analysis of their leisure time allocations and preferences. Those children who watched TV after school tended to watch more TV overall, use media more and develop a preference for sedentary leisure activities. Factor analysis of these leisure preferences yielded a model which accounted for 34 per cent of the variance in all leisure activities. 20 per cent of the variance was accounted for by TV related items, 9 per cent by their liking for and participation in active sports and 3 per cent by the time they spent video gaming or using the Internet. Moreover the preference for other sedentary activities like reading, listening to music and indoor play was strongly correlated with the routine of watching TV after school ($r = .442$), whereas their preference for sports and outdoor play was negatively correlated with TV after school ($r = .347$). Yet fewer than 10 per cent of this sample uses media for more than three hours per day – often considered the cut-off point associated with health risks – possibly because of restrictions imposed on media time by parents.

As I have said, most of children's sedentary leisure is accounted for by TV viewing, although other screen media contribute as well. Children who watched a lot of TV *and* who played video games spent significantly less time in moderately active leisure. Even given their light viewing schedules, the study finds some evidence of a complex trade-off between a liking for sedentary leisure (media, indoor play, hanging out with friends and shopping) and time spent in active leisure (biking, hiking and sports). Yet a simple substitution of sedentary for active leisure is not found. Whereas 32 per cent of the most sedentary children are inactive (suggesting a displacement effect), 48 per cent of them are highly active. This means half of the sample is both watching TV and exercising regularly. And whereas 13 per cent of the least sedentary are inactive, 20 per cent of them are very active, indicating that they use the time away from media for exercise. Indeed, 16 per cent of all children were both moderately active and moderately sedentary.

When trade-offs between sedentary lifestyles and active leisure were examined separately by gender, it was found that gender differences are involved in displacement effects. Looking only at the most sedentary children we see that 35 per cent of females are inactive but only 16 per cent of boys are. Yet it is also evident that many active children include some TV viewing in their daily routines; 25 per cent of active girls and 33 per cent of active boys are also heavy viewers. TV viewing seems to displace active leisure for the heaviest viewing girls only. Whereas 12 per cent of the inactive males were heavy viewers, 38 per cent of the inactive girls were. Moreover 85 per cent of the girls who watch a normal amount of TV are moderately active yet only 15 per cent of the heavy viewing girls are moderately active. If parents fail to support their natural tendency to play or fail to curtail their sedentary leisure, girls are more likely to displace active living with sedentary substitutes.

Lifestyle risks, TV and discretionary power

As we have seen in Chapter 8, parents' management of lifestyle risks vary. Those who value active leisure negotiate media use more, whereas food-oriented families are both more concerned about media and restrict media use more. Children who watch more TV tend to be less physically active, watch more TV after school, like TV food ads more and have lower health rating for the foods they eat while watching as well as for the snacks they choose themselves. But the challenge is to enable children to make healthy decisions for themselves. Obviously, no parenting style is without its problems. Parents don't apply the same strategies all the time and each can backfire. It became evident through this analysis that restrictions and freedom are two dimensions of consumer socialization and each operates differently. Yet the evidence shows that freedom to choose, clear rules and educational efforts can all have protective impact on children's lifestyle choices. Children who choose snacks because parents prefer them or because of their nutritional value do choose healthier foods when they purchase with their own money. Moreover, allowing children to choose is not always a bad strategy. Children who are allowed to watch TV during breakfast, to snack while viewing and to exert influence on parents while shopping are significantly more likely to choose a snack based on taste rather than on nutrition, but their tastes are in fact healthier than those who don't.

The research reported in the previous chapter suggested that the way children choose to spend their pocket money is related to their TV viewing. Those that watch TV often buy more toys but fewer snack foods – a result that might indicate their preferences in spending are influenced by the weight of advertising for playthings and media. The implication is that TV advertising can, from a risk point of view, be as responsible for developing sedentary lifestyles as fast food diets. Parenting style seems to have little impact on children's discretionary choices other than the fact that children in permissive families spend more of their own money on active leisure rather than toys. This suggests that when children are allowed to choose leisure freely, they prefer to spend on active rather than sedentary play. It is interesting to note, therefore, that although this choice is not related to parents' valuing of sports and active leisure, parents of children who spend their own money on play are significantly less concerned about the displacement effects of TV on children's exercise and social life. In giving some children the chance to choose outdoor play, permissive parents may be supporting healthy choices in their children to moderate heavy viewing. Although permissive families empower children to take risks (their children watch TV more, snack while watching, eat dinner in front of the TV and successfully use pester power), they are no more likely to make discretionary food purchases.

Un-confounding the multiple risk factors associated with teen empowerment

I have argued that panicked journalism and advocacy sciences emphasized the health risks associated with children's consumption of fast food because children are deemed 'vulnerable' to marketing. Yet as children get older, they gain discretionary powers to consume. As they enter their teens the mitigating influences of family diminish. Unlike younger children whose daily routines are regimented by family surveillance and lifestyle restrictions, teens' lifestyles vary with their social circumstances and leisure preferences. Some stay home listening to music and smoking dope while others are out at the mall shopping or playing on sports teams. Discretionary snacking and eating out of the home are more widely practised in the teen population. No longer under the tight control of their parents, most teenagers have sufficient money and freedom to establish their own lifestyles. The debates about obesity have emphasized the fact that most teens are advertising literate, have some knowledge of marketing and are responsible for some of their own spending. But are they competent consumers fully capable of managing the risk-cost-benefits calculus required in the risk society?

As children graduate from childhood into their teens, the incidence of obesity rises from 9 to 14 per cent. Many studies indicate that TV viewing increases during the early teens too. The YRBS data show the persistence of high levels of TV watching in American teens. 39 per cent of teens watched TV more than 3 hours per day which increased their rates of obesity from 12.4 to 17.9 per cent (odds ratio for excessive TV use is 1.55). Heavy TV viewing is also associated with other risky choices. Heavy TV viewers develop a liking of screen entertainments, play video games and spend more time with media. They eat less fruit and vegetables, participate in sports less and fail to sustain 60 minutes of active leisure five times a week. In watching TV more, they are also exposed to food advertising and they are far more likely to drink soft drinks daily. Yet, as we have seen, advertising provides a limited explanation of teens' weight status. This is not to imply that TV advertising is not a risk factor but rather to point out that its impact on the teen diet is marginal and their own potential to mitigate risks is considerable.

Researchers have shown that eating sufficient fruit and vegetables and getting exercise can be protective factors mitigating TV's effects. The YRBS data provide evidence that those who eat fruit and vegetables daily are 1.6 per cent less likely to be at risk of obesity (OR = .86). Analysis indicates that regular vigorous exercise can be a protective factor in weight gain (see Figure 9.4). So, too, playing team sports (OR = .692) and being active on a daily basis (OR = .713) are both protective factors potentially counteracting the increased sedentariness associated with heavy TV viewing. Thanks to parental guidance and media panic, many teens are aware of the risks that are associated with TV, namely a junk food diet and lack of exercise. A healthy

Risk factor	Per cent obese	Per cent obese	OR (odds ratio for risk factor)
Drink 4 + sodas	17.8	14.2	1.2
Eat 5 + fruit and vegetables daily	15.9	14.3	1.13
Play team sports	12.5	17.1	.692
Active 60 minutes	11.9	16.0	.713

Figure 9.4 Protective factors in the US teen population

	Lighter viewers	Heavy viewers
Total media use 6 + hrs/ day	34.4	78.5
Video games 3 + hrs/ day	18	35.6
Drank soda 1 / day	28.4	43.4
Ate 5 + fruit and vegetables	22.3	21.1
Played on sports teams	57.1	49.9
Active 60 minutes	35.7	30

Figure 9.5 Risky behaviours also related to heavy TV viewing

diet and regular activity are lifestyle decisions that most teens know reduce the risks of obesity. Yet most of them are 'discretionary risk takers'. Eight in ten (80 per cent) teens do not eat the five recommended servings of vegetables a day, 68 per cent do not get sufficient physical activity and 54.3 per cent use media for more than 6 hours every day. It can therefore be legitimately said that many teens put themselves at risk through lifestyle choices they make for themselves.

In this sense, the obesity risks experienced by teen populations is coincidental with the lessening of family supervision and their own increasing discretionary power over their leisure and snacks. The YRBS data also suggests that the decline in protective behaviours is especially linked to teens' TV viewing (see Figure 9.5). Analysis of this data set also shows that teens who watch TV more significantly exercise less and drink more soft drinks. This suggests that while teens may be aware of the health benefits of fruit and exercise, they may not understand that TV viewing itself fosters sedentary leisure and encourages ritualized snacking in front of the TV or cultivates a sedentary lifestyle in the long run. As noted previously, while soft drink consumption is only marginally related to obesity, its excessive consumption is highest among heavy viewing teens. Those teens who watch TV most put themselves at risk by consuming fewer fruit and vegetables (OR = 1.13) – perhaps because of the TV snacks they substitute for fruit.

But few hard and fast rules can be formulated about the obesogenic choices of teens because the mitigating behaviours are not uniformly experienced across the teen population (see Figure 9.6). Gender, ethnic background and SES define important aspects of households in which discretionary risk patterns develop most. Indeed the continuation of protective behaviours into the teen years seems to depend on social circumstances and family background: African and Hispanics are at greater risk of obesity (18.5 per cent) compared with white teens (10.8 per cent at risk), largely because of their heavier TV viewing and lack of salad eating. White teens tend to be more active and play more sports counteracting their tendency to watch TV more and eat fruit and vegetables less. So, too, girls are generally at lower risk of obesity (11 per cent) than boys (18 per cent), although they are less active and eat fewer fruit and vegetables – patterns which are accentuated among the heaviest viewing teens. For this reason, I caution readers against reductionist readings of the complex consequences of teen empowerment implied in the interactions between time spent in TV viewing, demographics and discretionary risk taking.

The teens' development of a pattern of sedentary leisure is perhaps the most interesting and complex of this interactions. I have noted that sedentary entertainment is a lifestyle preference that 51 per cent of teens choose. Moreover males seem to develop sedentary patterns most (see Figure 9.7). These 'screenagers' who use media more than 6 hours per day were more at risk (17.5 per cent) than moderate media users (11.5 per cent). The protective effect of moderate screen use had an OR of .611 and girl screenagers more than doubled their risks of obesity suggesting that screen dependence displaces activity most in females.

There is little evidence that digital media use has supplanted TV viewing. Although it has been occasionally suggested that a fascination with sport on TV and identification with sports celebrities can inspire active participation, the evidence suggests the opposite is generally true. Heavy viewers not only play on fewer sports teams than light viewers but are less likely to be active more than 60 minutes each day. Teens who watch more TV gradually find their interest in active leisure (and the time available to pursue sports) diminished. Yet the displacement of activity for sedentary leisure is gendered. While heavy TV viewing barely interferes with male rates of sports participation (40 per cent vs. 37 per cent who don't play), among females 56 per cent of heavy viewers compared with

	Afro/Hispanic	White	OR for at risk group
5 + fruit/vegetables	23.5	18.9	1.16 White at risk
Daily soda	35.8	33.6	1.10 A/H at risk
TV 3 + hrs.	54.5	27.4	1.18 A/H at risk
Video games 3 + hrs.	27.2	22	1.16 A/H at risk
Team sports	50.6	58.6	1.16 A/H at risk
Active 60 min.	29.1	37.2	1.18 A/H at risk
Ate no salad	44.9	30.5	1.38 A/H at risk
Exercise to lose weight	55.9	62.4	1.14 A/H at risk
Eat to lose weight	34.2	43.4	1.19 A/H at risk
Overweight	18.5	10.8	1.36 A/H at risk

	Female	Male	OR for at risk group
5 + fruit/vegetables	20	24	1.15 female at risk
Daily soda	30	39	1.2 male at risk
TV 3 + hrs.	38	41	1.12 male at risk
Video games 3 + hrs.	201	29	1.24 male at risk
Team sports	48	60.5	1.29 female at risk
Active 60 min.	25	42	1.44 female at risk
Ate no salad	33	41	1.18 male at risk
Exercise to lose weight	64	56	1.18 male at risk
Eat to lose weight	51	29	1.55 male at risk
Overweight	11	18	1.28 male at risk

Figure 9.6 Risky behaviours also related to ethnicity and gender

46 per cent of light viewers, do not participate in sports teams. It would seem that TV viewing not only fails to inspire the sporting life but accentuates the propensity among girls to discontinue playing on sports teams in favour of media.

	Lite Meda Use	Screenagers	Total
Boys	15.1%	21.4%	17.9%
Girls	6.7%	14.4%	11.1%

Figure 9.7   Screenagers at risk: Interrelation of gender and media use in teen obesity

	> 3 hours TV	< 3 hours TV	OR TV
Female teens	14.5	9.3	1.66
Male teens	21.1	15.8	1.42

	Active / TV	Not active /TV	Active/ No TV	Not active/ No TV
Female	11.9/	15.3	5.6	10.6
Male	18.0	23.5	13.8	18.2
OR activity (female)	.751		.498	
OR activity (male)	.713		.712	

Figure 9.8   Gender differences in activity levels as a protective factor in the relationship between TV and obesity

So too, the protective benefits of regular exercise is gender dependent (see Figure 9.8). Only 25.1 per cent of girls report daily 60-minute workouts compared with 42 per cent of boys. Yet risk analysis suggests that girls who exercise regularly are protecting themselves more from obesity by significantly lowering their BMIs. But for males, there is no similar weight reduction resulting from daily vigorous exercise. Although males exercise vigorously more often, the benefits of exercise are less noticeable. Exercise seems to be a protective factor for girls more than for boys, which perhaps explains why, although 21 per cent of male heavy viewers are obese, only 14.5 per cent of female heavy viewers are. The extremely low rates of obesity (5.6 per cent) among highly active girls who also view little TV implies 'protective' effects of resisting the lure of media are considerable.

Indeed, male teens seem to have a reputation for being risk takers. However savvy they seem, few teens seem to take seriously the long-term health risks associated with cigarettes, food, sex or drugs. Indeed, for US teens, risk taking seems to be part of their lifestyles: 18.5 per cent carry a weapon, 23 per cent smoke regularly, 35.9 per cent get into fights each year, 43.3 per cent drink regularly and 46.8 per cent engage in intercourse – often with no protection or contraception. When risk analysts tally the mortality risks, they find that car accidents, homicide and suicide are the major killers of the young. Compared to car accidents, gangs and drugs, eating fries and drinking Coke while watching TV seems like, well, small potatoes.

Clearly their growing awareness of lifestyle risks is having an impact on teens' lives. Although, like cigarettes and drugs, the health consequences of being overweight disappear into the fog that envelopes the end of their lifespan, the psychological consequences of adiposity are abundantly evident to them. Whether they read newspapers or not, most teens are keenly aware that their weight gain is a social problem. Nearly three in 10 (29.6 per cent) teens define themselves as overweight, although this perception is not scientifically accurate. Whereas 83.6 per cent of teens with BMI > 95 percentile see themselves as overweight, 75 per cent of normal BMI see themselves as normal weight. Girls are much more likely to misapprehend their weight status than boys.

Although the press's highlighting of obesity creates stress and anxiety, it also propels behavioural adjustments. YRBS data also indicate that many teens are attempting to lose weight by managing their diet and by exercise. Six in ten (59 per cent) teens in this survey report exercising to lose weight, 39 per cent eat less to lose weight and 5.6 per cent take a pill to lose weight. These weight control attempts differ according to gender, ethnicity, weight status and self-concept. Naturally those who feel overweight are more likely to report attempts at weight reduction than those who say their weight is normal. Six in ten (61 per cent) overweight teens eat less to lose weight and 77.8 per cent exercise to lose weight. Far fewer of normal weight teens report consciously doing either. The methods differ based on gender, too: girls are more likely to use dieting and pills to control weight gain whereas boys prefer exercising. Seven in ten (70.7 per cent) overweight females eat less to lose weight whereas only 56.8 per cent of overweight males do. But when it comes to exercise, male teens are keener. Eight in ten (80.6 per cent) obese males control their weight through staying active. Their attempts at weight regulation depend on many demographic factors such as age, ethnicity and SES. Afro and Hispanic males are least likely to use either method although they are most at risk.

Obesity is itself a psychological risk factor (see Figure 9.9). Obese teens are significantly more likely to feel depressed and to contemplate suicide: 17.5 per cent of obese teens consider suicide whereas 14.6 per cent of teens with normal BMI do. And here perceptions matter more than reality since 20.3 per cent of teens who feel overweight consider suicide – nearly double the 11.6 per cent of those contemplating suicide who see their weight as

Suicidal thoughts last month		Value
Female	Odds Ratio (obese/normal)	.424
	Low media users	.570
	Screenagers	1.345
	No. of valid cases	6230
Male	Odds Ratio (obese/normal)	.655
	Low media users	.816
	Screenagers	1.245
	No. of valid cases	6270

Figure 9.9   Obesity as a psychological risk factor related to gender (suicidal thoughts)

normal. TV viewing interacts with perceptions of weight status: Heavy viewers of normal weight see themselves as obese more than light viewers (26.6 vs. 24 per cent). Playing on sports teams is the only mitigating factor as it makes teens less likely to consider suicide.

Taken together, the research reported above supports the notion that today's youth acquire considerable consumer power. By the time they are teens they spend more money than previous generations, they are more knowledgeable about a wider range of brands and marketing techniques and they have plenty of say in what their families consume. In many cases, even young children can research their purchases on the Internet, consult with peers and save continuously for a treasured purchase. Yet to say that youth have been empowered by the marketplace to define themselves and their lifestyles, relative to earlier generations, does not imply that they are fully rational consumer subjects. Despite parents' efforts at media regulation and consumer socialization, not all children are sceptical about advertising, are cognitively capable of comparing different products on multiple attributes or knowledgeable about health and safety risks associated with long-term consumption of risky goods, like guns, fast foods, tobacco, alcohol and drugs. And as their families expand their scope, teens, like adults, become discretionary risk takers. In this respect, I suggest that it is time to put the 'responsible and choosing' child consumer back in the context of the complex process of lifestyle socialization. *Children come to make their own risky consumer choices, but not in contexts of their own choosing.* Both family negotiations and the market culture have been significantly galvanized by this medical controversy, which has made the fast food diets and sedentary lifestyles of youth into the mirror of adult lifestyles.

A precautionary politic of hope: Turning off the screen not the ads

Epidemiologists have shown that ethnicity, gender, region and socio-economic status are all sociocultural factors related to the distribution of weight gain in paediatric populations. Indeed, the scientific literature is quite clear that what puts youth at risk is unhealthy lifestyle. Child obesity results from an imbalance of energy intake over expenditure, sustained over long periods. Imbalance results from the regular consumption of energy-dense foods or from reduced activity levels, or both. This is why familial choices put children at risk – or mitigate them. Even a snack of 120 calories more a day eaten while watching cartoons can result in 1 kilogram of excess weight when sustained for over a year and without a parallel increase in energy expended.

Recognizing the constellation of health risks associated with heavy media consumption, Gortmaker et al. (1996) evaluated the effectiveness of the two-year Planet Health programme, which targeted decreasing television viewing among grade 6 and 7 students. This research explored the argument that if heavy TV viewing put teens at risk, then lessening TV consumption should reduce those risks. Controlling for baseline obesity, these researchers found that the programme reduced the overall prevalence of obesity among girls, but not boys. The intervention reduced television hours among both girls and boys, resulting in both lower total energy intake and increased fruit and vegetable consumption among girls. Yet it was only among girls that there was a significant reduction in the prevalence of obesity for each hour less of viewing. The researchers, however, were not able to determine if this benefit accrued from higher energy expenditure or improved diet. Moreover, it was unclear why reduced media consumption did not have a similar effect on the weight status or activity levels of boys.

A study from Stanford University, researching the relationship between television viewing and weight, set out to measure body weight differences between two sets of third and fourth graders. One group was taught how to lessen their time watching television and playing video games. The second group received no such instruction. For the first group, the instruction sought to establish a seven-hour-a-week limit on television and video game time. It was theorized that watching less television could free up to 14 hours for children to do something else – particularly engage in active leisure. The results showed that the children who watched less television and played fewer video games had a significant reduction in measures of obesity, such as BMI. The children who watched their usual amount of television experienced both BMI gain and skin fold thickness increase. The only difference between the two groups was the amount of television and video game playing they engaged in (Robinson 1999).

A follow-up study undertaken in California used an in-school media education programme designed to intervene in the sedentary lifestyle of children, which reduced the time students spent watching films, TV and playing video games by one-third. Robinson's (2000) controlled experiment revealed not only that media consumption was reduced by the media education treatment but that rates of weight gain were significantly slower (measured by BMI and skin fold thickness) in the treatment compared to control schools. Robinson's study confirmed that a school-based prevention strategy that reduces TV viewing can lessen the risks of overweight in children. Yet on closer examination, measurement issues leave it uncertain why students at the experimental schools gained weight more slowly than the control group. Although lower rates of BMI growth were found at the experimental school, these changes occurred without significant reduction in daily servings of high fat foods, highly advertised foods, snacking or increases in activity levels. Only the reduced number of meals or snacks eaten in front of the television was associated with slower weight gain. Unfortunately, Robinson does not report what percentage of children ate while viewing or analyse what happens in families that don't regularly eat in front of the TV.

Adapting Robinson's media education strategy for Canadian schools, Kline (2005) undertook a six-week media risk reduction intervention involving 178 students in North Vancouver elementary schools. These students voluntarily reduced their media use by 80 per cent during the Tune Out the Screen test week. Their media use, snacking habits and free time activities (active leisure and sedentary play) were monitored by means of a week-long media audit and activity diary..

Using each subject as their own control, this before–after comparison found children's overall media use was dramatically reduced through voluntary 'tune out' by 100 minutes Kline et al. (2006). The programme provided not only education about the lifestyle choices related to health but the subjects were given support for active play. The results showed that with family, peer and teacher encouragement, the sedentary time made available each day by children's reduced TV viewing was often converted to active outdoor leisure. Children were twice as likely to choose active outdoor pursuits as passive indoor pastimes when give the opportunity to choose. The study indicated that in children aged 7–10, time spent with video games and TV tends to be at the expense of active leisure. The heaviest media consumers, therefore, experienced greater benefit from turning off their TV sets and video games. Moreover, by measuring leisure preferences, the study found no evidence that those children who were heavy viewers of sports and identified with sports heroes had less sedentary lifestyles, or responded differently during the 'tune-out' week. Unfortunately no measures of energy intake, food preferences or body mass were gathered in this study. But the finding here corroborates those of others (Veugelers and Fitzgerald 2005) demonstrating the simple point that because heavy media use is related to weight status for multiple reasons, anything that reduces the time children spend using media is bound to have positive implications for their weight status – exposing them to fewer food commercials, releasing free time for active leisure and limiting the habit of snacking or dining while watching.

10
Conclusion

Following Ulrich Beck, I have tried to trace the part played by 'environmental risk analysis' in the discursive politics of globesity. Paralleling Beck's emphasis on ecological advocacy in the environmental politics, I have set out to document the growing importance of risk sciences within the discursive politics of child empowerment through a case study of the 'globesity pandemic'. Beck's optimism about reflexive modernity was founded on his belief that the struggles over environmentalism were ultimately producing awareness of the unsustainability of the industrial economy. Although Beck well understood that the market economy was a complex system of risk distribution, he failed to pay attention to the complicity of citizens in risk allocation decisions through their consumption practices. What I have called lifestyle risks are produced by corporations but also consumed by citizens in the course of their daily choices. As the case of global warming illustrates, mitigating climate change depends not only on climate science but its acceptance within a democratic politics of lifestyle change. So too with the health issues flagged by globesity, which as my comparative case study has shown, depended on anxieties about media-saturated domesticity and the discursive politics galvanized by food marketing to children.

This case study started by noting the importance of epidemiological analysis as the trigger for this scientific advocacy in both the US and the UK. I have traced how the health advocates' epidemic framing successfully propelled weight gain up the risk agenda. In the process, some risks became misinterpreted, and alternative ways of addressing the health problems marginalized. In the press the advocate's emphasis on a bad diet overstated the risks of child obesity and deflected attention from the protective role of active play for children's health. Some have argued, therefore, that the potential of reflexive modernization is thus undermined by sensationalistic journalism which distorts the public's perception of risks. Yet the trends in BMI were dramatized and the scientific terms of calories, weight status and 'risk factor' have entered into the popular lexicon. Nutritional recommendations (five servings of fruit and vegetables a day; 35 per cent caloric intake from fat) and healthy eating generally have been widely promoted, and the long-term costs of weight gain to the health system have found their way onto the policy agenda. As an impetus to science education, the globesity pandemic seems to have been a success. The once hidden population health perspective on weight gain entered the daily lexicon. Ordinary citizens can be expected to know about the 'lifestyle risks' associated with daily fast food and soft drink consumption – if they didn't know before.

Risk science is complex. Measures like BMI provide a limited way of measuring the multiple interacting pathogenic and mitigating processes which contribute to ill health. Epidemiology itself also pathologizes body morphology and medicalizes discourses on lifestyle choices. To risk science, obesity is simply a diagnostic category of body morphology, but to obese individuals it is experienced as a psychological risk. As noted earlier, there are a number of good psycho-physiological reasons why obese people are more likely to experience stress, depression and feelings of being out of control. As body weight increases, it takes more effort to be active, self-esteem erodes, stress and hypertension increase and the resulting depression can lead to comfort eating. Worrying about one's body can be a risk factor too, compounding the health problems experienced by the overweight.

Press debates about obesity pathologized overweight as an abnormality and singled out children as the most at risk. In doing so it both normalized a particular ideal body and censured deviation from the norms. It therefore contributed to the broader social perception of the body and the ideas surrounding healthy children's development, both by the medical professionals who wield the diagnosis and by individuals who experience the force of this medical injunction in the context of public risk controversy. Individuals who are overweight, especially women already concerned about beauty, can suffer a lack of self-esteem, which in turn often contributes to stress and depression. Stress and depression are also medical conditions, which can have important health consequences too as we saw in teen populations, not only taking a toll on their subjective well-being but contributing to health care costs. The medicalization of weight gain can be particularly problematic for children. An 'iatrogenic' effect – that is risks induced by the diagnostic category – can itself be a problem. In 2008 this became an issue in the UK, as intensified monitoring of BMI in the schools was considered a potential for victimization of children as 'fatties' (Hawkes 2008).

Perhaps more problematically, the attention to vulnerable children minimized the perceived risks to other populations – particularly parents and teenagers who are deemed competent to make their own lifestyle choices. As Canadian data show, however, when it comes to diet, risks are highest among the middle-aged baby boomers, not their children. While 25 per cent of adults in the 31–50-year old category exceed the recommended level of 35 per cent of energy from fat, only 7 per cent of children exceed this recommendation. Moreover evidence shows that fast food consumption worsens during adolescence reaching its zenith during the teen and early adult demographics. The same pattern is noted for physical activity which declines during adolescence, particularly for girls. Similar trends are noted in fruit and vegetable consumption. The implication of this is that by accentuating the risks associated with children, the press drew attention away from the bad lifestyle choices that supposedly informed adults make. Risk analysis tells us that young children seem to have the healthiest lifestyles. They eat better and are more active than any other population segment.

Panic politics and risk communication

Although the gap between public perceptions and expert sciences has dominated the discussion of risk communication so far, I think there is more to be said from this case study about the dynamics of risk communication. Newspapers, we have seen, not only became an effective channel of risk communication but journalists were the gatekeepers that selected, filtered and politicized the science by championing mitigation. I have used Cohen's theory of moral panic to emphasize how a deep anxiety about children's health and a legal question about children's market competences combined to frame the debates about mitigation. Backstage, advocacy sciences strategically escalated the debate by portraying vulnerable children as victims. Epidemiological evidence had indicated that those who watched TV most were at greater risk of obesity. Repeated studies of food advertising on TV indicated that in both the UK and the US children are exposed to an energy-dense diet. Surely, the advocates argued, this contributes to their bad health. As the press coverage reached its crescendo, the opposition between industry and health advocates re-ignited the long-simmering political struggle over food promotion to children. On one side were white-coated moral entrepreneurs and on the other the corporate suits asking government to rule on who is to blame for child obesity – marketers or parents.

Moral panic is a communication dynamic with consequences for both public risk perception and the politics of marketing. In the US, opportunistic lawyers launched class action lawsuits against food industry Goliaths, while young film-makers like Morgan Spurlock made 'biting' documentaries about the health effects of an unremitting diet of McDonald's. In the UK, Jamie Oliver campaigned to reform school menus while Sustain lobbied to banish advertising from the TV screen. Children's food marketers, chastened by the accusations, withdrew soft drinks from schools and promised to launch healthy lifestyle campaigns. Although parental anxieties baited the hook, it was children's uncertain status as 'informed consumers' that made them the lightning rod for the mounting debate about mitigating their unhealthy lifestyles which framed the dénouement of the globesity pandemic. In the process children were wrongly identified as the central victims (when it is their parents who needed the bariatric and triple bypass surgery), the food industry was blamed for children's bad diet (when parental indulgence and sedentary lifestyles were equally important risk factors) and the more complex problem of our lifestyle imbalance was reduced to a medical choice between exercise or diet pills. Ultimately ministers and policymakers were called on to formulate evidence-based policy. As the globesity epidemic gathered steam, the journalists' focus shifted from the metabolic systems underlying weight gain to the marketing ones.

Moral panic should not be viewed as an epi-phenomenon of parental anxiety but a risk communication dynamic galvanizing policy debates about risks to the young. Although both countries witnessed a dramatic increase in journalistic coverage of child obesity, the political fallout depended on the ideologies governing the market economy which grants choice to consumers, speech rights to corporations and assigns the costs of caring for children's health and well-being to the state. Lifestyle risk taking is accepted as a necessary part of our market economy. Yet in the case of children the assumption of 'informed consent' is questioned for reasons of their developmental immaturity. Children, by law, cannot be held responsible for their choices until they are fully competent consumers performing a cost-risk-benefit analysis. Hardly surprising, therefore, that food marketing on television targeting children reignited the long political struggle in both countries to regulate children's food marketing on television. Children's empowerment revealed itself as the Achilles heel of the neoliberal ideology. In the process, medical science became implicated, not only in the diagnosis of adiposity but in the policy deliberations about the influence of children's marketing.

Risk communication and marketing

Nutritional researchers had long noted how skewed the TV diet was. The literature showed that around the world a narrow range of core brands targeted children by habitually deploying the tried and true children's marketing techniques – animation, brand characters, cross marketing and fun appeals to capture their attention and play to their tastes. By focusing on the food industry's targeting of children, health advocates forced policymakers in the UK at least to realize that what was at stake was governmental responsibility for protecting children. In the US, bans on food advertising (following the model of cigarettes) were rejected because they constituted a suppression of commercial free speech. Self-regulation became the mantra of responsible food marketing. Yet in the UK Tony Blair's government launched a comprehensive policy directed at obesity prevention, which included a ban on food advertising targeting children under 16, better school meals, health promotion measures for children, nutrition education in schools and media literacy. Through a comparative content analysis of food advertising from 2004–7 in North America and the UK, I questioned whether corporate self-regulation was sufficient to rectify the bias in the food promotional system. Marketers' promises to positively promote healthy living and nutritional literacy were limited whereas the threat of a ban had already changed British targeting strategies and risk communication. By 2007, when the ban came into effect, North American children's time slots possessed a higher density of the 'bad five' food ads, risk messages less focused on health and more intensive child-oriented marketing techniques. Despite gestures such as removal of soft drinks from the schools, North American children were still exposed to an imbalanced diet of snacks, confections and cereals during their TV viewing.

Risk analysis was used not only to assess children's exposure to food advertising on TV but also to estimate the impact of the TV diet on their health in both countries. Considerable research effort has been devoted to measuring advertising's influence on children's dietary preferences, choices and requests for food. Reviews of advertising effects however showed that despite the unhealthy bias in the global food marketing system, the magnitude of advertisings' impact on children's health was marginal. Critics used this finding to argue there was no scientific basis for market regulation, suggesting instead, that it was bad parenting which was responsible for rising child obesity. My own review of the effects literature suggested that this criticism is both valid and ideologically loaded. It is true only insofar as parents have the capacity to mitigate their children's exposure to advertising by teaching advertising literacy, by controlling TV viewing and through their attempts to educate children about lifestyle choices. Yet instead of asking why 10 per cent of children are obese, I argue, we should be asking why 90 per cent of them are healthy. Blaming bad parenting therefore obfuscates the protective factors in children's lives which helps in explaining why the impact of the TV diet isn't greater.

Reporting a study of Vancouver children aged 8–12 I have noted that the influence of exposure to food advertising on brand knowledge and preferences is significant. Those who watch TV more, pay attention to, remember and form preferences for brands that are heavily advertised on TV. Moreover brand preferences are the basis of many of their requests to their parents. In this sense, advertising's consequences are both direct (on their brand preferences) and indirect (on their brand requests). In this respect, I found that the benefits of advertising literacy and cognitive defences may have been overstated, given that promotion influences children's consumption through the formation of preferences and liking within a food category. Yet the effects of this promotional effort on diet remains modest, at least until their teen years, because food choice is largely under the control of parents. Although children have a say in many diet decisions, their influence over snacks is greatest. My research shows that it is only when children are empowered to choose their TV snacks and make discretionary purchases that the cumulative weight of food advertising is clearly in evidence.

Marketing is a modality of lifestyle communication which interacts with familial and peer influences, constituting a constantly evolving part of the matrix of consumer socialization. As the food industry claimed, although children do have power to shape family lifestyle choices – a power that grows as they get older and more adept at social influence – parents ultimately buy most of the foods for the family and prepare their school meals and dinners. My research therefore confirms what has been long suspected: children develop a liking for the heavily marketed energy-dense snacks and drinks and buy them only in so far as *they are given a choice*. Moral panic had a kernel of truth: there were unseen lifestyle risks associated with children's consumer empowerment. The precautionary principle for regulating food marketing seems justified given marketers' impact on young children's discretionary consumption, not because it contributes to obesity but because children do not have sufficient knowledge and capacity to manage their own lifestyle risks. This is not to say that we should expect a ban on food marketing to radically improve children's health. As the industry advocates also pointed out, the health risks associated with heavy TV viewing confounds the contribution of advertising with other media-related risk factors which also contribute to and mitigate children's weight gain – particularly through the cultivation of sedentary leisure.

Media, power and consumer socialization

In Part III I reviewed the risk analysis of children's media-saturated lifestyles which showed that that one factor, excessive TV use, is associated with a constellation of lifestyle practices that result in energy imbalance. Exposure to television advertising is only one of these, and it makes a relatively modest contribution to their weight status, largely through its impact on kids' TV snacking and discretionary purchases of treats. Yet the epidemiological studies also show TV watching is consistently associated with weight gain because it displaces active leisure (especially in girls) and escalates the ritualized snacking that accompanies heavy TV watching. In this sense the behaviours most sanctioned by parents as part of children's empowerment – discretionary consumption, snacking and play time – are all complexly woven into the lifestyle choices practised in the media-saturated family. I have therefore suggested that one of the problems of research into the risk factors in the obesogenic family was that it distracted the researcher away from the protective family dynamics that reduced lifestyle risks.

Parents' supervision of food, money and media define the primary ways that young children are granted freedom to choose. But consumer socialization is a paradoxical form of learning that strives to both protect and prepare children to make healthy lifestyle choices for themselves. Three parenting styles – negotiative, permissive and mandated – were found to characterize their risk communication practices. My survey of Canadian parental strategies for consumer socialization confirmed that most families grant children some consumer power from a young age: they cultivate a taste for the healthy foods in the high chair, they provide safe educational toys for the first birthday and they give pocket money to teach them how to spend wisely at the store. As they get older, parents also grant children a say in family purchases using trips to the supermarket, co-viewing of television and family meals to discuss their preferences and pleasures associated with consumption.

Granted growing consumer power, children too develop strategies for getting more of what they want. They stabilize their tastes, learn to communicate their likes and dislikes to their parents and save money for special purchases. Their knowledge of the market economy expands through shopping trips, exposure to advertising and forays to the mall. They are able to search through catalogues and negotiate with parents. Although young children are restricted in their TV viewing, snacking and use of their own money, many gain increasing scope to make lifestyle choices as they get older. By age 8, many have TV in the bedroom and have meals in front of the TV. They are also granted choice in their TV snacks, treats and purchases with their pocket money. Although no parenting style proved superior, there was evidence that their approach to managing risk communication in the family had consequences for children's discretionary choices – for the foods they snacked on, the toys they bought and the activities that preoccupied their free time.

Because parents are aware of the debates about obesity, most also engage in efforts to inform, guide and limit children's exposure to those lifestyle risks associated with TV. In Canada at least, many parents attempt to instill in children a lifestyle which keeps them active and well. Young children had some knowledge of the risks: they know that junk food and being a couch potato is not good for them. By age 12, 25 per cent of children exhibit basic nutritional awareness and the majority have developed a taste for healthy foods. With age, of course, for many the patterns change. Given the constant negotiation and the restraints on their media use, young children often are more active and eat better than their elders. Media comes to preoccupy their lives, and as such brings another constellation of risk factors. Their diets get worse and their leisure becomes more sedentary as they get older. Unfortunately, parents seem more vigilant about restricting TV content than time spent viewing and TV snacks. Coupled with their media literacy, my research showed that TV puts those children more at risk, in families where parents grant considerable freedom to use media, to snack while viewing and to spend money on whatever they want. Little wonder that by 18 they are twice as likely to be overweight as at 10.

Risk communication as discursive politics

Although both countries were galvanized to respond to the obesity pandemic, their discursive politics of public health responsibility diverged.

What Kline (2006) calls the implicit medicalization of health care ensured that in the US very limited discussion of social, cultural or environmental origins of obesity took place. Kline argues that the American public's understanding of obesity as a lifestyle risk rests upon this medical ideology which 'limits governmental responsibility for addressing it, while systemic frames invite governmental action' (2006: 57). Grounded in neoliberal ideology, American policymakers failed to acknowledge the special status of child consumers. Without advertising restrictions, it was through PSAs and calls for corporate responsibility that Americans have sought to put the finger in the dyke of weight gain.

By contrast, nutrition has been part of Britain's public health policy for children from the end of the First World War, when Britain implemented school meals. With a long history of public health the UK had this advantage over the US when the obesity epidemic spilt onto the front pages and calls for an advertising ban escalated. Marketing communication was made part of the public health response by Tony Blair because his government recognized that 'the capacity of the NHS to treat us simply won't keep pace with the state of the country's health'. The debate over child obesity therefore not only resulted in a ban on children's advertising but in the realization that since the causes of obesity are multiple, a systemic solution is required. In January 2008 the Labour government launched a novel public health initiative which integrated media policy, health promotion, food regulation, school initiatives and parenting support in an effort to reduce child obesity. Time will tell whether this strategy works, but I believe that the policymakers in Britain have finally understood the idea of systemic risks in the consumer culture.

This is not to deny children agency. My analysis of the family dynamics recognizes that children are agentive, but not fully empowered consumers. The knowledge they have of the market is partial and biased, and the consumer power they have acquired is not absolute or independently exercised. Overall, children under eight at least cannot generally be viewed as sovereign consumers, but rather as *becoming consumer subjectivities within a complex matrix of socializing influences*. With this picture in mind, some protection in the marketplace may be justified. In this respect, the question of who is responsible for children's consumer socialization in the risk society is an important one, and the cooperation of the schools, parents and responsible corporations may be the best way to achieve responsible and informed young consumers.

By way of conclusion I argue the need to rethink the complex and volatile dynamic of consumer empowerment in the risk society. Children need a proactive consumer awareness that is informed by the risk-price-benefits associated with daily consumption. To this end, I have urged a rethinking of the competences that children need for life in the consumer society where the calculus of happiness is countermanded by the minimization of risk. As we have seen, from a very young age, parents conscientiously engage in trying to shape children's food preferences and cultivate the skills and attitudes that their children need to survive in the mediated marketplace. Product knowledge, taste discrimination and healthy discretionary choices are all considered important responsibilities of parents. Unfortunately, there is no guarantee that a parent's anxious attempts to either prepare or protect their children can stop the historical vector of the media-centric household. In this respect Britain's coordinated involvement of health advocacy, responsible food marketing, parental lifestyle management and schools' consumer education seems to be the best approach to reducing the risks associated with increasing child consumerism. The book therefore concludes by noting how experiments in educating young people about the risks of sedentary lifestyles and excessive junk food consumption have proven effective. I conclude by arguing that risk literacy in the schools could help arm young consumers with the knowledge they need to manage the multiple lifestyle risks of food and leisure for themselves.

Final words

As Gilles Lipovetsky (Lipovetsky et al. 2005) has written, a deep malaise has accompanied the transition from what he calls 'postmodern' to 'hypermodern' times. 'Anxieties about the future are replacing the mystique of progress', he argued (2005: 25). 'A sense of insecurity has invaded all minds: health has imposed itself as a mass obsession; terrorism, catastrophes and epidemics are regularly front-page news' in the risk society (39). At the outset of this book I stated my ambition to both theoretically and empirically contribute to Beck's argument about the central role that risk analysis now plays in the uncertain dynamics of reflexive modernization. Lifestyle risks are doubly controversial – as science and as blame. As we have seen, in the public sphere of the promotional market, sensationalism and advocacy sciences jointly propelled public debate about the health risks, obesity, diabetes and heart failure associated with eating too much 'fast food'.

Building on Bill Leiss's communication analysis of risk controversies, I have analysed the lifestyle risks associated with children's consumer empowerment. This case study of risk communication has emphasized the part health advocates played in the debates about the causes and reduction of child obesity. As I have shown, the epidemiological report issued by the WHO set the stage for the widening struggle over children's overweight bodies which not only raised awareness of children's weight gain but precipitated the mobilization of a coalition of health/parenting advocates against 'big food's' PR professionals. It was not ecology but epidemiology that detected the systemic risks; it was not environment but health that was endangered; and it was not industrial waste that was the problem but the mass marketing of food that dynamized the discursive politics of this new environmental advocacy.

I believe that globesity therefore signals a turning point in environmentalism as foodie paternalism redefined the lifestyle politics of the consumer culture (Shah et al. 2007: 222). Food, after all, is more than nutrition. Eating is a culturally privileged consumer activity deeply linked to our ideologies and values, our lifestyles and our religions. Provisioning our families is crucial to our modern identities, to our ethnic sensibilities and to our cultural capital, as well as our individual self-esteem and social attractiveness. Risk controversies like BSE, GMO, swine flu had already drawn public attention to the regulatory uncertainties surrounding health inspection, nutrition labelling and the marketing of food (Lien 2004). By way of consequence, eating was no longer associated with simply taste and cost, argued Marion Lien, but to 'issues of risk and distrust' (Lien 2004: 3). Media thus fostered a growing awareness that 'food risks' bound the outside (agribusiness) and the human inside (consumer well-being) into a seamless environmental anxiety about what we feed our families.

Moral panic dramaticizes and distorts the controversy surrounding all lifestyle risks to children, and perhaps that is a good thing. Indeed this study of the globesity pandemic suggests there may be positive consequences to public anxiety provoked by obesity. However overstated, panic has helped put children's health back on the agenda of child socialization. As my survey of parenting styles indicated, the debates about globesity reverberated through the Canadian family system, accentuating the anxieties that parents felt about children's nutritional choices and sedentary lifestyles. In the throes of growing concerns about snacks and fast food, many more parents became receptive to educating their children about nutrition, teaching advertising literacy and discouraging sedentary lifestyles. This, I conclude, is a reason for hope, because however slowly, Canadian parents are beginning to see lifestyle risks as an essential part of children's empowerment in the consumer marketplace. Indeed, the fate of reflexive modernity may hinge on the average family's everyday discussion of what children should eat, how much time they watch TV and their regular participation in active outdoor play.

Notes

1 Introduction: Growing Up in the Risk Society

1. Most of the data for the news analysis were gathered online and through Lexis-Nexis searches. Referencing of news stories will be found in an online appendix to this book at http://www.sfu.ca/media-lab/Globesity.

3 Putting the Pan in the Pandemic

1. For reasons of a readable narrative, I have not used formal citation in my frame analysis of the press debates. References are available at the online appendix.
2. Stop Commercial Exploitation of Children (SCEC) changed its name to Campaign for a Commercial Free Childhood (CCFC) in November 2004. I have referenced this organization according to its current name.

4 The TV Diet: Advertising as a Biased System of Risk Communication

1. The protocol and categories used can be found in the online appendix.

8 Panicked Parenting: Managing Children's Lifestyle Choices in the Risk Society

1. See the online appendix for questionnaire.

References

Achenreiner, G. and John, D. (2003) 'The Meaning of Brand Names to Children: A Developmental Investigation', *Journal of Consumer Psychology*, 13(3): 205–19.

Adams, J., Hennessy-Priest, K., Ingimarsdottir, S., Sheeshka, J., Ostbye, T. and White, M. (2009) 'Food Advertising during Children's Television in Canada and the UK', *Archives of Disease in Childhood*, 94: 658–62.

Advertising Age (2005) 100 Leading National Advertisers, 50th annual report, June.

Advertising Age (2006) Domestic Advertising Spending by Category, 26 June, 77(26): S-8: 7.

Advertising Education Forum (AEF) (2005) 'A Report on the US Workshop on Perspectives on Marketing, Self-Regulation and Childhood Obesity', *AAN Quarterly*, October, 2–4.

Advertising Standards Authority (2009) *Food and Soft Drinks Advertising Survey 2009*, available at http://asa.org.uk/General/Search.aspx?s=ASA.

Altheide, D. (2002) *Creating Fear: News and the Construction of a Crisis*, Berlin, Germany: Aldine de Gruyter.

American Association for the Advancement of Science (AAAS) (2002) http://www.aaas.org/news/releases/2002/topten.shtml.

American Obesity Society (2008) http://www.obesity.org/information/childhood_overweight.asp.

Anderson, A., Petersen, A. and Mathew, D. (2005) 'Communication or Spin? Media Relations in Science Journalism', in Stuart Allan (ed.) *Journalism: Critical Issues*, New York: Open University Press: 188–98.

Apovian, C. (2004) 'Sugar-Sweetened Soft Drinks, Obesity and Type 2 Diabetes', *Journal of the American Medical Association*, 292: 978–9.

Ashton, D. (3 March 2004) 'Food Ads don't Make Kids Unfit', *The Guardian*, 22 January 2003.

Atkin, C. (1975) 'Effects of Television Advertising on Children: First Year Experimental Evidence', Report no. 1, Michigan State University.

Atkin, C. (1978) 'Observation of Parent-Child Interaction in Supermarket Decision-Making', *Journal of Marketing*, October: 41–5.

Atkin, D., Greenberg, B. and Baldwin, T. (1991) 'The Home ecology of Children's Television Viewing: Parental Mediation and the New Video Environment', *Journal of Communication*, 41(3): 40–53.

Australian Division of General Practice (ADGP) (2003) 'What are we Feeding our Children? A Junk Food Advertising Audit', Australian Divisions of General Practice, February.

Azcuenaga, M. (1997) 'The Role of Advertising and Advertising Regulation in the Free Market', Federal Trade Commissioner Speech, Turkish Association of Advertising, Istanbul, 8 April.

Bahn, K. D. (1986) 'How and When Do Brand Perceptions and Preferences First Form? A Cognitive Developmental Investigation', *Journal of Consumer Research*, 13 (December): 382–93.

Barker, M. and Petley, J. (1997) *Ill Effects: The Media/Violence Debate*, London: Routledge.

Bar-On, M. (2000) 'The Effects of Television on Child Health: Implications and Recommendations', *Archives of the Diseases of Childhood*, 83(4): 289–92.

Bar-Or, O. (2000) 'Juvenile Obesity, Physical Activity, and Lifestyle Changes: Cornerstones for Prevention and Management', *Physician & Sports Medicine*, 28(11): 51–2, 55–6, 58.

Barr-Anderson, D., Larson, N., Nelso, M., Neumark-Sztainer, D. and Story, M. (2009) 'Does Television Viewing Predict Dietary Intake Five Years Later in High School Students and Young Adults?' *International Journal of Behavioural, Nutrition and Physical Activity*, 6(7): 1–8.

Bauer, K., Larson, N., Nelson, M., Story, M. and Neumark-Sztainer D. (2009) 'Fast Food Intake among Adolescents: Secular and Longitudinal Trends from 1999 to 2004', *Preventive Medicine*, 48: 284–7.

Beatty, S. and Salil, T. (1994) 'Adolescent Influence in Family Decision Making: A Replication with Extension', *Journal of Consumer Research*, 21(2): 332–41.

Beck, U. (1992) *The Risk Society*. London: Sage.

Beck, U. (1995) *Ecological Politics in an Age of Risk*, Cambridge: Polity Press.

Beck, U. (1998) 'Politics of Risk Society', in Jane Franklin (ed.) *Politics of Risk Society*, Cambridge Polity: 9–22.

Belch, G., Belch, M. and Ceresino, G. (1985) 'Parental and Teenage Influences in Family Decision Making', *Journal of Business Research*, 13: 163–76.

Bellisle, F. and Rolland-Cachera, M. (2001) 'How Sugar-Containing Drinks Might Increase Adiposity in Children', *Lancet v. n.*357: 490.

Benton, D. (2004) 'Role of Parents in the Determination of the Food Preferences of Children and the Development of Obesity', *International Journal of Obesity*, 28: 858–69.

Berey, U. and Pollay, R. (1968) 'The Influencing Role of the Child in Family Decision Making', *Journal of Marketing Research*, 5 (February): 70–2.

Berger, P., Berger, B. and Kellner, H. (1974) *The Homeless Mind*, London: Vintage.

Berkey, C., Rockett, H., Field, A. Gillman, M., Frazier, L., Camargo, C. and Colditz G. (2000) 'Activity Dietary Intake, and Weight Changes in a Longitudinal Study of Preadolescent and Adolescent Boys and Girls', *Pediatrics*, 105:4.

Berry, T., Wharf-Higgins, J. and Naylor, P. (2007) 'SARS Wars: An Examination of the Quantity and Construction of Health Information in the News Media', *Health Communication*, 27(1): 35–44.

Birch, L. and Fisher, J. (1998) 'Development of Eating Behaviors among Children', *Pediatrics*, 101(3): 539–50.

Borzekowski, D. and Robinson, T. (1999) 'Viewing the Viewers: Ten Video Cases of Children's Television Viewing Behaviors', *Journal of Broadcasting & Electronic Media*, 43(4): 506–28.

Borzekowski, D. and Robinson, T. (2001) 'The 30-Second Effect: An Experiment Revealing the Impact of Television Commercials on Food Preferences of Preschoolers', *Journal of the American Dietetic Association*, 101: 42–6.

Boseley, S. (3 March 2003) 'Obesity Epidemic Blamed on Food Firms', *The Guardian*.

Botterill, J. and Kline, S. (2007) 'From McLibel to McLettuce', *Society and Business Review*, 2(1): 74–95.

Boumtje, P., Huang, C., Lee, J. and Lin, B. (2005) 'Dietary Habits, Demographics, and the Development of Overweight and Obesity among Children in the United States', *Food Policy* 30(2): 115–28.

Boush, D., Friestad, M. and Rose, G. (1994) 'Adolescent Skepticism toward TV Advertising and Knowledge of Advertiser Tactics', *Journal of Consumer Research*, June: 165–75.

Boyce, T. (2007) 'The Media and Obesity', *Obesity Reviews*, 8 (1): 201–5.

Boynton-Jarrett, R., Thomas, T., Peterson, K., Wiecha, J., Sobol, A. and Gortmaker S. (2003) 'Impact of Television Viewing Patterns of Fruit and Vegetable Consumption among Adolescents', *Pediatrics*, 112(6): 1321–6.

Brody, G. H., Stoneman, Z., Lane, S. and Sanders, A. (1981) 'Television Food Commercials Aimed at Children, Family Grocery Shopping and Mother-Child Interactions', *Family Relations*, 30: 435–9.

Brook, S. (15 Nov 2004) 'Advertisers Hit Back Over Food Ad Ban', *The Guardian*.

Brosius, H. and Kepplinger, H. (1990) 'The Agenda Setting Function of Television News: Static and Dynamic Views', *Communication Research*, 17(2): 183–211.

Brucks, M., Armstrong, G. and Goldberg, M. (1988) 'Children's Use of Cognitive Defenses against Television Advertising: A Cognitive Response Approach', *Journal of Consumer Research*, 14: 471–82.

Buckingham, D. (2009a) 'The Appliance of Science: The Role of Evidence in the Making of Regulatory Policy on Children and Food Advertising in the UK', *International Journal of Cultural Policy*, 15(2): 201–15.

Buckingham, D. (2009b) 'Beyond the Competent Consumer: The Role of Media Literacy in the Making of Regulatory Policy on Children and Food Advertising in the UK', *International Journal of Cultural Policy*, 15(2): 217–30.

Buijzen, M., Bomhof, E. and Schuurman, J. (2008) 'A Test of Three Alternative Hypotheses Explaining the Link between Children's Television Viewing and Weight Status', *Journal of Children & Media*, 2 (1): 67–74.

Buijzen, M., Schuurman, J. and Bomhof, E. (2008) 'Associations between Children's Television Advertising Exposure and their Food Consumption Patterns: A Household Diary Survey Study', *Appetite*, 50: 231–9.

Bundred, P., Kitchiner, D. and Buchan, I. (2001) 'Prevalence of Overweight and Obese Children between 1989 and 1998: Population Based Series of Cross Sectional Studies', *British Medical Journal*, 322: 1–4.

Burggraf, K. (2001) 'Eating Disorder Symptomatology and Media, Family, Psychological, and Maturational Variables: A Longitudinal Study of Young Females', *Dissertation Abstracts International*, 61(12-B): 6734.

Byrd-Bredbenner, C. (2002) 'Saturday Morning Children's Television Advertising: A Longitudinal Content Analysis', *Family and Consumer Sciences Research Journal*, 30: 382–403.

Byrd-Bredbenner, C. and Grasso, D. (1999) 'A Comparative Analysis of Television Food Advertisements and Current Dietary Recommendations', *American Journal of Health Studies*, 15(4): 169–80.

Byrd-Bredbenner, C. and Grasso, D. (2001) 'The Effects of Food Advertising Policy on Televised Nutrient Content Claims and Health Claims', *Family Economics and Nutrition Review*, 13(1): 37–49.

Cairns, G., Angus, K. and Hastings, G. (2009) 'The Extent Nature and Effects of Food Promotion to Children: A Review of the Evidence to December 2008', report prepared for the World Health Organization, December 2009. Institute for Social Marketing, University of Stirling and the Open University: UK.

Calvert, S. (2008) 'Children as Consumers: Advertising and Marketing', *Journal of Communication*, 18(1): 205–34.

Campbell, K., Waters, E., O'Meara, S. and Summerbell, C. (2001) 'Interventions for Preventing Obesity in Childhood: A Systematic Review', *Obesity Reviews*, 2(3): 149–57.

Campos, P. (24 April 2004) 'The Big Fat Con Story', *The Guardian*.

Carlson, L., Grossbart, S. and Walsh, A. (1990) 'Mothers' Communication Orientation and Consumer Socialization Tendencies', *Journal of Advertising*, 19(3): 27–38.

Carlson, L., Grossbart, S. and Stuenkel, J. (1993) 'The Role of Parental Socialization Types on Differential Family Communication Patterns Regarding Consumption', *Journal of Consumer Psychology*, 1(1): 31–52.

Carruth, B., Goldberg, D. and Skinner, J. (1991) 'Do Parents and Peers Mediate the Influence of Television Advertising on Food Related Purchases?' *Journal of Adolescent Research*, 6(2): 253–71.

CCFC (2000–10) 'Campaign for a Commercial-Free Childhood', press release, downloaded from http://www.commercialfreechildhood.org./press.htm.

Cebrzynski, G. (8 January 2007) 'Responsibility of Parents has been Forgotten in Furor over Ads' Effect on Childhood Obesity', *Nation's Restaurant News*, 16.

Centers for Disease Control and Prevention (CDC) (2004) 'Overweight among US Children and Adolescents', *National Health and Nutrition Examination Survey*, Retrieved 15 March 2007, from http://www.cdc.gov/nchs/data/nhanes/databriefs/overweight.pdf.

Centers for Disease Control and Prevention (CDC) (2007) NHANES III, http://wwwn.cdc.gov/nchs/nhanes/bibliography/Pubs.aspx?CatID=53&name=Overweight/Obesity.

Center for Science in the Public Interest (2006) 'Parents and Advocates Will Sue Viacom and Kellogg', accessed on 18 January 2008, http://www.cspinet.org/new/200601181.html.

Chamberlain, L., Wang, Y. and Robinson, T. (2006) 'Does Children's Screen Time Predict Requests for Advertised Products? Cross-Sectional and Prospective Analyses', *Archives of Pediatric and Adolescent Medicine*, 160: 363–8.

Chaplin, L. and John, D. (2005) 'The Development of Self-Brand Connections in Children and Adolescents', *Journal of Consumer Research*, 32(1): 119–29.

Chapman, K., Nicholas, P. and Supramaniam, R. (2006) 'How Much Food Advertising is there on Australian Television?' *Health Promotion International*, 21: 172–80.

Chapman, S. (2001) 'Advocacy in Public Health: Roles and Challenges', *International Journal of Epidemiology*, 30: 1226–32.

Chernin, A. (2008) 'The Effects of Food Marketing on Children's Preferences: Testing the Moderating Roles of Age and Gender', *The Annals of the American Academy of Political and Social Science*, 615: 101–22.

Chinn, S. and Rona, R. (2001) 'Prevalence and Trends in Overweight and Obesity in Three Cross Sectional Studies of British Children, 1974–1994', *British Medical Journal*, 32(6): 24–6.

Chopra, M., Galbraith, S. and Darnton-Hill, I. (2002) 'A Global Response to a Global Problem: The Epidemic of Overnutrition', *Bulletin of the World Health Organization*, 80(12): 952–58.

Chou, S., Rashad, I. and Grossman, M. (2005) 'Fast-Food Restaurant Advertising on Television and its Influence on Childhood Obesity', Working Paper 11879, Nat Bureau of Economic Research.

Chou, S. Rashad, I. and Grossman, M. (2008) 'Fast-Food Restaurant Advertising on Television and its Influence on Childhood Obesity', *The Journal of Law and Economics*, 51(4): 599–618.

Christensen, P. (2004) 'The Health-Promoting Family: A Conceptual Framework for Future Research', *Social Science & Medicine*, 59: 377–87.

Christopher, F., Fabes, R. and Wilson, P. (1989) 'Family Television Viewing: Implications for Family Life Education', *Family Relations*, 38(2): 210–14.

Clarke, B. (2003) 'The Complex Issue of Food, Advertising and Child Health: An Interview with Jeremy Preston', *Advertising and Marketing to Children*, Oct–Dec: 13–16.

Clarke, M., Heaton, M. and Isrealsen, C. (2005) 'The Acquisition of Family Financial Roles and Responsibilities', *Family and Consumer Sciences Research Journal*, 33(4): 321–40.

Cloud, J. (2 December 2002) *Time*, http://www.time.com/time/magazine/article/0,9171,1003804,00.html.

Cohen, S. (1972) *Folk Devils and Moral Panics: The Creation of the Mods and Rockers*, London: MacGibbon & Kee.

Colb, S. (29 January 2003) 'Why Suing McDonald's could be a Good Thing', CNN, http://www.cnn.com/2003/LAW/01/29/findlaw.analysis.colb.mcdonalds/.

Connor, S. (2006) 'Food-Related Advertising on Preschool Television: Building Brand Recognition in Young Viewers', *Pediatrics*, 118(4): 1478–85.

Cook, D. (2000) 'Exchange Value as Pedagogy in Children's Leisure: Moral Panics in Children's Culture at Century's End', *Leisure Sciences*, 23: 81–98.

Coon, K., Goldberg, J., Rogers, B. and Tucker, K. (2001) 'Relationships between Use of Television during Meals and Children's Food Consumption Patterns', *Pediatrics*, 107(1): 1–9.

Coveney, J. (2002) 'What does Research on Families and Food Tell us? Implications for Nutrition and Dietetic Practice', *Nutrition & Dietetics*, 59(2): 113–19.

Cozens, C. (14 June 2002) 'McDonald's and Coke Fund Healthy Eating Drive', *The Guardian*.

Crespo, C., Smith, E., Troiano, R., Bartlett, S., Macera, C. and Anderson, R. (2001) 'Television Watching, Energy Intake, and Obesity in US Children: Results from the Third National Health and Nutrition Examination Survey, 1988–1994', *Archives of Pediatric and Adolescent Medicine*, 155(3): 360–5.

Critcher, C. (2006) *Moral Panics and the Media*, Maidenhead: Open University Press.

Cullen, K., Ash, D., Warneke, C. and de Moor, C. (2002a) 'Intake of Soft Drinks, Fruit Flavored Beverages, and Fruits and Vegetables by Children in Grades 4 through 6', *American Journal of Public Health*, 92 (1): 475–7.

Cullen, K., Lara, K. and de Moor, C. (2002b) 'Children's Dietary Fat Intake and Fat Practices Vary by Meal and Day', *Journal of the American Dietetic Association*, 102: 1773–8.

Cullen, K., Baranowski, T., Owens, E., Marsh, T., Rittenberry, L. and de Moor, C. (2003) 'Availability, Accessibility, and Preferences for Fruit, 100% Fruit Juice, and Vegetables Influence Children's Dietary Behavior', *Health Education and Behavior*, 30: 615–26.

Cummings, H. and Vandewater, E. (2007) 'Relation of Adolescent Video Game Play to Time Spent in Other Activities', *Archives of Pediatric and Adolescent Medicine*, 161(7): 684–9.

Davis, A. (2000) 'Public Relations, News Production and Changing Patterns of Source Access in the British National Media', *Media, Culture & Society*, 22(1): 39–59.

Dennison, M., Barbara A., Erb, M., Tara, A. and Jenkins, P. (2002) 'Television Viewing and Television in Bedroom Associated with Overweight Risk among Low-Income Preschool Children', *Pediatrics*, 109: 1028–35.

Derbaix, C. and Bree, J. (1997) 'The Impact of Children's Affective Reactions Elicited by Commercials on Attitudes Toward the Advertisement and the Brand', *International Journal of Research in Marketing*, 14: 207–29.

Dibb, S. and Gordon, S. (2001) *TV Dinners: What's being Served up by the Advertisers?* London: Sustain.

Dietz, W. (1986) 'Prevention of Childhood Obesity', *Pediatric Clinics of North America*, 33(4): 823–33.

Dietz, W. (1991) 'Factors Associated with Childhood Obesity', *Nutrition*, 7(4): 290–1.

Dietz, W. (1996) 'The Role of Lifestyle in Health: The Epidemiology and Consequences of Inactivity', *Proceedings of the Nutrition Society*, 55(3): 829–40.

Dietz, W. and Gortmaker, S. (1985) 'Do we Fatten our Children at the Television Set? Obesity and Television Viewing in Children and Adolescents', *Pediatrics*, 75(5): 807–12.

Dixon, C. (2004) 'Children's Likes and Dislikes', *Brand Strategy*, July/Aug, http://findarticles.com/p/articles/mi_go2028/is_200407/ai_n6554269/.

Dong, L., Block, G. and Mandel, S. (2004) 'Activities Contributing to Total Energy Expenditure in the United States: Results from the NHAPS study', *International Journal of Behavioral Nutrition and Physical Activity*, 1(4): 1–11.

Dotson, M. and Hyatt, E. (2005) 'Major Influence Factors in Children's Consumer Socialization', *The Journal of Consumer Marketing*, 22(1): 35–41.

Douglas, M. (1994) *Risk and Blame*, London: Routledge.

Drotner, K. (1992) 'Modernity and Media Panics', in M. Skovmand and K. Schrøder (eds) *Media Cultures: Reappraising Transnational Media*, London: Routledge: 42–62.

Dubow, J. (1995) 'Advertising Recognition and Recall by Age – Including Teens', *Journal of Advertising Research*, 35(5): 55–60.

Durant, R., Baranowski, T., Johnson, M. and Thompson, W. (1994) 'The Relationships among Television Watching, Physical Activity, and Body Composition of Young Children', *Pediatrics*, 94: 449–55.

Eberstadt, M. (2003) 'The Child-Fat Problem', *Policy Review*, 117.

The Economist (13 December 2003) 'Filling the World's Bellies'.

Eisenmann, J., Bartee, T. and Wang, M. (2002) 'Physical Activity, TV Viewing, and Weight in US Youth: 1999 Youth Risk Behavior Survey', *Obesity Research*, 10(5): 379–85.

Ekstrom, K., Tansuhaj, P. and Foxman, E. (1987) 'Children's Influence in Family Decisions and Consumer Socialization: A Reciprocal Review', *Advances in Consumer Research*, 14: 283–7.

Endicott, C. (14 November 2005) 'Global Marketing', *Advertising Age*, http://www.google.ca/search?hl=en&client=firefox-a&hs=e6H&rls=org.mozilla%3Aen-US%3Aofficial&q=advertising+age+Nov+14+2005+global&aq=f&aqi=&aql=&oq=&gs_rfai=

Engle, M. (2004) 'Regulating Food Advertising to Children: An Historical Perspective', presentation, IOM Meeting on Food Marketing and the Diets of Children and Youth, Washington, DC, 14 October.

Ewen, S. (1996) *PR: A Social; History of Spin*, New York: Basic Books.

Ewing, M., Napoli, J. and Plessis, E. (1999) 'Factors Affecting In-Market Recall of Food Product Advertising', *Journal of Advertising Research*, 39(4): 29–38.

Fang, J., Wylie-Rosett, J., Cohen, H., Kaplan, R. and Alderman, M. (2003) 'Exercise, Body Mass Index, Caloric Intake, and Cardiovascular Mortality', *American Journal of Preventive Medicine*, 25(4): 283–9.

FAO/WHO (2002) 'Joint FAO/WHO Obesity: 5.1 Recommendations for Preventing Excess Weight Gain and Obesity' available at www.who.int/dietphysicalactivity/publications/trs916/en/gsfao_obesity.pdf.

Faulkner, G., Finlay, S. and Roy, S. (2007) 'Get the News on Physical Activity Research: A Content Analysis of Physical Activity Research in the Canadian Print Media', *Journal of Physical Activity and Health*, 4(2): 180–92.

Federal Trade Commission (FTC) (1978) *Staff Report on Television Advertising to Children*, Washington, DC: US Government Printing Office.

Federal Trade Commission (FTC) (1981) *In the Matter of Children's Advertising*, Washington, DC: US Government Printing Office.

Field, A., Camargo, C., Taylor, B., Berkey, C., Roberts, S. and Colditz, G. (2001) 'Peer, Parent and Media Influences on the Development of Weight Concerns and Frequent Dieting among Preadolescent and Adolescent Girls and Boys', *Pediatrics*, 107(1): 54–60.

Finklestein, E., Fiebelkorn, I. and Wang, G. (2003) 'National Medical Spending Attributable to Overweight and Obesity: How Much and who's Paying', *Health Affairs*, http://content.healthaffairs.org/cgi/content/abstract/hlthaff.w3.219.

Fischhoff, B. (2005) 'Risk Perception and Communication', in D. Kamien (ed.) *Handbook of Terrorism and Counter-Terrorism*, New York: McGraw-Hill: 463–92.

Fischhoff, B., Lichtenstein, S., Slovic, P., Derby, S. and Keeney, R. (1981) *Acceptable Risk*, New York: Cambridge University Press.

Fitch, K., Pyenson, B., Abbs, S. and Liang, M. (2004) 'Obesity: A Big Problem getting Bigger', *Milliman*, http://www.milliman.com/pubs/Healthcare/content/research_reports/Obesity-Big-Problem-Getting-Bigger.pdf.

Flegal, K., Ogden, C., Wei, R., Kuczmarski, R. and Johnson, C. (2001) 'Prevalence of Overweight in US Children: Comparison of US Growth Charts from the Centers for Disease Control and Prevention with other Reference Values for Body Mass Index', *American Journal of Clinical Nutrition*, 73(6): 1086–93.

Flurry, L. (2007) 'Children's Influence in Family Decision-Making: Examining the Impact of the Changing American Family', *Journal of Business Research*, 60(4): 322–30.

Folta, S., Goldberg, J., Economos, C., Bell, R. and Meltzer, R. (2006) 'Food Advertising Targeted at School-Age Children: A Content Analysis', *Journal of Nutrition Education and Behavior*, 38: 244–8.

Food Advertising Unit (FAU) (30 June 2006) 'The Food, Soft Drink and Advertising Industries' Response to Ofcom's Option 4 Challenge', http://www.adassoc.org.uk/aa/index.cfm/newsroom/.

Food Advertising Unit (FAU) (2006) 'Annual Report', http://www.ofcom.org.uk/consult/condocs/foodads_new/responses/fau.pdf.

Food and Drug Administration (FDA) (2004) 'Brief Summary: Disclosing Risk Information in Consumer-Directed Print Advertisements', US Department of Health and Human Services, January, DDMAC.

Food Commission (2005) *Marketing of Foods to Children*, http://www.which.co.uk.

Food Standards Agency (6 December 2005) 'Nutrient Profiling Model Delivered to Ofcom', press release, http://www.food.gov.uk/news/newsarchive/2005.dec.

Fox, N. (1999) 'Postmodern Reflections on "Risk", "Hazards" and Life Choices', in D. Lupton (ed.) *Risk and Sociocultural Theory: New Directions and Perspectives*, Cambridge: Cambridge University Press: 12–33.

Francis, L. and Birch, L. (2006) 'Does Eating during Television Viewing Affect Preschool Children's Intake', *Journal of the American Dietetics Association*, 106(4): 598–600.

Fromm, E. (1947) *Man for Himself: An Inquiry into the Psychology of Ethics*, New York: Holt, Rinehart and Winston.

Furedi, F. (1997) *Culture of Fear: Risk-Taking and the Morality of Low Expectation*, London: Cassell.

Galst, J. and White, M. (1976) 'The Unhealthy Persuader: The Reinforcing Value of Television and Children's Purchase-Influencing Attempts at the Supermarket', *Child Development*, 47: 1089–96.

Gantz, W., Schwartz, N., Angelini, J. and Rideout, V. (2007) *Food for Thought: Television Food Advertising to Children in the United States*, The Kaiser Family Foundation: 15–6, http://www.kff.org/entmedia/7618.cfm.

Garriguet, D. (2004) *Overview of Canadian's Eating Habits*, Health Statistics Division Ottawa, Catalogue 82-620-MIE No. 2.

Gentile, J. and Walsh, D. (2002) 'A Normative Study of Family Media Habits', *Journal of Applied Developmental Psychology*, 23(2): 157–78.

Gibbins, J. and Reimer, B. (1999) *The Politics of Postmodernity*, London: Sage.

Giddens, A. (1998) 'The Risk Society: The Context of British Politics', in Jane Franklin (ed.) *The Politics of Risk Society*, Cambridge: Polity: 23–34.

Gitlin, T. (1987) *The Sixties: Years of Hope and Rage*, NY: Bantam.

Globe and Mail (2 April 2007) 'Concern about Childhood Obesity is Shading into Hysteria', A 12.

Goldberg, M. and Gorn, G. (1974) 'Children's Reactions to Television Advertising: An Experimental Approach', *The Journal of Consumer Research*, 1(2): 69–75.

Goldberg, M., Gorn, G. and Gibson, W. (1978) 'TV Messages for Snack and Breakfast Foods: Do they Influence Children's Preferences?' *Journal of Consumer Research*, 5(2): 73–81.

Gordon-Larson, P., Adair, L., Nelson, M. and Popkin, B. (2004) 'Five-Year Obesity Incidence in the Transition Period between Adolescence and Adulthood: The National Longitudinal Study of Adolescent Health', *American Journal of Clinical Nutrition*, 80(3): 569–75.

Gorn, G. and Goldberg, M. (1982) 'Behavioral Evidence of the Effects of Televised Food Messages on Children, *Journal of Consumer Research*, 9(2): 200–5.

Gortmaker, S., Must, A., Sobol, A., Peterson, A., Colditz, G. and Dietz, W. (1996) 'Television Viewing as a Cause of Increasing Obesity among Children in the United States, 1986–1990', *Archives of Pediatric and Adolescent Medicine*, 150(4): 356–62.

Gostin, L., Arnos, P. and Brandt, A. (1997) 'FDA Regulation of Tobacco Advertising and Youth Smoking: Historical, Social and Constitutional Perspectives', *Journal of the American Medical Association*, 277(5): 410–18.

Gracey, D., Stanley, N., Burke V., Corti, B. and Beilin, L. (1996) 'Nutritional Knowledge, Beliefs and Behaviours in Teenage School Students', *Health Education Research*, 11(2): 187–204.

Greenberg, M. (1989) 'Risk, Drama, and Geography in Coverage of Environmental Risk by Network Television', *Journalism Quarterly*, 66(2): 267–276.

Groom, N. (16 July 2004) 'McDonald's CEO Says Can't Stop Ads for Kids', Reuters, http://www.reuters.com/article/idUSN1636984920070716.

Grossbart, S. and Crosby, L. (1984) 'Understanding the Bases of Parental Concern and Reactions to Children's Food Advertising', *Journal of Marketing* 48(Summer): 79–92.

The Guardian (17 September 2002) 'Childhood Obesity at Epidemic Levels'.

Hackett, R. and Zhao, Y. (2005) *Democratizing Global Media: One World, Many Struggles*, New York: Rowman & Littlefield.

Halford, J., Gillespie, J., Brown, V., Pontin, E. and Dovey, T. (2004) 'Effect of Television Advertisements for Foods on Food Consumption in Children', *Appetite*, 42(2): 221–5.

Hammond, K., Wylie, A. and Casswell, S. (1999) 'The Extent and Nature of Television Food Advertising to New Zealand Children and Adolescents', *Australian and New Zealand Journal of Public Health*, 23(1): 49–55.

Hancox, R. J. and Poulton, R. (2006) 'Watching Television is Associated with Childhood Obesity: But is it Clinically Important?' *International Journal of Obesity*, 30: 171–5.

Harabin, R., Coote, A. and Allen, J. (2003) *Health in the News: Risk Reporting and Media Influence*, London: King's Fund Publications, www/kingsfund.org.uk/Publications.

Hardy, L., Bass, S. and Booth, M. (2007) 'Changes in Sedentary Behavior among Adolescent Girls: A 2.5 Year Prospective Cohort Study', *Journal of Adolescent Health*, 40(2): 158–65.

Harris, J., Kaufman, P., Martinez, S. and Price, C. (2002) 'The US Food Marketing System', *Agricultural Economic Report*, no. 811, Washington, DC: US Department of Agriculture Economic Research Service.

Harrison, K. and Marske, A. (2005) 'Nutritional Content of Foods Advertised during the Television Programs Children Watch Most', *American Journal of Public Health*, 95: 1568–74.

Hart, K., Bishop, J. and Truby, H. (2002) 'An Investigation into School Children's Knowledge and Awareness of Food and Nutrition', *Journal of Human Nutrition and Dietetics*, 15: 129–40.

Hastings, G., Stead, M., McDermott, L., Forsyth, A., MacKintosh, A., Rayner, M., Godfrey, C., Caraher, M. and Angus, K. (2003) 'Review of Research on the Effects of Food Promotion to Children', report commissioned by Food Standards Agency, September, http://www.foodstandards.gov.uk/multimedia/pdfs/promofoodchildrenexec.pdf.

Hawkes, C. (2004) *Marketing Food to Children: The Global Regulatory Environment*, Geneva: World Health Organization.

Hawkes, N. (5 August 2008) 'Government Bans the Word "Obese" to Describe Overweight Children', *The Times*.

Hayes, M., Ross, I., Gasher, M., Gutstein, D., Dunn, J. and Hackett, R. (2007) 'Telling Stories: News Media, Health Literacy and Public Policy in Canada', *Social Science and Medicine*, 64(9): 1842–52.

Health Development Agency (2003) see Vlad, *British Medical Journal*, 327: 1308 December 4. BMJ 2003; 327: 1308 doi: 10.1136/bmj.327.7427.1308-d (Published 4 December 2003).

Hernandez, B., Gortmaker, S., Colditz, G., Peterson, K., Laird, N. and Parra-Cabrera, S. (1999) 'Association of Obesity with Physical Activity, Television Programs and other Forms of Video Viewing among Children in Mexico City', *International Journal of Obesity*, 23(8): 845–54.

Hill, A. (2002) 'Developmental Issues in Attitudes to Food and Diet', *Proceedings of the Nutrition Society*, 61: 259–66.

Hill, J. and Radimer, K. (1997) 'A Content Analysis of Food Advertisements in Television for Australian Children', *Australian Journal of Nutrition and Dietetics*, 54(4): 174–81.

Hill, J., Wyatt, H., Reed, G. and Peters, J. (2003) 'Obesity and the Environment: Where Do we Go from Here?' *Science*, 299: 852–7.

Hitchings, E. and Moynihan, P. (1998) 'The Relationship between Television Food Advertisements Recalled and Actual Foods Consumed by Children', *Journal of Human Nutrition and Dietetics*, 11: 511–17.

Hobbs, R. (2004) 'Does Media Literacy Work? An Empirical Study of Learning how to Analyze Advertisements', *Advertising & Society Review*, Vol. 5, Issue 4, 1–28.

Hofferth, S. and Sandberg, J. (2001) 'Changes in American Children's Time, 1981–1997', in S. Hofferth and T. Owens (eds) *Children at the Millennium: Where Did we Come from, Where are we Going?* New York: Elsevier Science.

Holt, D., Ippolito, P., Desrocher, D. and Kelley, C. (2007) 'Children's Exposure to TV Advertising in 1977 and 2004', Information for the Obesity Debate, Federal Trade Commission, Washington, DC: US Government Printing Office.

Hopman, W., Berger, C., Joseph, L., Barr, S., Prior J., Harrison, M., Poliquin, S., Towheed, T., Anastassiades, T., Goltzman, D. and the CaMos Research Group (2007)

'Changes in Body Mass Index in Canadians over a Five-Year Period: Results of a Prospective, Population-Based Study', *BMC Public Health*, 7: 150–61.

Isler, L., Popper, E. and Ward, S. (1987) 'Children's Purchase Requests and Parental Responses: Results from a Diary Study', *Journal of Advertising Research*, October–November (27): 28–39.

Jackson, S. and Scott, S. (1999) 'Risk Anxiety and the Social Construction of Childhood', in D. Lupton (ed.) *Risk and Sociocultural Theory*, Cambridge: Cambridge University Press.

James, J., Thomas, P., Cavan, D. and Kerr, D. (2004) 'Preventing Childhood Obesity by Reducing Consumption of Carbonated Drinks: Cluster Randomized Controlled Trial', *British Medical Journal*, 328: 1237.

Janz, K., Burns, T., Torner, J., Levy, S., Paulos, R., Willing, M. and Warren, J. (2001) 'Physical Activity and Bone Measures in Young Children: The Iowa Bone Development Study', *Pediatrics*, 107: 1387–93.

Jeffrey, D., McLellarn, R. and Fox, D. (1982) 'The Development of Children's Eating Habits: The Role of Television Commercials', *Health Education Behavior*, 9(78): 174–89.

John, D. (1999) 'Consumer Socialization of Children: A Retrospective Look at Twenty Five Years of Research', *Journal of Consumer Research*, 26(3): 183–213.

Jolliffe, D. (2004) 'Extent of Overweight among US Children and Adolescents from 1971 to 2000', *International Journal of Obesity*, 28: 4–9.

Kaiser Family Foundation (2010) 'Generation M: Media in the Lives of Eight to Eighteen Year Olds'. Menlo Park, California. Available online at www.kff.org/entmedia/entmedia030905pkg.cfm Accessed on 10/2006.

Kasperson, R. (1992) 'The Social Amplification of Risk: Progress in Developing an Integrative Framework', in S. Krimsky and D. Golding (eds) *Social Theories of Risk*, Westport: Praeger: 153–78.

Keirle, K. and Thomas, M. (2000) 'The Influence of School Health Education Programmes on the Knowledge and Behaviour of School Children towards Nutrition and Health Research', *Science and Technological Education*, 18 (2): 173–90.

Keller, M. and Kalmus, V. (2009) 'Between Consumerism and Protectionism', *Childhood*, 16 (3): 355–75.

Kim, S. and Willis, A. (2007) 'Talking about Obesity: News Framing of who is Responsible for Causing and Fixing the Problem', *Journal of Health Communication*, 12(3): 359–76.

Klesges, R., Shelton, M. and Klesges, L. (1993) 'Effects of Television on Metabolic Rate: Potential Implications for Childhood Obesity', *Pediatrics*, 91: 281–6.

Kline, K. (2006) 'A Decade of Research on Health Content in the Media: The Focus on Health Challenges and Socio-Cultural Context and Attendant Informational and Ideological Problems', *Journal of Health Communication*, 11(1): 43–59.

Kline, S. (1984) 'Environmental Agenda Setting: An Ideological Analysis of the News Coverage of the Energy Crisis', in N. Evernden (ed.) *The Paradox of Environmentalism*, Toronto: Faculty of Environmental Studies.

Kline, S. (1993) *Out of the Garden: Toys, TV and Children's Culture in the Age of Marketing*, London: Verso.

Kline, S. (2005) 'Countering Children's Sedentary Lifestyles: An Evaluation Study of a Media Risk Education Approach', *Childhood*, 12(2): 239–58.

Kline, S. (2010) 'Children as Competent Consumers', in D. Marshall (ed.) *Understanding Children as Consumers*, London: Sage: 239–57.

Kline, S., Stewart, K. and Murphy, D. (2006) 'Media Literacy in the Risk Society: An Evaluation of a Risk Reduction Strategy', *Canadian Journal of Education*, 29(1): 131–53.

Koplan, J., Liverman, C. and Kraak, V. (eds) (2005) 'Preventing Childhood Obesity: Health in the Balance', Committee on Prevention of Obesity, Children and Youth Food and Nutrition Board Institute of Medicine of the National Academies, Washington, DC: National Academies Press.

Koplan, J., Liverman, P., Kraak, C., Vivica, W. and Shannon, L. (eds) (2006) *How do we Measure Up? Progress in Preventing Childhood Obesity Food and Nutrition*, Board Institute of Medicine of the National Academies, Washington, DC: National Academies Press.

Kotz, K. and Story, M. (1994) 'Food Advertisements during Children's Saturday Morning Television Programming: Are they Consistent with Dietary Recommendations?' *Journal of the American Dietetic Association*, 94: 1296–300.

Kozel1, C., Kane, W., Hatcher, M., Hubbell, A., Dearing, J., Forster-Cox, S., Thompson, S., Pérez, F. and Goodman, M. (2006) 'Introducing Health Promotion Agenda-Setting for Health Education Practitioners', *Californian Journal of Health Promotion*, 4(1): 32–40.

Kunkel, D., Wilcox, B., Cantor, J., Palmer, E., Linn, S. and Dowrick, P. (2004) 'APA Task Force Report on Advertising and Children: Psychological Issues in the Increasing Commercialization of Childhood', Washington: American Psychological Association.

Kuribayashi, A. (2001) 'Actual Nutritional Information of Products Advertised to Children and Adults on Saturday', *Children's Health Care*, 30(4): 309–22.

Laurson, K. Eisenmann, J. and Moore, S. (2008) 'Lack of Association between Television Viewing, Soft Drinks, Physical Activity and Body Mass Index in Children', *Acta Paediatrica*, 97: 795–800.

Lawrence, R. (2004) 'Framing Obesity: The Evolution of News Discourse on a Public Health Issue', *The Harvard International Journal of Press/Politics*, 9(3): 56–75.

Leatherdale, S. and Wong, S. (2009) 'Association between Sedentary Behavior, Physical Activity and Obesity: Inactivity among Active Kids', *Preventing Chronic Disease*, 6(1): A26.

Leiss, W. (2001) *In the Chamber of Risks: Understanding Risk Controversies*, Montreal: McGill-Queen's University Press.

Leiss, W. and Chociolko, C. (1994) *Risk and Responsibility*, Montreal: McGill-Queen's Press.

Leiss, W. and Powell, D. (1996) *Mad Cows and Mother's Milk: The Perils of Poor Risk Communication*, Montreal: McGill-Queen's University Press.

Lewis, M. and Hill, A. (1998) 'Food Advertising on British Children's Television: A Content Analysis and Experimental Study with Nine-Year Olds', *International Journal of Obesity*, 122(3): 206–14.

Lien, M. (2004) 'The Politics of Food as Risk', in M. Lien and B. Nerlich (eds) *The Politics of Food*, Oxford: Berg: 1–32.

Lin, B., Guthrie, J. and Frazo, E. (1999) 'Quality of Children's Diets at and away from Home, 1994–96', *Food Review*, 22(1): 2–10.

Linn, S. (2004) *Consuming Kids*, New York: The New Press.

Lipovetsky, G., Charles, S. and Brown, A. (2005) *Hypermodern Times*, Cambridge: Polity.

Livingstone, M. and Bovill, M. (1999) *Children and their Changing Media Environment: A European Comparative Study*, London: Routledge.

Livingstone, S. and Helsper, E. (2004) *Advertising Foods to Children: Understanding Promotion in the Context of Children's Daily Lives*, prepared for OFCOM, http://www.ofcom.org.uk.

Lobstein, T. and Dibb, S. (2005) 'Evidence of a Possible Link between Obesogenic Food Advertising and Child Overweight', *Obesity Reviews*, 6: 203–8.

Lowry, R., Wechsler, H., Galuska, D., Fulton, J. and Kann, L. (2002) 'Television Viewing and its Association with Overweight, Sedentary Lifestyle, and Insufficient

Consumption of Fruits and Vegetables among US High School Students: Differences by Race Ethnicity and Gender', *Journal of School Health*, 72: 413–21.

Lyle, D. (14 July 2004) 'Obesity across Borders', speech, UK All Party Parliamentary Obesity Group Meeting, London: http://www.eaca.be/default.asp?s=SAP.

Mangleburg, T. (1990) 'Children's Influence in Purchase Decisions: A Review and Critique', *Advances in Consumer Research*, 17: 813–25.

Manning, P. (2001) *News and News Sources: A Critical Introduction*, Thousand Oaks, CA: Sage.

Marquis, M., Filion, Y. and Dagenais, F. (2005) 'Does Eating while Watching Television Influence Children's Food-Related Behaviours?' *Canadian Journal of Dietetic Practice and Research*, 66(1): 12–8.

Marshall, D., O'Donohoe, S. and Kline, S. (2007) 'Families, Food and Pester Power: Beyond the Blame Game?' *Journal of Consumer Behaviour* (July–August): 162–81.

Marshall, D., O'Donahoe, S. and Kline, S. (2008) 'Television Promotion of Children's Snacks: Food for Thought', in K. Ekberg and B. Tufte (eds) *Child and Teen Consumption*, Nordicom Goteborg University.

Marshall, S., Biddle, S., Gorely, T., Cameron, N. and Murdey, I. (2004) 'Relationships between Media Use, Body Fatness and Physical Activity in Children and Youth: A Meta-Analysis', *International Journal of Obesity*, 28: 1238–46.

Martin, M. (1997) 'Children's Understanding of the Intent of Advertising: A Meta Analysis', *Journal of Public Policy and Marketing*, 16(2): 205–16.

Matheson, D., Killen, J., Wang, Y., Varady, A. and Robinson, T. (2004) 'Children's Food Consumption during Television Viewing', *American Journal of Clinical Nutrition*, 79(6): 1088–94.

McAllister, M. and Giglio, J. (2005) 'The Commodity Flow of US Children's Television', *Critical Studies in Media Communication*, 22(1): 25–44.

McCombs, M. and Ghanem, S. (2001) 'The Convergence of Agenda Setting and Framing', in O. Reese, M. Gandy and A. Grant (eds) *Framing Public Life: Perspectives on Media and our Understanding of the Social World*, New Jersey: Lawrence Erlbaum: 67–82.

McCombs, M. and Shaw, D. (1972) 'The Agenda Setting Function of the Press', *Public Opinion Quarterly*, 36: 176–87.

McDonald, G. (1980) 'Family Power: The Assessment of a Decade of Research, 1970–1979', *Journal of Marriage and the Family*, 42(November): 841–54.

McGinnis, J., Appleton-Gootman, J. and Kraak, V. (eds) (2006) *Food Marketing to Children and Youth: Threat or Opportunity?* Washington, DC: National Academies Press, Institute of Medicine.

McMaster University (3 November 2008) 'Media Coverage Affects how People Perceive Threat of Disease', *Science Daily*, http://www.sciencedaily.com– /releases/ 2008/10/081029121818.htm.

McNeal, J. (1964) *Children as Consumers*, Austin: Bureau of Business Research, University of Texas.

McNeal, J. (1999) *The Kids' Market: Myths and Realities*, Ithaca, NY: Paramount Market Publishing.

Media Tenor (2006) 'Media Analysis Data and Methodology', available at http://www.mediatenor.com/newsletters.php?id_news=171.

Mello, M. (2010) 'Federal Trade Commission Regulation of Food Advertising to Children: Possibilities for a Reinvigorated Role', *Journal of Health Politics Policy and Law*, 35(2): 227–76.

Monheit, A., Vistnes, J. and Rogowski, J. (2006) 'Overweight in Adolescents: Implications for Health Expenditures', Working Paper 13488, NBER, http://www.nber.org/papers/w13488.

Montgomery, K. (2007) 'Food Advertising to Children in the New Digital Marketing Ecosystem', in K. Ekstrom and B. Tufte (eds) *Children Media and Consumption*, Nordicom: Goteborg University: 179–94.

Morgenstern, M., Sargent, J. and Hanewinkel, R. (2009) 'Relation between Socioeconomic Status and Body Mass Index: Evidence of an Indirect Path via Television Use', *Archives of Pediatric and Adolescent Medicine*, 163 (8): 731–8.

Moschis, G. (1985) 'The Role of Family Communication in Consumer Socialization of Children and Adolescents', *The Journal of Consumer Research*, 11(4): 898–913.

Moschis, G. and Churchill, G. (1978) 'Consumer Socialization: A Theoretical and Empirical Analysis', *Journal of Marketing Research*, 15(November): 599–609.

Moschis, G. and Moore, R. (1979) 'Decision Making among the Young: A Socialization Perspective', *Journal of Consumer Research*, 6(September): 101–12.

Moschis, G. and Moore, R. (1982) 'A Longitudinal Study of Television Advertising Effects', *Journal of Consumer Research*, 9: 279–86.

Moschis, G., Moore, R. and Smith, R. (1984) 'The Impact of Family Communication on Adolescent Consumer Socialization', *Advances in Consumer Research*, 11: 314–19.

Muschert, G. (2007) 'The Columbine Victims and the Myth of the Juvenile Superpredator', *Youth Violence and Juvenile Justice*, 5(4): 351–66.

National Center for Health Statistics (NHANES), (2000) Reports, Maryland, United States: Public Health Service, available at http://www.cdc.gov/nchs/products/nhsr.htm.

Neilson, S. and Popkin, B. (2003) Patterns and Trends in Food Portion Sizes, 1977–1998, *Amer. Journal of Preventive Medicine*, 27(3): 205–10.

Neilson, S. and Popkin, B. (2004) 'Changes in Beverage Intake 1977–1998', *Journal of the American Medical Association*, 289(4): 450–3.

Neville, L., Thomas, M. and Bauman, A. (2005) 'Food Advertising on Australian Television: The Extent of Children's Exposure', *Health Promotion International*, 20(2): 105–12.

Nicklas, T., Baranowski, K. and Berenson, G. (2001) 'Eating Patterns, Dietary Quality and Obesity', *Journal of the American College of Nutrition*, 20: 599–608.

Obermiller, C. and Spangenberg, E. (2000) 'On the Origin and Distinctness of Skepticism toward Advertising', *Marketing Letters*, 11(4) 311–22.

O'Dougherty, M., Story, M. and Stang, J. (2006) 'Observations of Parent-Child Co-Shoppers in Supermarkets Children's Involvement in Food Selections, Parental Yielding and Refusal Strategies', *Journal of Nutrition Education and Behavior*, 38(3): 183–8.

Ofcom (2005) *Children's Food Choices, Parents' Understanding and Influence, and the Role of Food Promotions*, Appendix 5: DGA content analysis, London: Ofcom.

Ofcom (2006) *Television Advertising of Food and Drink Products to Children: Options for New Restrictions*, London: Ofcom.

Østbye, T., Pomerleau, J., White, M., Coolich, M. and McWhinney, J. (1993) 'Food and Nutrition in Canadian "Prime Time" Television Commercials', *Canadian Journal of Public Health*, 84: 6, 367–9.

Page, R. and Brewster, A. (2007) 'Emotional and Rational Product Appeals in Televised Food Advertisements for Children: Analysis of Commercials Shown on US Broadcast Networks', *Journal of Child Health Care*, 11(4): 323–40.

Parry, V. (3 June 2004) 'On Road to Perdition: The Death of an Overweight 3-Year-Old Opened the Doors to a Wave of Simplistic Hysteria about Obesity', *The Guardian*.

Pecheux, C. and Debraix, C. (1999) 'Children and Attitude toward the Brand: A New Measurement Scale', *Journal of Advertising Research*, July/Aug: 19–27.

Pelman v. McDonald's Corp. (22 January 2003) WL 145584.

Phelps, J. and Hoy, M. (1996) 'The Aad-Ab-PI Relationship in Children: The Impact of Brand Familiarity and Measurement Timing', *Psychology & Marketing*, 13(1): 17.

Philo, G. (2007) 'News Content Studies, Media Group Methods and Discourse Analysis: A Comparison of Approaches', in E. Devereaux (ed.) *Media Studies: Key Issues and Debates*, LA: Sage: 100–33.

Phipps, S., Burton, P. and Osberg, L. (2006) 'Poverty and the Extent of Child Obesity in Canada, Norway and the United States', *Obesity Reviews*, 7(1): 5–12.

Pirouznia, M. (2001) 'The Influence of Nutrition Knowledge on Eating Behavior – the Role of Grade Level', *Nutrition and Food Science*, 31(2): 62–7.

Powell, L., Szczypka, G. and Chaloupka, F. (2007) 'Adolescent Exposure to Food Advertising on Television', *American Journal of Preventative Medicine*, 161: 553: 560.

Prasad, K., Rao, T. and Sheikh, A. (1978) 'Mother vs. Commercial', *Journal of Communication*, Winter (4): 91–6.

Pringle, H. (14 January 2004) 'Why Banning Advertising to Children would be Naïve?' *Media Week*, available at www.ipa.co.uk.

Rawnsley, A. (22 October 1998) 'The Mad Cow Scandal was Such an Outrage that it Could Never be Allowed to Happen Again – Could It?' *The Guardian*.

Reece, B., Rifon, N. and Rodriguez, K. (1999) 'Selling Food to Children: Is Fun Part of a Balanced Breakfast?' in M. Macklin and L. Carlson (eds) *Advertising to Children: Concepts and Controversies*, Thousand Oaks, CA: Sage Publications: 189–208.

Reid, A. (5 March 2004) 'The Ad-Flab Debate', *Campaign*: 20–1.

Reid, L. (1979) 'Viewing Rules as Mediating Factors of Children's Responses to Commercials', *Journal of Broadcasting*, 23: 15–26.

Reid, L. and Frazer, C. (1980) 'Children's Use of Television Commercials to Initiate Social Interaction in Family Viewing Situations', *Journal of Broadcasting*, 24: 149–59.

Rhee, K. (2008) 'Childhood Overweight and the Relationship between Parent Behaviors, Parenting Style and Family Functioning', *The Annals of the American Academy of Political and Social Science*, 615(11): 217–35.

Richards, E. (2004) 'Pelman v McDonalds', Louisiana State University Legal Website, *biotech.law.lsu.edu/cases/food/Pelman_v_McDonalds_SDNY_brief.htm*.

Rieken, G. and Yavas, U. (1990) 'Children's General, Product and Brand Specific Attitudes towards Television Commercials: Implications for Public Policy and Advertising Strategy', *International Journal of Advertising*, 9: 136–48.

Riesman, D., Denney, R. and Glazer, N. (1950) *The Lonely Crowd: A Study of the Changing American Character*, New Haven: Yale University Press.

Roberts, B., Blinkhorn, A. and Duxbury, J. (2003) 'The Power of Children over Adults when Obtaining Sweet Snacks', *International Journal of Paediatric Dentistry*, 13: 76–84.

Roberts, M. and Pettigrew, S. (2007) 'A Thematic Content Analysis of Children's Food Advertising', *International Journal of Advertising*, 26(3): 357–67.

Robertson, T. and Rossiter, J. (1974) 'Children and Commercial Persuasion: An Attribution Theory Analysis', *Journal of Consumer Research*, 1: 508–12.

Robertson, T. and Rossiter, J. (1977) 'Children's Responsiveness to Commercials', *Journal of Communication*, 27(1): 101–6.

Robinson, T. (1999) 'Reducing Children's Television Viewing to Prevent Obesity', *Journal of the American Medical Association*, 282: 1561–7.

Robinson, T. (2000) 'Can a School-Based Intervention to Reduce Television Use Decrease Adiposity in Children in Grades 3 and 4?' *Western Journal of Medicine*, 173(1): 40.

Robinson, T., Borzekowski, D., Matheson, D. and Kraemer, H. (2007) 'Effects of Fast Food Branding on Young Children's Taste Preferences', *Archives of Pediatric and Adolescent Medicine*, 161 (8): 792–7.

Robinson, T. and Killen, J. (1995) 'Ethnic and Gender Differences in the Relationships between Television Viewing and Obesity, Physical Activity, and Dietary Fat Intake, *Journal of Health Education*, 26 (2 Suppl.): S91-8.

Rosengren, A., Hawken, S., Ounpuu, S., Sliwa, K., Zubaid, M., Almahmeed, W., Blackett, K., Sitthi-Amorn, C. Sato, H. and Yusuf, S. (2004) 'Association of Psychosocial Risk Factors with Risk of Acute Myocardial Infarction in 11119 Cases and 13648 Controls from 52 Countries: Case-Control Study', *Lancet*, 11–17 September, 364(9438): 953–62.

Rossiter, J. and Robertson, D. (1974) 'Children's Television Commercials: Testing the Defenses', *Journal of Broadcasting*, 23: 33–40.

Rossiter, J. and Robertson, D. (1976) 'Canonical Analysis of Developmental, Social, and Experiential Factors in Children's Comprehension of Television Advertising', *Journal of Genetic Psychology*, 129: 317–27.

Roy, S., Faulkner, G. and Finlay, S. (2007) 'Fit to Print: A Natural History of Obesity Research in the Canadian News Media', *Canadian Journal of Communication*, 32(3): 575–97.

Sanders, L. (8 March 2005) 'McDonald's Unveils Global Ad Campaign Aimed at Children: Marketing Effort Responds to Obesity Controversy', *Ad Age*, http://adage.com/article?article_id=45281.

Sanders, T. (2007) 'Select Committee Castigated for Citing Death of 3 Year-Old Girl in Obesity Report', *The British Medical Journal* , 25 May: 1503.

Sandman, P., Weinstein, N. and Klotz, M. (1987) 'Public Response to the Risk from Geological Radon', *Journal of Communication*, 37 (3): 93–108.

Schlosser, E. (2001) *Fast Food Nation: What the All-American Meal is Doing to the World*, New York: Allen Lane.

Schor, J. (2004) *Born to Buy*, New York: Scribner.

Schudson, M. (1989) 'The Sociology of News Production', *Media, Culture & Society*, 11: 263–82.

Shah, D., McLeod, D., Kim, E., Lee, S., Gotleib, M., Ho, S. and Breivik, H. (2007) 'Political Consumerism: How Communication and Consumption Orientations Drive "Lifestyle Politics"', *The Annals of The American Academy of Political and Social Science*, 611: 211–35.

Slovic, P. (1992) 'Perception of Risk: Reflections on the Psychometric Paradigm', in S. Krimsky and D. Golding (eds) *Social Theories of Risk*, New York: Praeger: 117–52.

Slovic, P. and Weber, E. (2002) *Perception of Risk Posed by Extreme Events: Risk Management Strategies for an Uncertain World*, New York: Palisades.

Smiciklas-Wright, H., Mitchell, D. Mickle, S. Cook, A. and Goldman, J. (2002) 'Foods Commonly Eaten in the United States, 1989–91 and 1994–96: Are Portion Sizes Changing?' US Department of Agriculture, *NFS Report*, No. 96-5:252, http://www.ars.usda.gov/sp2userfiles/place/12355000/pdf/portion.pdf.

Smith, P. and Best A. (2007) 'Unravelling the Web of Discourse Analysis', in E. Devereaux (ed.) *Media Studies: Key Issues and Debates*, Thousand Oaks, CA: Sage: 78 99.

Snider, D. (2004) http://www.hhs.gov/asl/testify/t041005a.html.

Sorenson, S., Manz, J. and Berk, R. (1998) 'News Media Coverage and the Epidemiology of Homicide', *American Journal of Public Health*, 8(10): 1510–14.

Spigel, L. (1998) 'Seducing the Innocents', in H. Jenkins (ed.) *The Children's Culture Reader*, New York: New York University Press.

Spock, B. (1964) *Baby and Child Care*, New York: Pocket Books.

Squires, S. (3 November 1998) 'Obesity-Linked Diabetes Rising in Children', *Washington Post*: Z07, available at www.usda.gov/cnpp/WP%20Obesity%20Article.htm (date accessed 10 November 2001).

Stettler, N., Signer, T. and Suter, P. (2004) 'Electronic Games and Environmental Factors Associated with Childhood Obesity in Switzerland', *Obesity Research*, 12, 896–903.

Story, M. and Faulkner, P. (1990) 'The Prime Time Diet: A Content Analysis of Eating Behavior and Food Messages in Television Program Content and Commercials', *American Journal of Public Health*, 80(6): 738–40.

Story, M. and French, K. (2004) 'Food Advertising and Marketing Directed at Children and Adolescents in the USA', *International Journal of Behavioral Nutrition and Physical Activity*, 1: 3, http://www.ijbnpa.org/content/1/1/3

Stratton, P. (1994) 'The Myths about Children's Dietary Choices', *Admap*, December 1: 20–4.

Stratton, P. (1997) 'Influences on Food Choice within the Family', in G. Smith (ed.) *Children's Food: Marketing and Innovation*, London: Blackie Academic & Professional: 1–19.

Subrahmanyam, K., Kraut, R., Greenfield, P. and Gross, E. (2000) 'The Impact of Home Computer Use on Children's Activities and Development', *The Future of Children: Children and Computer Technology*, 10 (2): 123–44, http://www.princeton.edu/futureofchildren/publications/journals/.

Sustain Alliance (3 March 2004) *Sustain Calls for Adban*, London: Sustain Alliance for Better Food and Farming.

Sustain Alliance (2004a) *Children's Food and Health: Why Legislation is Urgently Required to Protect Children form Unhealthy Food Advertising and Promotions*, London: Sustain Alliance for Better Food and Farming.

Sustain Alliance (2004b) *Children's Food Bill: For Better Food and a Healthier Future*, London: Sustain Alliance for Better Food and Farming, www.sustainweb.org/child_index.asp.

Sustain Alliance (2005) *The Children's Food Bill: Why we Need a New Law, not More Voluntary Approaches*, London: Sustain Alliance for Better Food and Farming.

Swinburn, B., Egger, G. and Raza, F. (1999) 'Dissecting Obesogenic Environments: The Development and Application of a Framework for Identifying and Prioritising Environmental Interventions for Obesity', *Preventive Medicine*, 29: 563–70.

Talib, N. (2007) *The Black Swan*, New York: Random House.

Taras, H., Sallis, J., Patterson, T., Nader, P. and Nelson, J. (1989) 'Televisions' Influence on Children's Diet and Physical Activity, *Journal of Developmental and Behavioral Pediatrics*, 10: 176–80.

Taras, H., Zive, M., Nader, P., Berry, C., How, T. and Boyd, C. (2000) 'Television Advertising and Classes of Food Products Consumed in a Paediatric Population', *International Journal of Advertising*, 19:487–93.

Taveras, E., Sandora, T., Shih, M., S., Ross-Degnan, D., Goldmann, D. and Gillman, M. (2006) 'The Association of Television and Video Viewing with Fast Food Intake by Preschool-Age Children', *Obesity*, 14(Nov): 2034–41.

Taylor, J., Evers, S. and MacKenna, M. (2005) 'Determinants of Healthy Eating in Children and Youth', *Canadian Journal of Public Health*, 96(3): S20–S26.

Teinowitz, I. (6 December 2005) 'Children and Food Study Slams Marketing Industry', *Ad Age.com*, http://adage.com/article?article_id=47672.

Terkildsen, N., Schell, F. and Ling, C. (1998) 'Interest Groups, the Media, and Policy Debate Formation: An Analysis of Message Structure, Rhetoric, and Source Cues', *Political Communication*, 15(1): 45–61.

Thompson, K. (1998) *Moral Panics*, London: Routledge.

Treichler, P., McGee, D., Karnik, N. and Ruiz, M. (1998) 'The Legacy of AIDS: Global Media Coverage of Infectious Diseases', paper presented at International Conference on AIDS, *Int Conf AIDS*, 12: 731 (abstract no. 34231).

Tremblay, M. and Willms, J. (2003) 'Is the Canadian Child Obesity Epidemic Related to Physical Inactivity?' *International Journal of Obesity*, 27, 1100–5.

Tuchman, G. (1972) 'Objectivity as Strategic Ritual: An Examination of Newsmen's Notions of Objectivity', *American Journal of Sociology*, 77(4): 660–79.

Tuchman, G. (1978) *Making News: A Study in the Construction of Reality*, New York: The Free Press.

Tucker, L. (1986) 'The Relationship of Television Viewing to Physical Fitness and Obesity', *Adolescence*, 21(84): 797–806.

Tulloch, J. and Lupton, D. (2003) *Risk and Everyday Life*, London: Sage.

UK National Diet and Nutrition Survey (2000) 'Young People Aged 4 to 18 Years', *Report of the Diet and Nutrition Survey*, Volume 1, http://www.statistics.gov.uk/ssd/surveys/national_diet_nutrition_survey_children.asp.

Valkenburg, P. and Buijzen, M. (2005) 'Identifying Determinants of Young Children's Brand Awareness: Television, Parents and Peers', *Applied Developmental Psychology*, 26, 456–68.

Valkenburg, P. and Cantor, J. (2002) 'The Development of a Child into a Consumer', in S. Calvert, A. Jordan and R. Cocking (eds) *Children in the Digital Age: Influences of Electronic Media on Development*, Westport, CO: Praeger: 201–14.

Vandewater, E., Shim, M. and Kaplovitz, A. (2004) 'Linking Obesity and Activity Level with Children's Television and Video Game Use', *Journal of Adolescence*, 27: 71–85.

Veerman, L., Beeck, E., Barendregt, J. and Mackenbach, J. (2009) 'By How Much Would Limiting TV Food Advertising Reduce Childhood Obesity?' *European Journal of Public Health*, 19 (4): 365–9.

Ventura, A. and Birch, L (2007) 'Review: Does Parenting Affect Children's Eating and Weight Status?' *International Journal of Behavioral Nutrition and Physical Activity*, 15(5): 1–12.

Veugelers, P. and Fitzgerald, A. (2005) 'Effectiveness of School Programs in Preventing Childhood Obesity', *American Journal of Public Health*, 95(3): 432–5.

Wackman, D. Wartella, E. and Ward, S. (1977) 'Learning to be Consumers: The Role of the Family', *Journal of Communication*, 27 (1): 138–51.

Walsh, C. (April 4 2004) 'Things Go Bitter with Coke', *The Observer*: B5.

WARC (25 January 2007) 'US Taskforce to Mull Ads and Child Obesity', *WARC News*, http://www.warc.com.

Ward, S (1972) *Children and Promotion: New Consumer Battleground?* Cambridge, MA: Marketing Science Institute.

Ward, S. (1974) 'Consumer Socialization', *Journal of Consumer Research* 1(September): 1–16.

Ward, S. and Wackman, D. (1972) 'Children's Purchase Influence Attempts and Parental Yielding', *Journal of Marketing Research*, 9(November): 316–19.

Ward, S., Wackman, D. and Wartella, E. (1977) *How Children Learn to Buy: The Development of Information Processing Skills*, Beverly Hills, CA: Sage.

Wardle, J., Gutherie, C., Sanderson, S., Birch, L. and Plomin, R. (2001) 'Food and Activity Preferences in Children of Lean and Obese Parents', *International Journal of Obesity*, 25(7): 971–7.

Warren, R., Wicks, R., Wicks, J., LeBlanc, F. and Chung, D. (2008) 'Food and Beverage Advertising on US Television: A Comparison of Child-Targeted Versus General Audience Commercials', *Journal of Broadcasting & Electronic Media*, 52(2): 231–46.

246   *References*

Weintraub, E., Bolls, P., Fujioka, Y. and Engelbertson, J. (1999) 'How and Why Parents Take on the Tube', *Journal of Broadcasting & Electronic Media*, 43(2): 175–92.

Weiss, E. and Kien, C. (1987) 'A Synthesis of Research on Nutrition Education at the Elementary School Level', *Journal of School Health*, 57(1): 8–13.

Which? (2006) *Childcatchers: The Tricks used to Push Unhealthy Food to your Children*, http://www.which.co.uk.

Wiecha, J., Peterson, K., Ludwig, D., Kim, J., Sobol, A. and Gortmaker, S. (2006) 'When Children Eat What they Watch: Impact of Television Viewing on Dietary Intake', *Journal is Archives of Pediatrics and Adolescent Medicine*, 160(4): 436–42.

Wilcox, B., Cantor, J., Dowrick, P., Kunkel, D., Linn, S. and Palmer, E. (2004) *Report of the Task Force on Advertising and Children: Recommendations*, Washington, DC: American Psychological Association.

Wilson, N. and Blackhurst, A. (1999) 'Food Advertising and Eating Disorders: Marketing Body Dissatisfaction, the Drive for Thinness, and Dieting in Women's Magazines', *Journal of Humanistic Counseling, Education & Development*, 38, 111–23.

Williams, Christine (2006) *Inside Toyland: Working Shopping and Social Inequality*, Berkley: University of California Press.

Wilson, N., Quigley, R. and Mansoor, O. (1999) 'Food Ads on TV: A Health Hazard for Children?' *Australian and New Zealand Journal of Public Health*, 23: 647–50.

Wilson, N., Signal, L., Nicholls, S. and Thomson, G. (2006) 'Marketing Fat and Sugar to Children on New Zealand Television', *Preventive Medicine*, 42: 96–101.

Winman, A. (1983) 'Parental Influence and Children's Responses to Television Advertising', *Journal of Advertising*, 12(1): 12–18.

Wintour, P. (30 March 2004) 'Jowell Rejects Legislation to Combat Obesity', *The Guardian*.

Woloshin, S. and Schwartz, L. (2002) 'Translating Research into News', *Journal of the American Medical Association*, 287(21): 2856–8.

Wootan, M. (2003) *Pestering Parents: How Food Companies Market Obesity to Children*, Center for Science in the Public Interest: 62.

World Health Organization (WHO) (1997) 'Obesity: Preventing and Managing the Global Epidemic', report on a WHO Consultation on Obesity, 3–5 June 1997. Geneva: WHO/NUT/NCD/98.1:1998.

World Health Organization (WHO) (2000) *Obesity: Preventing and Managing the Global Epidemic*, Geneva: World Health Organization, Technical Report Series 894, available at http://www.who.int/nutrition/publications/obesity/WHO_TRS_894/en/index.html.

World Health Organization (WHO) (2002) *Diet, Physical Activity and Health*, Geneva: World Health Organization, v. 1, Resolution WHA55.23.

World Health Organization (WHO) (2002) *The World Health Report: Reducing Risks, Promoting Healthy Life*, Geneva: World Health Organization.

World Health Organization (WHO) (2003) *Diet, Nutrition and the Prevention of Chronic Diseases*, Geneva: World Health Organization, Report Series, No. 916, available at http://www.who.int/dietphysicalactivity/publications/trs916/en/.

Yates, B. (2001) 'Media Literacy and Attitude Change: Assessing the Effectiveness of Media Literacy Training on Children's Responses to Persuasive Messages within the ELM', presentation, Annual Convention of the Broadcast Education Association, Las Vegas, 20–23 April: 33.

Young, B. (2003a) 'Does Food Advertising Make Children Obese?' *International Journal of Marketing and Advertising to Children* 4(3): 21–6.

Young, B. (2003b) 'Does Food Advertising Influence Children's Food Choices? A Critical Review of Some of the Recent Literature', *International Journal of Advertising*, 22: 441–59.

Youth Risk Behaviour Survey (2007) data available at http://www.cdc.gov/HealthyYouth/YRBS/data/index.htm.

Yusuf, S., Hawken, S., Ounpuu, S., Dans, T., Avezum, A., Lanas, F., McQueen, M., Budaj, A., Pais, P., Varigos, J. and Lisheng, L. (2004) 'Effect of Potentially Modifiable Risk Factors Associated with Myocardial Infarction in 52 Countries (the INTERHEART study): Case-Control Study', *Lancet*, 364: 937–52.

Zaninotto, P., Wardle, H., Stamatakis, E., Mindell, J. and Head, J. (2006) 'Forecasting Obesity to 2010', National Centre for Social Research, http://www.dh.gov.uk/assetRoot/04/13/18.29/0413.

Zimmerman, F. and Bell, J. (2010) 'Associations of Television Content Type and Obesity', *American Journal of Public Health*, 100(2): 334–40.

Index

Lightning Source UK Ltd.
Milton Keynes UK
UKOW06n0305270216

269217UK00012B/508/P